TOWARD NEW HORIZONS FOR WOMEN IN DISTANCE EDUCATION

RADICAL FORUM ON ADULT EDUCATION SERIES
Edited by Jo Campling, Series Consultant: Colin Griffin.

Curriculum Theory in Adult Lifelong Education
Colin Griffin

Learning Liberation — Women's Response to Men's Education
Jane L. Thompson

Adult Education and Community Action
Tom Lovett, Chris Clarke and Avila Kimurray

Mutual Aid Universities
Edited by Eric Midwinter

Post-education Society
Norman Evans

University Adult Education in England and the USA:
A Reappraisal of the Liberal Tradition
Richard Taylor, Kathleen Rockhill and Roger Fieldhouse

Adult Education and Socialist Pedagogy
Frank Youngman

Adult Education and the Working Class
Kevin Ward and Richard Taylor

Educational Responses to Adult Unemployment
Barbara Senior and John Naylor

Class, Ideology and Community Education
Will Cowburn

Radical Approaches to Adult Education
Tom Lovett

Learning for Life: Politics and Progress in Recurrent Education
Edited by F. Molyneux, G. Low and G. Fowler

TOWARD NEW HORIZONS FOR WOMEN IN DISTANCE EDUCATION

International Perspectives

Edited
by
Karlene Faith

Ministry of Education, Ontario
Information Services & Resources Unit,
13th Floor, Mowat Block, Queen's Park,
Toronto M7A 1L2

Foreword by Elizabeth Burge

ROUTLEDGE
London and New York

First published in 1988 by
Routledge
a division of Routledge, Chapman and Hall
11 New Fetter Lane, London EC4P 4EE

Published in the USA by
Routledge
a division of Routledge, Chapman and Hall, Inc.
29 West 35th Street, New York NY 10001

© 1988 Karlene Faith and in the names of the authors

Printed and bound in Great Britain by
Biddles Ltd, Guildford and King's Lynn

All rights reserved. No part of this book may be reprinted or reproduced or utilised in any form or by any electronic, mechanical, or other means, now known or hereafter invented, including photocopying and recording, or in any information storage or retrieval system, without permission in writing from the publishers.

British Library Cataloguing in Publication Data

Toward new horizons for women in distance
    education : international perspectives. —
    (Radical forum on adult education series).
    1. Women. Further education. Distance study
    I. Faith, Karlene II. Series
    376

ISBN 0-415-00565-5

This book was word-processed on a MacIntosh Plus, formatted using MagnaType, and typeset on a Linotron 100. It was illustrated and laid out in camera-ready form at Simon Fraser University through Computing Services and the Centre for Distance Education/Instructional Media Centre (Office of Continuing Studies).

Simon Fraser University
Burnaby, British Columbia
V5A 1S6, Canada.

CONTENTS

PREFACE   i

ACKNOWLEDGEMENTS   iii

FOREWORD, *Elizabeth Burge*   vii

INTRODUCTION   1

1. Naming the Problem, *Karlene Faith*   3

THE GENDER FACTOR IN DISTANCE EDUCATION   19

2. Canada: The West Coast, *June Sturrock*   25

3. Gender-Related Patterns in Choice of Major Subject or Degree Course at FernUniversität (West Germany), *Christine von Prümmer and Ute Rossié*   39

4. Women as Distance Learners in Israel, *Yael Enoch*   67

5. Teaching Art at a Distance in New Zealand, *Jeanne Macaskill*   82

6. Distance Education as a Means of Enhancing Self-Esteem Among Adult Female Students In Sweden, *Birgitta Willén*   93

7. Atlantic Canada Perspectives, *Diana R. Carl, Erin M. Keough and Lorraine Y. Bourque*   107

ISSUES OF EQUITY   121

8. Women in Papua New Guinea: Distance Education as a Means for Educational Advancement, *Angela Mandie-Filer*   129

9. Female Imagery in Course Materials: Kenya, *I. Barbara Matiru and Debbie Gachuhi*   137

10. Women in Distance Education at the University of the South Pacific, *Marjorie Crocombe, Joan Teaiwa, Arlene Griffen, Ruby Va'a, Eileen Tuimaleali'ifano, Penelope Schoeffel, Adi Davila Toganivalu*   152

11. The Indian Experience, *Gomathi Mani, Kamalini H. Bhansali; and Jyoti H. Trivedi*   172

12. By Print and Post: Vocational Training for Isolated Women (Australia), *Paulene Heiler and Wendy Richards*   190

13. Women in Turkey and the Potential for Open Learning, *Ülkü S. Köymen*   205

14. Problems and Possibilities: Canadian Native Women in Distance Education, *Barbara Spronk and Donna Radtke*   214

15. Negotiating a New Model for Aboriginal Teacher Education: ANTEP—A Case Study (Australia), *Loene Furler and Carol Scott*   229

FACING NEW CHALLENGES   249

16. A Reconsideration of the Attraction of the Dutch Open University for Female Students, *Jo Boon and Gerry Joosten*   254

17. Towards a More Women-Centred Approach for Distance Education Curriculum (The Netherlands), *Nelly Oudshoorn*   264

18. Extramural Teaching and Women's Studies: "Women in Society" Course (New Zealand), *Shelagh Cox and Bev James*   275

19. Sowing Seeds: Initiatives for Improving the Representation of Women (United Kingdom), *Gill Kirkup*   287

PIONEERS IN DISTANCE EDUCATION   313

20. Bridging the Gap: The Contributions of Individual Women to the Development of Distance Education to 1976, *Diana R. Carl*   316

INDEX   339

PREFACE

by

Karlene Faith

This book was the inspiration of Elizabeth Burge, Head of the Instructional Resources Development Unit of the Ontario Institute for Studies in Education and an internationally respected innovator in distance education. Liz presented the idea to Jo Campling, Editor of the Radical Forum in Education series for Croom Helm publishers, who was enthusiastic. Liz then communicated the idea to members of the Women's International Network (WIN) of the International Council for Distance Education (ICDE), at meetings in Melbourne, Australia in August 1985. Delegates from Fiji, Israel, Sweden, Turkey, Canada, Kenya, Australia, West Germany and New Zealand immediately volunteered to contribute articles; following the ICDE meetings, further offers came from distance educators in Papua New Guinea, India, England and the Netherlands. There was a clear consensus that a need existed for documentation of women's work in this rapidly expanding phenomenon in global educational systems. During the past decade women have produced a substantial body of work related to women's needs and experiences as students and practitioners within conventional educational settings. Distance educators have benefited from this research while realizing that the experience of women in distance education is likewise relevant to the interests of educators in more traditional contexts.

Given that this would be the first published book on women in distance education, and given the nascent stage of the research in this area, it was agreed that we would take a case study approach, with each author independently identifying the relevant issues within her own professional and regional context. The contributors to this volume are strikingly varied in terms of cultural, national, religious, educational, family and class backgrounds. They do not represent unified ideological perspectives, feminist or otherwise. Their levels of experience vary, as do the foci of their expertise. And yet, their remarkable diversity notwithstanding, there are common themes which recur again and again, demonstrating global and cross-cultural convergences of women's concerns. One of my keenest challenges as an editor, in this regard, was to reduce thematic repetition without removing from the reader's view the realization that, however variable the particulars, the contributors echo one another's general perceptions and theoretical conclusions. Whether or not they represent a global "feminist" awakening, their collective voices make an unambiguous statement about universal similarities in female experience and response. Even taking into account cultural, social, political and economic variables, it is clear from this volume of articles that women throughout the world are expanding their horizons; for many women, distance education is the vehicle for this development. Indeed, perhaps the most provocative and paradoxical observation to be made concerning distance education is that while, on the one hand, it encourages individual development and choice, on the other hand, it colludes with traditional gender roles and expectations by facilitating women's confinement to the home.

* * *

On a different note, the clearest distinction between distance education (that is, home study) and face-to-face classroom instruction is in methodology, and new technologies have been a factor in the rapid growth of the worldwide distance education movement. At the same time, global inequities of resources and different cultural styles of communication preclude any universal prescriptions for appropriate methodologies in distance education. Therefore, for example, while Canadian authors in this volume attest to the value placed in their country on high-tech telecommunications systems, authors from other nations suggest that dependency on the written word for interaction with students is not perceived as a negative limitation. The question as to whether some "delivery systems" are more effective than others (taking goals and context into account) is one that female distance educators share with their male colleagues, and it is hoped that articles in this volume will help stimulate further evaluative research in this area.

ACKNOWLEDGEMENTS

The compilation of the manuscript for this book has been an outstanding team endeavour conducted under the generous auspices of Simon Fraser University (SFU) in British Columbia, Canada. Dr. J. Colin Yerbury, Director of the SFU Centre for Distance Education within the Office of Continuing Studies, offered vital encouragement and facilitated access to university resources. I am very grateful to him, as I am to all other individuals whose talents and generosity of time and spirit made this project feasible. I offer my special thanks to:

- Elizabeth Burge, whose contacts and expertise enhanced the book's development and whose long-distance friendship, counsel and sense of humour kept my confidence afloat.

- Barbara Lange, who typed every word, made every needed change (time and again), caught errors on my behalf, coded the entire word-processed manuscript in preparation for typesetting, and cooperated in every way beyond the call of duty. And, through it all, she managed to get married and host her wedding.

- Laura Coles, upon whom I depended at every stage of the book's development. Her keen editorial skills proved indispensable both substantively in a number of chapters and in copy-editing throughout. Laura also prepared the index and she coordinated the multi-faceted final stages of the production, ensuring synchrony among all the other members of the team. Her myriad professional skills combined with her gentle demeanor lightened the load for everyone concerned. Laura's participation was all the more remarkable because she had to commute to the university by ferry from her country home on the B.C. coast.

- Dr. June Sturrock, my esteemed colleague and valued friend, who rallied to my aide on many occasions during the year in which the book was developed. She listened sensitively to my concerns and found solutions for them. She contributed a chapter, and her knowledge, insight and editorial acumen improved my own work and that of several other contributors.

- Elizabeth Carefoot, a respected independent artist as well as an illustrator with the SFU Instructional Media Centre, who applied her considerable talents to the book's design and layout and whose bright spirit and enthusiasm for the project made our collaboration a joyful one. (It is also worth mentioning that Elizabeth has a reputation as one of Canada's most renowned belly dancers!)
- Rupindera Rai, who provided library assistance and who skillfully and patiently instructed me on how to use the word-processor.
- Kay Uno, who respectfully and expertly handled the reams of correspondence and telegrams exchanged between our office and contributors from many nations, and whose clear eye for detail saved me from some potential embarrassments.
- Members of the Executive of the International Council for Distance Education—notably Elizabeth Burge, Gisela Pravda and Maureen Smith, and ICDE President, Kevin Smith—for their strong support of the Women's International Network and this project.
- Charles Chadwick and Ken Wallace of the British Council in Ottawa, and Barbara Davis in London, for facilitating contacts in England.
- Jo Campling, the series editor, whose belief in the project led us to the respected imprint of Croom Helm.
- Sue Joshua, Croom Helm in-house editor, who kindly responded to all my questions and who patiently accommodated delays in the manuscript's completion.
- Keith Harry, Documentation Officer, and Nazira Dytham, Information and Documentation Assistant, at the International Centre for Distance Learning (The United Nations University), and Manfred Delling of West Germany, for valued bibliographic assistance.
- Dr. Simon Verdun-Jones, Director of the SFU School of Criminology, whose respect for the value of distance education and

Acknowledgements

international collaboration provided me with needed encouragement and time away from routine course development responsibilities.

- The staff of the SFU Centre for Distance Education—Catherine Porter, Christine Dempster, Debbie Sentance, Teresa Book, Carol Lane, Leila Hargreaves, Deanne Mackie, Mindy Ferrier, Lesley Rougeau and Karen Saxton, and administrators Dawn Howard and Hannah Hadikein—for their collegial and practical support, and Eddy Chan, SFU photographer, who graciously took our pictures.

- Ellen Sangster, of the SFU Computing Services Typesetting Service who, with assistance from Jill Whaley, transformed the completed draft of the book into a camera-ready manuscript and who assured the project's favourable completion in miracle time.

I am especially grateful to each of the women who authored articles for this collection—for their promptness in submitting their work, their flexibility in responding to editorial suggestions, their patience with Canada's peculiar postal system, their many personal kindnesses to me, and above all for the good work they do and the thought and care they bring to it. Our hope is that this collective effort will be for some readers an enlightening introduction to distance education, and that it will also benefit our colleagues around the world with a deeper appreciation of women's concerns and contributions to the field.

Finally, for sheer inspiration I thank my longtime and long-distance friend Leslie, who through many years of unavoidable isolation has succeeded in completing two Bachelor of Arts degrees and is now headed for a Master's degree—and has done it all as a first-rate distance education student. – K.F.

FOREWORD

by

Elizabeth Burge

> **Elizabeth J. Burge** worked as a librarian and library designer in Australia and was educated at the University of Adelaide, the Salisbury College of Advanced Education and the Ontario Institute for Studies in Education (OISE). She is currently head of the Instructional Resources Development Unit of OISE, which is the Graduate School of Education of the University of Toronto. She is also responsible for the development of distance mode M.Ed. courses run by OISE throughout Ontario. Her field development, teaching and writing interests centre around developing stronger links between theory and practice relating to the design of adult learning. Liz has been active in the ICDE, of which she is Vice-President, the Women's International Network, of which she is the Chair, and the Canadian Association for Distance Education.

"Light a candle, don't curse the dark."

The old exhortation is an appropriate metaphor for this book. After over one hundred years of formal distance education, we confront the darkness of the unwritten experience of women as distance mode learners and educators. This book is the first known published compilation of the experience of women in international distance education. This initial candle therefore has its own style, values and intensity—all of which Karlene Faith addresses in the context-setting first chapter.

But the book has more significance than in being a record of past achievement and future concerns. Its emergence is very close in time to two important fiftieth anniversaries, each of which is part of our personal and professional histories.

I

In 1938, *Three Guineas* was published, authored by the English feminist and writer Virginia Woolf. In a first-person style that claimed the legitimacy of a woman's perception of the world, she argued strongly that women's access to education was essential for their economic independence. This independence in turn, Woolf believed, was essential for a critical intellectual autonomy in the world. Education, however, as it had been structured up to the mid-1930s in the United Kingdom, was inhibiting both access to and development of independence because of the limits of its intellectual resources for learning. "Language structures, categories of analysis, and criteria of what was worth knowing [arising from male domination of knowledge production and use] was so androcentric as to severely handicap women's capacity for self-understanding and communication" (Pierson, 1984:7). Woolf argued for "finding new words and creating new methods" (1986:164). She wanted a new and radically different education, one that would produce a different kind of person who valued a civilized existence, in balance between private and public worlds: "Let it be built on lines of its own... Let the pictures and books be new... or it should teach the art of understanding other people's lives and minds" (p. 39).

Woolf's arguments have, since 1938, supported those writers and educators who value feminist approaches and those who argue against gender bias and for a balance of "feminine" and "masculine" in our world (e.g., Nelson, 1977; Salner, 1985). Rich (1979) has described their activities as "a feminist renaissance," and her description is an appropriate context for the writers of this present book:

> that in the struggle to discover women and our buried or misread history, feminists are doing two things: questioning and re-exploring the past, and demanding a humanization of intellectual interests and public measures in the present. In the course of this work, we are recovering lost sources of knowledge and of spiritual vitality, while familiar texts are receiving a fresh critical appraisal, and the whole process is powered by a shift in perspective far more extraordinary and influential than the shift from theology to humanism of the European Renaissance (p. 126).

McCormack, for example, has suggested recently that the new academic freedom will be one of "affirmative access" — "the right to speak and be heard in a language that is your own, to define an

Foreword

agenda and set priorities, and to set standards of performance" (1986:2).

This kind of access is needed because we know that the female experience of education differs from the male experience (Belenky et al., 1986). That difference cannot be explained adequately by arguments about inherent male and female characteristics, but rather by the impacts of very early gender-based socialization, the consequent sets of achievement expectations, and conditions of schooling. "Women's ways of knowing" and some of their preferred ways of learning are challenging educators to rethink how they can help women learn (Clinchy et al., 1985).

The contributors to this book illustrate what Martin calls a "gender-sensitive" approach: "Taking gender into account when it makes a difference and ignoring it when it does not, such an ideal allows us to build into curricula, instructional methods, and learning environments ways of dealing with trait genderization and with the many and various other gender-related phenomena that enter into education today" (1986:10).

Women distance educators are still taking initial steps toward recognizing the presence of women and girls as learners. At the research level, as evidenced in this book, there is new attention to context-embedded phenomena. Some procedural limitations of research designs and rigid scientific procedures (Scheuneman, 1986) have been challenged. One doesn't want to over-simplify the "context-embedded/context-removed" distinction, but it points to a need for an integration of different epistemological approaches and a recognition that gender-related and feminist issues in writing and research must be acknowledged (Miller and Swift, 1980; Poff, 1985; Eichler, in press). Scheuneman argues that the needed integration of male and female perspectives in educational research parallels the integration of male and female behaviour in our personal lives; my argument is that the professional arena of distance education research and practice needs to show integrated perspectives much more than it has to date. But this is a long-term goal. A shorter-term goal has to be a wider recognition of the experience of women students and educators: a naming of the realities and the problems. Developing new concepts or new definitions of old concepts is needed before "feminist explanatory models and feminist epistemology" (Poff, 1985) can be built as sturdy foundations for distance education practices.

II

Across the Atlantic and west to the Pacific, in Victoria, British Columbia, distance educators gathered in 1938 for the first conference of the then International Council for Correspondence Education (ICCE). Thirty of the eighty-eight listed delegates were women. Since then twelve more international conferences have been held with large increases in the number of delegates. The 13th world conference in Melbourne attracted approximately six hundred listed delegates—more than a 65% increase over the 1938 attendance. But that steady growth has not applied to women delegates. Judging from published figures for eight of the thirteen conferences, one of the best years for women's attendance was 1957, when 51% of the delegates were women. At the largest conference, in Melbourne in 1985, 24% of the 596 listed delegates were women. With so many women involved at the grassroots level in distance education internationally—as educators and administrators as well as learners—their low conference attendance figures have to be illustrative of the same barriers and realities for women that Woolf had seen fifty years earlier.

The WIN candle was lit at the 1982 world conference of the ICCE in Vancouver, B.C. where 25% of the 374 delegates were women, and the host was Audrey Campbell. They helped change the name International Council for Correspondence Education to the International Council for Distance Education (ICDE), to reflect positive and innovative distance education methods. But they also experienced some conference realities that were not felt as positive or innovative: for example, exclusive "he-man" language and other indicators of marginalization and male control of knowledge production and transmission. Students and teachers alike were referred to as he or him—very rarely as she or her.

Balancing these discomforts were reassurances—the indicators of respect for and belief in each others' experience as women educators, and strong shared commitment to distance education and to providing radical means of helping people learn.

Before the 1982 conference ended, the Women's International Network (WIN) had been established. While its goals are specific to women, it operates as an integral part of the ICDE and shows that the organization is losing its androcentric bias (at least some of it!). Six goals emerged from a post-conference survey of all female ICDE members (Burge, 1983):

Foreword

- sharing of ideas and experience on a regular basis
- developing a professional and personal support system
- analyzing women's roles in distance education
- conducting research and disseminating results
- meeting new colleagues and staying in contact
- addressing the needs of female distance learners

These goals have been met through newsletters, workshops, individual networking, activity at ICDE world conferences, and now through this book. It is fair to say that since 1982 WIN has shown signs of progressing through Janeway's three stages of understanding power relationships—disbelief and questioning, bonding and organizing for action (1980).

WIN's presence at the 1985 ICDE conference in Melbourne was a landmark event. Greater recognition of issues affecting women was evident; there was serious attention paid to non-sexist language guidelines for writers, and inclusive language was used in the conference sessions. WIN held special sessions on issues relating to women; these sessions were notable for their intensity and for the recognition that a lot of research into women in distance education is needed.

While talk about women distance learners and educators has been plentiful, writing and research has not. In all the issues of two journals, *Teaching at a Distance* and *Distance Education,* since 1974 and 1980 respectively, only six articles have been overtly concerned with women (Peacock et al., 1978 and 1979; Swarbrick, 1978 and 1980; Thornton, 1986; Tremaine and Owen, 1984). The strong emergence of male writers to define and explain their perspectives on the field of distance education has not been paralleled by activity by female writers. The research lacks a balance between rigorous positivist (e.g., experimental) and rigorous naturalistic (e.g., ethnographic) epistemological paradigms. Neither has the research to date, with rare exception, been noted for extensive use and explorations of feminist epistemological frameworks (for discussions of this problem, see Gilligan, 1982; Poff, 1985; Salner, 1985; Belenky et al., 1986). Few studies have used Woolf's "new words" and "new methods" to explore how the construction of knowledge is built into the design of distance courses, the impacts of gender-based contexts on that construction, the particular experience of women-learners from phenomenological perspectives, and feminist research approaches. Kelly and Elliott have indicated the dearth of general published scholarship on women's education, up to 1982, and their summary is appropriate for us:

> The past decade has witnessed a proliferation of excellent research studies on very important topics concerning women—their roles and relative status, their participation in the work force and in politics, their contribution to economic development, and so forth. This scholarship is rich and highly relevant for understanding the significance of education to women's lives. However, most of it does not directly consider education. We learn little from this body of knowledge about why women attend school, what they learn in school, how education affects them, or whether education makes a contribution to improving their lives apart from class, ethnicity, and other social background factors (1982:1).

It is no accident that this book is set in a growing literature that values the experience of women students, teachers, researchers and administrators—a literature recently described as "The New Scholarship on Women and Education" *(Educational Researcher,* special issue, 1986).

The first flickerings of the candle that is this book grew in August 1984 when I discussed with Jo Campling of Croom Helm an idea for a book about women in international distance education. Jo's support of the idea and her encouragement to continue planning led to more detailed discussions a year later at a WIN meeting in Melbourne. We decided to proceed under the able editorship of Dr. Karlene Faith of Simon Fraser University, a criminologist and distance educator by profession, a feminist by conviction. Since September 1985, Karlene has sheltered, trimmed and nurtured the candle to increase its power and light. Without her skill, persistence against great odds, good humour and unshakeable belief in the legitimacy of women's needs and experience of the world, the candle would have flickered out. Without the support of Dr. Colin Yerbury and Simon Fraser University, Karlene would not have had access to all the institutional resources needed for her work.

Enjoy this book. Be impressed. It is unique as a first event and in its feminist style. It illuminates experience, it celebrates achievement, and it reveals inequities. It also seeks companions against the dark.

References

Belenky, M., B.M. Clinchy, N.R. Goldberger, and J.M. Tarule. (1986). *Women's Ways of Knowing: The Development of Self, Voice and Mind*. New York: Basic Books.

Burge, E.J. (1983). "Professional Networking: An ICDE Example." *ICDE Bulletin, 3,* 15–18.

Clinchy, B.M., M.F. Belenky, N. Goldberger and J.M. Tarule. (1985). "Connected Education for Women." *Journal of Education, 167,* 28–45.

Educational Researcher, (1986) 5:(6).

Eichler, M. (in press). *Nonsexist Research Methods: A Practical Guide*. Boston: Allen and Unwin.

Gilligan, C. (1982). *In a Different Voice*. Harvard, Mass.: Harvard University Press.

Janeway, E. (1980). *Powers of the Weak*. New York: Knopf.

Kelly, G.P. and C.M. Elliott. (Eds.). (1982). *Women's Education in the Third World: Comparative Perspectives*. Albany, New York: State University of New York Press.

Martin, J.R. (1986). "Redefining the Educated Person: Rethinking the Significance of Gender." *Educational Researcher, 15,* 6–10.

McCormack, T. (1986). "Feminism and the New Academic Freedom." Unpublished paper.

Miller, C. and K Swift. (1980). *The Handbook of Nonsexist Writing*. New York: Lippincott and Crowell.

Nelson, K.H. (1977). "Cognitive Styles and Sex Roles in Teaching-Learning Processes." Paper presented to the Annual Convention of the American Psychological Association, San Francisco, California, August 1977.

Peacock, G., M.S. Hurley and J.F. Brown. (1978). "New Opportunities for Women: A Group Entry Project at Newcastle upon Tyne." *Teaching at a Distance, 12,* 33–42.

Peacock, G., M.S. Jurley and J.F. Brown. (1979). "New Opportunities for Women: A Progress Project." *Teaching at a Distance, 16,* 68–69.

Pierson, R.R. (1984). "Historical Moments in the Development of a Feminist Perspective on Education." *Resources for Feminist Research, 13*(1), 1–9.

Poff, D.C. (1985). "Feminism Flies Too: The Principles of a Feminist Epistemology." *Resources for Feminist Research, 14*(3), 6–8.

Rich, A. (1979). "Toward a Women-Centered University." In *On Lies, Secrets and Silence: Selected Prose 1966–1978*. New York: Norton.

Salner, M. (1985). "Women, Graduate Education and Feminist Knowledge." *Journal of Education, 167*, 46–58.

Scheuneman, J.D. (1986). "The Female Perspective on Methodology and Statistics." *Educational Researcher, 15*, 22–23.

Swarbrick, A. (1978). "A Discourse on Method: Interviewing in a Preliminary Study of Women Graduates in the Yorkshire Region." *Teaching at a Distance, 12*, 62–64.

Swarbrick, A. (1980). "To Encourage the Others: Women Studying Technology." *Teaching at a Distance, 17*, 2–14.

Thornton, N. (1986). "A Model for Interinstitutional Collaboration: The Women's Studies Inter University Course Program." *Distance Education, 7*(2), 214–236.

Tremaine, M. and J. Owen. (1984). "The Female Majority: Women Who Study Extramurally." *Teaching at a Distance, 25*, 45–50.

Woolf, V. (1986). *Three Guineas*. London: Hogarth Press, (originally published by Hogarth Press in 1938).

INTRODUCTION

Chapter 1

NAMING THE PROBLEM

by

Karlene Faith

> **Karlene Faith** was born in Saskatchewan (Canada) in 1938. She studied at the Université de Poitiers (France), the Centre for the Study of Intercultural Documentation (Mexico) and the University of California in Santa Cruz (UCSC), where she received a B.A. in Anthropology (completing field work in Jamaica, West Indies) and a Ph.D. in the History of Consciousness. She taught courses at a number of universities in women's studies, criminology, music history and Third World studies and has published in these areas. She worked for the Peace Corps in Eritrea, East Africa; in California, she coordinated programmes in community schooling, women's studies, cross-cultural field studies and prison education. Since 1982 Karlene has been at Simon Fraser University (British Columbia) as Distance Education Coordinator for the School of Criminology, where she also teaches courses on women and criminal justice. She is the mother of four grown children and has one grandchild.

The desire for education... is a desire which springs from no conceit of cleverness, from no ambitions of the prizes of intellectual success as it is sometimes falsely imagined, but from the conviction that for many women to get knowledge is the only way to get bread, and still more from the instinctive craving for light which in many is stronger than the craving for bread (Josephine Butler, 1868).

Introduction

The challenges encountered by women within the distance education enterprise reflect universal educational inequities, which will be discussed in this introductory chapter. Approximately two-thirds of the world's illiterate adult population are women (UNESCO, 1984), and even in countries with a high literacy level women are significantly underrepresented in positions of educational authority. In most countries, curriculum development, instructional design and methodology, administration and textbook authorship are conducted primarily from the perspectives of male educators. At the primary school level 52% of the world's teachers are female (Taylor, 1985:77), but principals, superintendents and others in decision- and policy-making positions, at all levels of schooling, are predominantly male (Sexton, 1976:58; Acker and Piper, 1984; Sivard, 1985:21; Shakeshaft, 1986). School enrolments and educational attainment levels, as reported in a 1985 world survey, indicate a continuation of the biases against females, with a disturbing increase in the imbalances:

> In 1950 there were 27 million more boys than girls enrolled in primary and secondary levels of education; currently there are 80 million more boys than girls enrolled....In developing countries two-thirds of the women over the age of 25 (and about half the men) have never been to school (Sivard, 1985:5).

Student enrolments in many industrialized nations are now evenly balanced from elementary school through undergraduate university study. However, female participation at the graduate level declines sharply, and females commonly constitute fewer than 15% of all tenured university faculty positions (Roberts, 1984:7). Thus, even when the persevering female student succeeds in completing a Master's or Doctorate degree, she remains, to use Virginia Woolf's parlance, an Outsider (1938:106).

Conventionally, the historical exclusion of women from the respected ranks of the academy is blamed on women: women are deficient in natural intellectual ability; women are temperamentally unstable, and they lack motivation; women's domestic preoccupations preclude public life; and so on (see, for example, Newman, 1985 and Shapiro, 1987). Such perceptions of women were crystallized in the teachings of virtually all major religions and were further legitimized by the philosophical underpinnings of global political systems, aided and abetted even by great revolutionary thinkers such as Jean-Jacques Rousseau. In 1762, he wrote a critique of eighteenth-century schooling practices in which he proposed many of the ideas that were later to permeate progressive models of education in Europe and in North America. And while Rousseau surely advanced the necessity of a student-centred approach to teaching, he failed entirely to grasp the contradictions between his liberationist theories on the one hand and his teleological view of female destiny on the other. To wit:

> The whole education of women ought to relate to men. To please men, to be useful to them, to make herself loved and honored by them, to raise them when young, to care for them when grown, to

counsel them, to console them, to make their lives agreeable and sweet—these are the duties of women at all times, and [these duties] ought to be taught from childhood (1979:365). Throughout history women have vigorously challenged the concept of preordained female subservience. Not until the twentieth century, however, have women been able to organize world-wide initiatives toward rectifying the imbalances. Distance education is one of the educational arenas in which women in numbers are now speaking out.

Women and Distance Education

Distance education is a global and rapidly growing phenomenon which offers formal learning opportunities to people who would not otherwise have access to schooling. Teachers and students are separated by physical distance, and the means by which they communicate range from basic print materials and the use of postal service to highly sophisticated communications technologies. In the early twentieth century, children living in isolated regions benefited from government-sponsored home study programmes as a means of achieving an education. My own grandparents, Canadian pioneers and prairie homesteaders, relied greatly on home study for the education of their twelve children, and it was my grandmother who supervised this activity. Indeed, there was pressure on girls from pioneer families to be highly literate so that they could one day, in turn, educate their own children. The importance of women to the early home study enterprise was acknowledged by the noted Australian scholar Geoffrey Bolton, in his address to the 1985 meetings of the International Council for Distance Education in Melbourne. He states:

> One side-effect of correspondence education which appears to have been less widely publicised than it deserved was its reliance on the labour of wives and mothers as supervisors and teachers. The new democracies have always tended to regard the transmission of culture as an interest for women. It was taken for granted that as the men of the household would be fully occupied with their farm duties the children's mother would accept the responsibility of organising the receipt and despatch of correspondence materials, overseeing the students to ensure that they got on with their assignments diligently and regularly, and in general fitting in the role of surrogate monitors with the thousand and one tasks of a busy pioneer wife. Few mothers had previous teaching experience of any kind and many had limited formal education. It would not have been surprising if in the process

of helping their children with their education many mothers experienced some stimulus to their own intellectual interests (Bolton, 1986:17-18).

Geographic distance from educational institutions is no longer the single motivation for entering a distance education programme. Adults whose employment demands and/or family responsibilities preclude school attendance make up a major share of distance education enrolments. People who prefer guided or tutored independent study to classroom attendance likewise turn to distance education programmes. However, as the papers in this volume attest, adult distance learners more often share the single fact of having enrolled in a home study programme as the only or as the most viable option for advancing their education. And whereas in the past home study was perceived as inferior to "real" schooling, developments in recent decades of high-quality study materials, access to external library services, increasing sophistication in tutorial methods and myriad uses of technology have significantly advanced both the quality, we believe, and the reputation, certainly, of distance education. Economy and flexibility continue to be the most obvious characteristics of home study, but this method is no longer assumed to be less effective than classroom learning (see, for example, Daniel *et al.*, 1982). Over four hundred institutions in sixty-one countries now offer home study in twenty-six languages, serving over two million people in accredited programmes ranging from basic literacy to post-graduate studies (plenary session, ICDE, August 14, 1985, Melbourne).

The high level of enrolment by women in many home study programmes world-wide in part reflects the still-prevalent assumption that a woman's place is in the home. And whereas female students are commonly employed at least parttime, a significant share of them are indeed homemakers. For example, a study of enrolments at the Open University in England found that in 1975 women represented 42% of all new enrolments, and one-third of these women were occupationally self-defined as Housewife (McIntosh, 1976:vi-vii). The determination of such women to expand their knowledge and gain new skills is testimony to the global perception that females need and deserve to be educated no less than their brothers. Whether or not they get married and whether or not they become mothers, women are insisting as never before that their exclusion from educational domains is unacceptable.

This book documents case studies of the incremental progress in a number of distance education programmes in various countries.

Based on distance education literature, conference attendance and informal observation we can estimate that as many as a third of all distance educators globally are female. Student enrolments in distance education vary, but females constitute the majority in many programmes. The purpose of presenting these papers and case studies is primarily to document selected examples of women's contributions to and female participation within distance education. We are also concerned with how our presence is relevant to education in the larger context. We hope that this international forum will generate more discussion, exchange and publications.

The Quest for Equality

Given national disparities, as identified by the contributors to this volume, we cannot generalize about the status of females in education. We do know that women in virtually every country are promoting equal educational opportunities for females, and that initiatives since the 1960s have occurred in Africa, Asia, Latin America and the Middle East, as well as in Europe, North America, the Pacific, India and so on (Jayawardena, 1986; Kelly and Elliott, 1982; Sivard, 1986; Smock, 1981; Thomson, 1986). We also know, however, that in most countries females are still undereducated— relative both to males and to their own needs. Even in countries which show a commitment to providing more access to education for girls and women, much work remains to be done to improve the quality of education. The question has been raised as follows: "Does education enable women to widen their roles beyond the household, mitigating the impact of marriage, childbearing, and child rearing on women's participation and status in social, economic, and political life?" (Kelly and Elliott, 1982).

Global societal demands for democratization have accelerated in recent decades and, notwithstanding clear differentials of opportunity according to class position and other structural inequities, women in all parts of the world have awakened to the discriminations they have suffered simply because they are female. Whether they enter a study programme for personal enhancement or to improve their employment opportunities, the large numbers of women returning to school via distance education signify the importance of this learning mode as a means for women to expand their horizons.

The goals of social, economic and political empowerment are implicit in struggles for liberation. Whereas structural changes in power imbalances require major challenges to the status quo, on an individual basis "liberation" is often perceived as achievable through education. The rhetoric (if not always the reality) of western nations which prize individualism has traditionally emphasized that education is the ticket to success: that is, occupational choice, increased income and higher status. Educators in developing nations have likewise posited education as the route toward both individual advancement and constructive social change. Clearly education is no guarantee against poverty, social injustice and powerlessness, and wherever these exist women and children suffer the most. (See, for example, Sidel, 1986; Sivard, 1985; Thomson, 1986). Yet, to organize effectively against these conditions, education is universally perceived as essential.

Given this widespread confidence in education, it is not surprising that so many women have turned to it in an effort to improve their lives. Increased access to basic adult education programmes, vocational programmes and academic study through distance education reinforce this belief that individuals, and even whole societies, can transcend inherited limits through increased knowledge. Despite the undeniable drawbacks of many affirmative action admission and hiring policies, the effort to increase participation by women and other political minority groups conveys the clear message that to qualify as a democracy a society must give equal educational (and employment) opportunity to all members.

The ideal of equal opportunity is not, however, as straightforward as it might seem. To some it indicates a commitment to equal access to the existing system; to others it signifies a challenge to that system. Certainly, as many scholars have discussed at length, "equal" does not translate as "identical" (see especially Ayim, 1986, and Weiner, 1986). Fennema and Ayer convincingly argue that equal access to a male-biased education cannot be construed as an advance for women and that instead of calling for equality in education we should be seeking equity—allowing for curriculum diversity which addresses the needs of various student constituencies and which takes socially inherited inequities into account (Fennema and Ayer, 1984). Jane L. Thompson states unequivocally:

> It is not merely a question of improving the chances of women to compete in a man's world...but to demand a radical change in the nature of what is being offered. This implies at least an equal share in its control, at least an equal share in the determination of what

counts as valuable knowledge within it, and at least an equal recognition that what is important about women's experience of the world is as valid as men's. Without such *real* equalities, notions of "equality of opportunity" are essentially rhetorical (1983:93).

Each of the contributors to this volume is a distance educator who recognizes that women's status can be measured in part by their degree of access to education, even though educational attainment does not necessarily translate into equitable economic returns either in developing countries (Smock, 1981) or in those that are highly industrialized. In Canada, for example, the numbers of women enrolled in undergraduate education actually exceeds that of men (CCLOW, 1986a); however, the wage gap between men and women in Canada is greater than in any other industrialized nation except Japan (CCLOW, 1986b:7). As several chapters emphasize, male distance students are typically motivated by the expectation of greater occupational advantages. Many female students, on the other hand, are more likely to select courses for general interest, with little confidence that their newly acquired knowledge will significantly enhance their employment or promotion opportunities. This lack of confidence is related to class as well as to gender. In defining theoretical parameters within which women's lower status can be examined relative to education, Arlene McLaren succinctly sums up the dilemma:

> In class-structured societies, it is argued, schools are crucial in ensuring that children inherit the class positions of their families. Similarly, it is claimed in gender-structured societies, education is crucial in ensuring that males achieve positions of greater economic rewards, power, prestige and authority than females (1985:61).

The issues of gender and class are inseparable for women, given that a woman's class position is generally determined by her father's or husband's status and income. The reality that the vast majority of the world's females are dependent on resources acquired through and/or controlled by males is a commonplace explanation for the perpetuation of female subordination. Further, as Audrey Smock remarks in her cross-cultural study of women in education:

> It seems likely that the more pronounced the inequities in income distribution, the more highly stratified the society...and the more traditional the basis for social differentiation, the poorer the educational prospects would be for the majority of women, over and above the disadvantages they share with males from lower social and economic strata (1981:15).

Thus, women are caught in double (or triple) jeopardy: even when as individuals they overcome systemic economic (and/or racial) barriers, they still remain subject to those barriers that are engendered by sex discrimination.

Strategies for organizing against class disparities generally focus on male-dominated labour market issues or questions of foreign imperialism and only peripherally address issues of sexism (Yates, 1986; Sargent, 1981). The struggle for women's liberation, on the other hand, has been informed not only by the oppressive conditions of women's lives but also by a recognition that economic, racial, sexual and all other structural forms of discrimination against powerless groups are inherent in a patriarchal model of social organization. The revolutionary goal, therefore, is not merely to alleviate women's suffering just to the point at which their misery balances that of the men in their status group; rather, it is to challenge effectively the very foundations of status differentials. Educators may exaggerate the potential role of education in this process toward genuine democracy; knowledge and understanding do not necessarily lead to concerted social action. However, it is surely relevant, as Paulo Freire demonstrated so brilliantly, that education which encourages a critical consciousness can be a first step toward human liberation (1972). Indeed, it is almost routine within developing countries that at the inception of national independence women have fought for the right to be educated as a primary expression of female emancipation (Jayawardena, 1986). It is at this stage that, for many women, the question of how to combine study with mothering, homemaking and, often, an outside job, becomes problematic. For such women who are determined to advance their formal education, home study may be the only option.

The Student at Home

Women who enrol in distance education programmes, including those who are employed, commonly cite their responsibilities as mothers of young children as their reason for choosing home study. As increasing numbers of women enter the paid work force from necessity, the need for high-quality universal childcare facilities becomes indisputable. However, this need has not been met. In most countries it is expected that mothers will be somehow always home with their children, even if they must be employed to support them. Countries engaged in educational reform commonly introduce courses specifically for women on family care and nutrition, with the straightforward implications that 1) women have a sex-bound responsibility for these domestic activities, and 2) women do not share with men the same need for knowledge and skills required by public life or the paid labour force. Such sex-specific curriculum, based on gender-role traditions, may advance family health, which must be the first priority. However, it will not advance the fundamental struggle for equality. Ultimately, neither justice in the abstract nor a concrete commitment to human development can be seen as a priority within an approach to education which exclusively delegates females to the least socially empowering activities.

The conflict that many women experience between their need and desire to care for their families and their need to study, both for personal fulfillment and for job-related purposes, is particularly poignant for the single mother whose children are dependent on her earning capabilities. Even in two-parent families, with both adults working outside the home, the mother is expected to assume primary responsibility for children and housekeeping. Many women attempt to re-educate their husbands as to the fundamental inequity in such arrangements, apparently with little success. Moreover, husbands sometimes actively oppose their wives' efforts to gain an education. Although it is likely that most men, as well as women, are supportive of their spouse's educational aspirations, several female adult students have reported to me that their mates have refused to accommodate their need for quiet study time. Colleagues tell me about extreme cases where women's husbands have hidden or damaged their study materials and assignments in efforts to sabotage their educational ambitions. (I have never heard of a case where a woman did this to her husband; however, although it would be structurally anomalous, we cannot presume this does not happen.)

Related to the problems of family-responsibility imbalances, women often identify a need for more contact with others in similar circumstances. In this book, several authors address the issue of a support system and show how a number of distance education programmes have created opportunities for student interaction.

Female distance educators often feel isolated too. The 1985 meetings of the International Council for Distance Education (ICDE), held in Melbourne, Australia, were attended by almost 600 distance educators from over 60 countries. Under the inspired leadership of

Liz Burge, more than half of the approximately 150 women in attendance at this conference gathered at several meetings to meet each other and to strengthen the ICDE Women's International Network. The recognition, voiced in Melbourne, that women in the same profession need to increase communication with one another *as women* strengthened our resolve to develop this first book on women in distance education.

Feminist Perspectives

The contributors to this volume represent thirteen nations and a wide range of priorities as distance educators, yet all are concerned with the planning of curricula which not only respect female interests and experience but also challenge gender-dichotomous role and value systems, which place *de facto* limitations on girls' aspirations and expectations. Public education in many countries, for as long as a century, has demanded that girls shall have the same learning opportunities as boys. However, both the overt and the hidden curricula have issued clear messages that it is boys, not girls, who are being trained to conduct the world's business (Chisholm and Holland, 1986); girls only need to learn how to cook, clean and care for babies and other people. The basic premises of public education continue to reflect patriarchal imperatives. In 1978, Dorothy Smith, an oft-quoted Canadian scholar, articulated the problem as follows:

> Women have largely been excluded from the work of producing the forms of thought and the images and symbols in which thought is expressed and ordered. There is a circle effect. Men attend to and treat as significant what men say. The circle of men whose writing and talk was significant to each other extends backwards in time as far as our records reach. What men were doing was relevant to men, was written by men about men for men. Men listened and listen to what one another said....This is how a tradition is formed (1978:281).

The uses of language, definitions of meaning, construction and deconstruction of paradigms, underlying epistemological assumptions, interpretations of history, theory-making and practical learning methodologies have all been transmitted, within the diverse range of cultural and national contexts, through male-dominated conduits of judgement. Into this solid mass of patriarchal authority and tradition, twentieth-century feminists (including some males) have ventured—with some trepidation and considerable courage. Notable among such individuals is Dale Spender. In response to

Naming the Problem

those who take an individualistic and ahistorical view of feminist social analyses and who, therefore, feel personally and unfairly accused of perpetrating travesties against women in education, her comments are relevant.

Feminists have come to appreciate that the invisibility of women is not a problem of individual male historians or philosophers conducting a personal campaign to keep women out of their respective disciplines (although such individuals can still be found) but a *structural problem* which has been built into the production of knowledge. Because it has been primarily men who have determined the parameters, who have decided what would be problematic, significant, logical and reasonable, not only have women been excluded from the process *but the process itself can reinforce the 'authority' of men and the 'deficiency' of women* (1981:2).

Not every contributor to this book would identify as a feminist, given the political connotations and the negative stereotypes so often attached to that word. And yet, these educators are describing radical alternatives to the educational status quo. They are devising innovative approaches to doing their work, leading us toward new ways of learning and educating within inherited structures, asking questions that until recently would have been considered heretical, and leading us toward new horizons.

Whereas distance education curricula, as in conventional schooling, continue to be dominated by patriarchal constructions of knowledge, models for change are in the making. The architects of these changes no longer acquiesce to traditional assumptions about what must be taught, how it must be taught, or to whom. They gauge truth not only in terms of what is "proven" but also in terms of what is possible, assuming that truth must include experiential and subjective realities as well as objective and quantifiable data. They recognize that the practice of handing down one objective "truth" is both arrogant and limiting. In fact, they no longer uncritically accept "objectivity," as traditionally defined, as a viable concept (Spender, 1981:5-8). In this regard, Adrienne Rich quotes from filmmaker Michelle Clinton: "The culture assumes in general, that male films (read art, journalism, scholarship, etc.) are objective and female films are subjective; male subjectivity is still perceived as *the objective point of view* on all things, in particular women" (1979:14).

Articulate feminists must continually face the charge that their work is "biased," not objective, because their observations and analyses often include advocacy and perspectives drawn from personal experience. Individuals who are commited to preserving the status quo are surely likewise biased, whether or not they are prepared to recognize or acknowledge it. (This would include all those who ignore research that focuses on women, because they find the subject "too limiting"; such critics are apparently oblivious to the irony in this judgement.) The problem here involves not just the collection of accurate facts but also their interpretation and implementation: what Spender calls the "politics of knowledge" (1981:7).

In 1973, in the United States, a major report on women in higher education was conducted by the prominent Carnegie Commission on Higher Education. Presented at a time when little research had been done in this area, the report confirmed the negative situation experienced by women in higher education and gave impetus to institutions for making needed changes. Reflective of that need was the fact that of the nineteen esteemed members of the Commission, only two were female (Carnegie, 1973:viii). By the late 1980s, the voice of authority concerning women's predicament has shifted to those who are the subject of their own research. In the past half-decade, particularly in England and North America, many women writers have exhorted educators to examine masculinist or patriarchal traditions as they affect learning and teaching in primary and secondary schools, adult education, colleges and universities, and vocational training. This literature is a direct outgrowth of the development of feminist theory over the past two decades. It also reflects on the considerable skills and energies that women have used to establish new presses, organize conferences, design curricula, build programmes and associations—in short, to show that if women are to be included in the educational enterprise in a meaningful way, that enterprise must be transformed (see, for example, Bowles, 1984, and Spender, 1981).

But the transformation is complex and problematic. Peggy McIntosh (1984:26) identifies a "sequence of thinking" related to the History discipline that shows the complexity of this transformational process:

Phase 1: Womanless History;
Phase 2: Women in History;
Phase 3: Women as a Problem, Anomaly, or Absence in History;
Phase 4: Women as History;
Phase 5: History Reconstructed, Redefined, and Transformed to include us all.

This intellectual heritage first disregards the fact of female existence then identifies those few famous women who are included in history as relevant by virtue of being exceptional. Next it acknowledges female existence as a problem, a deviance or as irrelevant and, in effect, absent. Then the balance is turned on its head, with a feminist recognition that women have at all times been central players in human development. And finally, we have the challenge presented to us in its fullest dimension, whereby we search for means by which humanity can locate our wholeness as a species.

* * *

A horizon, according to Webster's dictionary, is "the apparent junction of earth and sky, from the observer's perspective." We can also think of it as a symbolic line separating the ideal from the reality. Our distance education horizons can reflect transformations and new partnerships if we change our attitudes toward and processes of knowledge and learning. Those who have been denied their history on the bases of sex, race, class and other categories of suppression and subordination would stand strongly together on the new horizon. The ultimate and radical result would be the eradication of systemic and categorical power imbalances and a fuller development of the human capacity for excellence.

> Elitism and oppression are both incompatible with excellence. Excellence emerges neither from already knowing everything nor from not knowing anything but rather from a trust in the possibility of finding out....Excellence could be defined as clearly communicated discoveries which have consequences for thought, feeling, behavior and society....One could define liberation work as the breakdown of elitism and oppression in the world between all peoples....Liberation and knowledge are not only compatible but interdependent. [Education] can offer relevant resources for the liberation of women and...the liberation of women is essential to humanizing our knowedge (Peterson, 1982:84-85).

References and Selected Bibliography

Acker, Sandra et al. (Eds.). (1984). *World Yearbook of Education 1984: Women in Education.* New York: Kogan Page.

Acker, Sandra and David W. Piper. (Eds.). (1984). *Is Higher Education Fair to Women?* Guildford, Surrey: SRHE and NFER-Nelson.

Ayim, Maryann. (1986). "Women's Rights: A Seamstress' Analysis." *Canadian Journal of Education,* 11(3), 215-30.

Bleier, Ruth. (1984). *Science and Gender: A Critique of Biology and its Theories on Women.* New York: Pergamon Press.

Bolton, Geoffrey. (1986). "The Opportunities of Distance." In *Flexible Designs for Learning: Report of the Thirteenth World Conference of the International Council for Distance Education* (pp.13-23). Melbourne: La Trobe University.

Bowles, Gloria. (1984). "The Uses of Hermeneutics for Feminist Scholarship." *Women's Studies International Forum,* 7(3), 185-88.

Butler, Josephine. (1868). *Education and the Employment of Women* (pp. 7-8). London: Macmillan, quoted in Cheris Kramarae and Paula A. Treichler. (1985). *The Feminist Dictionary* (p. 134). Boston: Pandora Press.

Carnegie Commission on Higher Education. (1973). *Opportunities for Women in Higher Education: Their Current Participation, Prospects for the Future, and Recommendations for Action.* New York: McGraw-Hill.

CCLOW. (1986a). *Decade of Promise: An Assessment of Canadian Women's Status in Education Training and Employment, 1976-1985.* Toronto: Canadian Congress for Learning Opportunities for Women.

CCLOW. (1986b). "Women's Education and Labour Force Participation: Canada and OECD Countries." Toronto: Canadian Congress for Learning Opportunities for Women.

Chisholm, Lynne A. and Janet Holland. (1986). "Girls and Occupational Choice: Anti-sexism in Action in a Curriculum Development Project." *British Journal of Sociology of Education,* 7(4), 353-65.

Daniel, John S., Martha A. Stroud and John R. Thompson. (Eds.). (1982). *Learning at a Distance: A World Perspective.* Edmonton: Athabasca University/ICDE.

Fennema, Elizabeth and M. Jane Ayer. (Eds.). (1984). *Women and Education: Equity or Equality.* Berkeley: McCutcheon.

Fowlkes, Diane L. and Charlotte S. McClure. (Eds.). (1984). *Feminist Visions: Toward A Transformation of the Liberal Arts Curriculum.* Tuscaloosa: University of Alabama Press.

Freire, Paulo. (1972). *Pedagogy of the Oppressed*. N. Y.: Herder and Herder.

Gardiner, Jean. (1986). "Working with Women." In Kevin Ward and Richard Taylor. (Eds.). *Adult Education and the Working Class: Education for the Missing Millions*. Wolfeboro, New Hampshire: Croom Helm.

Hutchinson, Enid and Edward Hutchinson. (1986). *Women Returning to Learning*. Cambridge: National Extension College.

Janeway, Elizabeth. (1980). *Powers of the Weak*. New York: Alfred Knopf.

Jayawardena, Kumari. (1986). *Feminism and Nationalism in the Third World*. London: Zed Books.

Kelly, Gail P. and Carolyn M. Elliott. (Eds.). (1982). *Women's Education in the Third World: Comparative Perspectives*. Albany, New York: State University of New York Press.

Komarovsky, Mirra. (1985). *Women in College: Shaping New Feminine Identities*. New York: Basic Books.

McIntosh, Naomi E., with Judith A. Calder and Betty Swift. (1976). *A Degree of Difference*. University of Surrey: Society for Research into Higher Education.

McIntosh, Peggy. (1984). "Interactive Phases of Curricular Re-Vision." In Bonnie Spanier, Alexander Bloom and Darlene Boroviak. (Eds.). *Toward a Balanced Curriculum: A Sourcebook for Initiating Gender Integration Projects*. Cambridge, Mass.: Schenkman Publishing Company.

McLaren, Arlene T. (1985). *Ambitions and Realizations: Women in Adult Education*. London: Peter Owen.

Newman, Louise Michele. (Ed.). (1985). *Men's Ideas/Women's Realities: Popular Science, 1870-1915*. New York: Pergamon Press.

Peterson, Gail. (1982). "The Struggle of an Academic Feminist: Elitism versus Excellence." *Women's Studies International Forum*, 5(1), 83-85.

Rich, Adrienne. (1979). "Toward a Woman-Centered University." In *On Lies, Secrets and Silence*. New York: W.W. Norton.

Roberts, Joan I. (1984). "Assimilation or Integration: The Woman Student, Women's Studies and the Transmission of Women's World View." *National Women's Studies Newsletter*, 2(3).

Rousseau, Jean-Jacques. (1979; originally published 1762). *Emile (or On Education)*. Translated by Allan Bloom. New York: Basic Books.

Sargent, Lydia. (1981). *Women and Revolution*. Montreal: Black Rose.

Schuster, Marilyn R. and Susan R. Van Dyne. (Eds.). (1985). *Women's Place in the Academy: Transforming the Liberal Arts Curriculum*. Totowa, New Jersey: Rowman and Allanheld.

Sexton, Patricia. (1976). *Women in Education*. Bloomington, Indiana: Phi Delta Kappa Educational Foundation.

Shakeshaft, Charol. (1986). *Women in Educational Administration*. Beverly Hills, California: Sage Publications.

Shapiro, Joan Poliner. (1987). "Women in Education: At Risk or Prepared?" *The Educational Forum, 51*(2), 167-83.

Sidel, Ruth. (1986). *Women and Children Last*. New York: Viking Press.

Sivard, Ruth Leger. (1985). *Women...A World Survey*. Washington, D.C.: World Priorities.

Smith, Dorothy. (1978). "A Peculiar Eclipsing: Women's Exclusion from Man's Culture." *Women's Studies International Quarterly, 1*(4), 281-96.

Smock, Audrey C. (1981). *Women's Education in Developing Countries: Opportunities and Outcomes*. New York: Praeger Publishers.

Spender, Dale. (1980). *Man Made Language*. London: Routledge and Kegan Paul.

Spender, Dale. (Ed.). (1981). *Men's Studies Modified: The Impact of Feminism on the Academic Disciplines*. Oxford: Pergamon Press.

Spender, Dale. (1982). *Invisible Women: The Schooling Scandal*. London: Writers and Readers Publishing Cooperative Society.

Spender, Dale. (Ed.). (1983). *Feminist Theorists: Three Centuries of Women's Intellectual Traditions*. London: The Women's Press.

Spender, Dale and Elizabeth Sarah. (Eds.). (1980). *Learning to Lose: Sexism and Education*. London: The Women's Press.

Taylor, Debbie. (Ed.). (1985). "Women: An Analysis—Education." In *Women: A World Report* (pp. 70-80). London: Methuen.

Thompson, Jane L. (1983). *Learning Liberation: Women's Response to Men's Education*. London and Canberra: Croom Helm.

Thomson, Aisla. (1986). *The Decade for Women*. Toronto: Canadian Congress for Learning Opportunities for Women.

UNESCO. (1984). "Statistical Yearbook." Paris: UNESCO.

Weiner, Gaby. (1986). "Feminist Education and Equal Opportunities: Unity or Discord?" *British Journal of Sociology of Education, 7*(3), 265-74.

Woolf, Virginia. (1938). *Three Guineas*. N. Y.: Harcourt, Brace and World.

Yates, Lyn. (1986). "Theorising Inequality Today." *British Journal of Sociology of Education, 7*(2), 119-34.

THE GENDER FACTOR
IN
DISTANCE EDUCATION

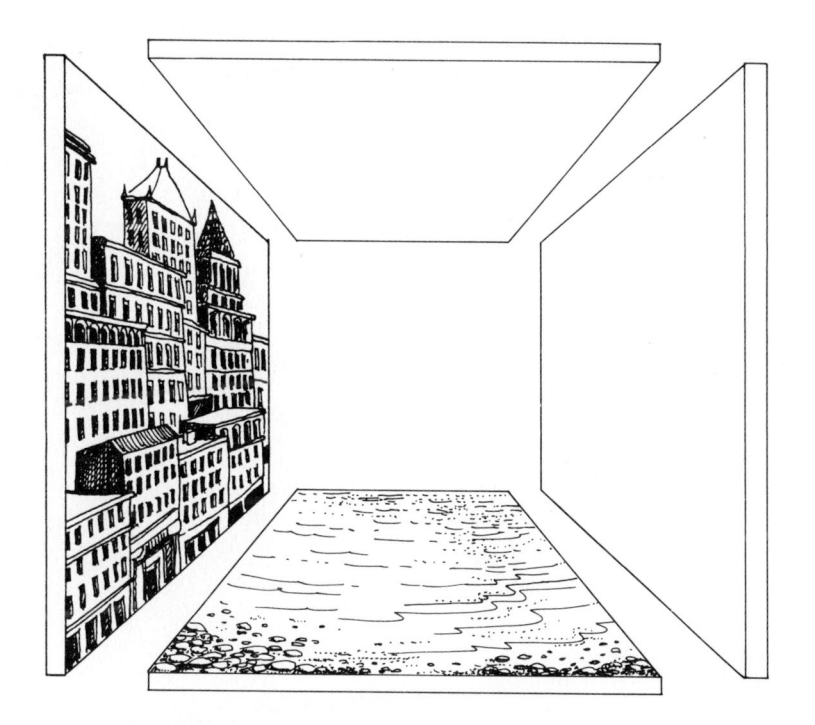

Editor's Introduction

Given that British Columbia hosted the first international meetings of distance educators, in 1938, and the first meetings of the Women's International Network (WIN), in 1982, it may be fitting that this first collection of articles by women in distance education was compiled in this Canadian province. In Chapter 2, to open this section, June Sturrock contributes an overview of women in distance education in B.C. She acknowledges both the advances that have been made toward validating the active presence of females in the provincial distance education enterprise and the obstacles that remain. Her discussion covers course development and delivery, the activity of professionals in various institutions who are expanding learning opportunities for women, and the students for whom these initiatives have direct relevance. In both her descriptive detail and the analysis she brings to her discussion, Sturrock conveys optimism that within British Columbia female students can expect increasing responsiveness to their distance learning needs. That optimism is based on work accomplished to date and, even more, on the sustained commitment to all students which Sturrock and many of her distance education colleagues in B.C. are demonstrating.

* * *

Females commonly constitute close to half of total enrolments in distance education programmes, for reasons discussed in a number of chapters. A notable exception is the FernUniversität in West Germany, a distance education university where females are a distinct minority. As discussed in Chapter 3, Christine von Prümmer and Ute Rossié have conducted an extensive survey among FernUniversität students to determine the effects of gender on course selection, including family and occupational factors.

Using an effective blend of survey data, analyses and comments from students, their study offers valuable perspectives for educators who are breaking out of gender stereotyping in curriculum planning. Rossié's and von Prümmer's findings can serve as a reference base for studies of other programmes.

* * *

Yael Enoch, of Israel, writes of another single mode distance education university—this one named (ironically, for our purposes) Everyman's University (EU), which serves 7,000 students per semester. In Chapter 4, Enoch discusses the issue of gender tracking in higher education in Israel, whereby females are not expected to advance their professional credentials beyond occupations considered appropriate for women. Her study reveals that female students generally enter EU with a higher previous educational attainment level than male students and they also earn higher marks. Significantly, in this regard, whereas most female students at EU make traditional course choices, avoiding mathematics and sciences, those women who do enrol in these nontraditional subjects outperform the male students. This point underscores the argument that female underrepresentation in math and science cannot be explained in terms of inherent sex-based limitations.

* * *

In Chapter 5 we travel to New Zealand, where Jeanne Macaskill has developed a unique approach to teaching art at a distance. Macaskill attributes the programme's success to the direct, personal encouragement which students receive; she identifies a lack of self-confidence as a key characteristic among women entering the programme and stresses the importance of building their confidence as a component of skill development. This emphasis on and validation of the subjective elements of education can be interpreted as typically "female"—given that females, in particular, have been traditionally socialized to acknowledge feelings and develop nurturant attitudes. Macaskill's work alerts us to the universal problems generated by teachers, female or male, who fail to take students' feelings into account, who consider emotional factors to be outside the purview of professional educators, or who lack the interpersonal skills to respond appropriately to students' needs.

* * *

The benefits of offering emotional support to students is a theme that is commonly expressed by educators seeking more holistic approaches to their interactions with students. Birgitta Willén, of Sweden, considers this theme in Chapter 6 in her study of distance education as it affects students' self-esteem. She points out that the social expectation that women will take full responsibility for family care "impedes their goals outside the domestic arena." Domestic responsibilities limit women's access to resources or institutions which could facilitate their extra-familial interests, and this, in turn, has the effect of limiting both women's aspirations and their sense of self-worth. Distance education is one means by which homemakers can reconcile their conflicting needs. Willén found that increased self-esteem was particularly evident among female students who began their studies in middle age. Increased knowledge, positive interactions with teachers and other distance learners, and expanded understanding of the value of higher education were identified as primary factors in gaining self-confidence. As Willén suggests, this confidence serves as an asset not only to the individual but also to society at large and to the processes of social change on which theories of equality are contingent.

* * *

This section begins with an overview of women in distance education on Canada's west coast and it ends, in Chapter 7, with a discussion of programmes on the east coast of Canada. Three authors, Diana R. Carl, Erin M. Keough and Lorraine Y. Bourque, present descriptions of their respective programmes and the challenges they face as distance educators, sharing in common a commitment to the uses of technology to expand learning opportunities. By virtue of their command over the various technologies, they serve as inspiration to women who may have well-conditioned fears of entering the technical realms of education.

In the first portion of Chapter 7, Carl describes her work at Mount Saint Vincent University in Nova Scotia, Canada's first women's university; although it became co-educational in 1971, the majority of students are still female. This university is also unique in that it uses television to bring classroom and distance students together in their study process. Further, there has not been a need at Mount Saint Vincent University to persuade colleagues of the importance of women's issues—a challenge commonly experienced in conventional institutions.

In her discussion of programmes at Memorial University in Newfoundland, Canada's most easterly province, Keough describes a number of initiatives of relevance to women. Memorial's Division of Extension has given priority to community development, including programmes supportive of women's employment and cultural interests. Notable among Memorial's accomplishments has been the acclaimed Telemedicine network, coordinated by Keough, which offers continuing education to health professionals in isolated areas.

In this chapter, one is easily impressed with the spirit of innovation characterizing women-centred programming in eastern Canada; Bourque reinforces this impression in her discussion of the work at the Université de Moncton in New Brunswick. This institution was "almost exclusively" male when it opened in 1963; now over half the graduates are female. This change wasn't happenstance but rather the consequence of administrators, notably the author herself, who facilitated the development of parttime programmes of special interest to women, utilizing teleconferencing and television to increase women's access to university study. As many as three-quarters of the university's distant learners are female, many of them re-entry students, and women have been the driving force in meeting the challenges of communications technology at this university.

* * *

From the chapters in this section we can conclude that women are indeed in the vanguard of identifying components of distance education—enrolment patterns, programme initiatives, curriculum planning, course delivery, and student support services—which illuminate the gender factor. – K.F.

― Chapter 2 ―

CANADA: THE WEST COAST

by

June Sturrock

June Sturrock, Ph.D., Programme Director of Course Development at Simon Fraser University's Centre for Distance Education, has lived in Vancouver for eighteen years. She has published papers on Shakespeare, Samuel Richardson, Wordsworth, Charlotte Yonge and Iris Murdoch, as well as on distance education, and she is presently completing a book entitled *Daughters of the Church: Conflicting Attitudes to Women in the Novels of Charlotte M. Yonge*. She is a publishing poet and has two daughters.

Author's Note: I should like to thank all the people who have provided information for this chapter, especially Catherine Kerr of the Open Learning Institute, Beverley Gropen and Garth Luck of the University of British Columbia, staff members of the Registrar's Office and University Extension Department at the University of Victoria, and my colleagues at Simon Fraser University, especially Karlene Faith.

Introduction

I recently managed to bring a little sunshine into the life of one of my British Columbian colleagues. While preparing this chapter, I phoned her to ask whether her institution (which shall be nameless) had a policy on non-sexist language. Her laughter lasted some time, but her answer, when it came, was brief enough: "Here?" she asked incredulously.

Evidently, then, in British Columbia as elsewhere, a strong resistance to change persists throughout all levels of the teaching profession, a resistance that is occasionally quite deliberate but usually no more than half-conscious. However, this Canadian province of mountains, islands, inlets, inaccessible communities and vast, chilly distances has, for these obvious geographical reasons, frequently been in the vanguard of change in distance education. This chapter deals with the effects of changing attitudes towards women in university distance education in B.C., in relation to distance education students, programme content, course content and style, and the professional concerns of women working in distance education.

British Columbian students of all ages and types are served by distance education administered by a wide range of institutions. For example, the provincial Ministry of Education deals with thousands of elementary and high school students: in 1982 its Correspondence Branch was described as "the largest elementary/secondary school in the province, with an approximate annual enrolment of 17,000 students" (Ruggles et al., 1982:18). The British Columbia Institute of Technology enrolled about 3,500 students in directed study courses in 1981. North Island College serves students throughout approximately 30,000 square miles on northern Vancouver Island and the adjacent mainland and is "the only non-campus based community college in Canada" (ibid., p.22); Emily Carr College of Art and Design also has a developing and innovative distance education programme. The Open Learning Institute (OLI), as well as offering university level courses, deals with Adult Basic Education, while the Knowledge Network of the West (KNOW) transmits educational television by satellite to learners of all ages and levels. These various distance education programmes, and numerous others as well, represent a concerted effort by educators to make formal study opportunities available to all British Columbian residents, extending to and including university-level education, which is the focus of this chapter.

In British Columbia, all three universities—the University of British Columbia (UBC), Simon Fraser University (SFU) and the University of Victoria (UVic)—offer courses through distance education. UBC has a Guided Independent Study programme organized through its Access Office; SFU's Centre for Distance Education comes under its Office of Continuing Studies; and UVic's distance education courses are offered by its Department of University Extension. OLI's University division operates entirely through distance learning, while the Knowledge Network also provides programming for university-level students who are taking courses through any of these four institutions. Since 1984, the institutions have been working together through the Open University Consortium of British Columbia (OUCBC). Women at all these institutions are concerned with distance education — as students, educators, instructional designers, administrators, advisers, artists and support staff.

Programme and Course Content

> It is quite clear that the universities and the intellectual establishment intend to keep women's experiences as far as possible invisible and women's studies a barely subsidized, condescendingly tolerated ghetto. The majority of women who go through undergraduate and graduate school suffer an intellectual coercion of which they are not even consciously aware. In a world where language and naming are power, silence is oppression, is violence. (Rich, 1979:204).

The silence of which Adrienne Rich writes so powerfully is no longer quite unbroken. Despite the generally unfavourable intellectual climate of the 1980s, a few more squeaks and even some bellows are audible in some areas of post-secondary education, and among these is distance education: more tutors flinch more obviously when they hear at orientation meetings that "the student must check to see that he has all his course materials." One important way in which distance education is slowly developing into a more inclusive and equitable system is in programme and course content. This is perhaps the most significant development, since only by changing our concept of what is and what is not intellectually valid can we begin to open our eyes to a more inclusive vision of our culture, a change of mind which is important for male and female students alike.

Because women are especially likely to need the flexibility and ease of access that distance education provides, educational institutions have a special responsibility to offer the courses women will need in their professional lives. Traditional female professions, such as nursing, teaching, childcare and social work, are reasonably well served in British Columbia. OLI, UVic and UBC all offer nursing courses, which are generally delivered through print and a video component, sometimes including a live interactive component: UVic has been especially active in this area; its range of courses are 60% television, 35% print-based, and 5% other (Ruggles *et al.*, 1982:20). Several nursing courses, such as UBC's two *Professional Issues in Nursing* courses, explicitly discuss nursing as an aspect of the traditional female role and the problems inherent in a traditional "woman's profession," such as comparatively low prestige, low salaries and lack of power. UVic also offers several courses in its *Social Work B.S.W. Programme.* Perhaps the most healthy area of university distance education in B.C. is education itself. All three universities offer courses in education, and some courses deal explicitly with issues concerning women in the profession. SFU's newly developed *Social Issues in Education* course, for instance, includes a unit entitled "Standing on the Sidelines: Sexism and Inequality" (from which I stole the epigraph to this section).

Besides these professional courses, there are some interesting developments in university-level distance education courses in general. SFU, which has an active on-campus women's studies programme, offers an introductory women's studies course, *Perspectives on Women,* through its Centre for Distance Education; the course includes overviews on women in paid work, women and housework, socialization, media images of women, pornography, rape and the history of feminist thought. The author of this course, Dr. Anita Clair Fellman, also created another credit course, *History of Women in North America from 1850 to the Present,* one of the earliest distance educations courses ever offered by SFU. The print materials for this course and for *Perspectives on Women* are now also being used by Athabasca University in Alberta in their Women's Studies Programme.

In other areas, too, scholars in various fields are working to make women's experience more visible. UBC, for instance, offers a course on the *History of the American West,* which devotes a unit to the role of women in the West; similarly, its course on contemporary social problems in China includes a full discussion of the role of women in contemporary China. At SFU, the School of Criminology offers *Minorities and the Criminal Justice System,* a course which is organized into three parts, the longest of which deals with women and the criminal justice system (women, though not a minority in terms of population, are very much a minority in the criminal justice system, on both sides of the law).

The concerns and accomplishments of women are emphasized in other B.C. courses, too. For instance, a fine arts course, *Contemporary Art in Canada,* is offered jointly by OLI and the Emily Carr College of Art and Design, with television components shown on the Knowledge Network; this course discusses fully the work of many of Canada's women artists. Another truly Canadian course offered by

OLI, *Composition and Native Indian Literature,* communicates strongly the female images and modes of understanding in the novels, poems and plays it discusses. More predictably, perhaps, OLI's *Sociology of the Family* course explicitly discusses the changing roles of women in the family, and three of its eight required texts deal exclusively with women or women's traditional concerns; its students learn, for instance, to distinguish "sex" and "gender," to define patriarchal ideology, and to recognize behaviour which reinforces conventional masculine and feminine stereotypes.

Although in some fields women's experience certainly is acknowledged and honoured, many of the university-level courses offered through distance education in B.C. reflect the traditional and persistent academic blindness to women's achievements, needs and perspectives. To demonstrate this fully, I would need to analyze critically dozens of courses, so I have merely drawn on a few examples, from my own original discipline. (I have not specified the institutions involved.) Students can, for instance, take a course on post-war British fiction without reading a single work by a woman (thus ignoring completely Muriel Spark, Doris Lessing, Iris Murdoch and half a dozen other distinguished writers); or they can choose a Modern American Fiction course which excludes women completely, or a Victorian poetry course which not only excludes women poets, but refers in its course outline to Dante Gabriel Rossetti merely as "Rossetti," thus sweeping into oblivion Dante Gabriel's sister, Christina, at least as considerable a poet. Such omissions are so much a product of traditional male-dominated cultural norms that one can easily remain desensitized to them. Educators, women and men alike, academic staff and instructional designers alike, must remain aware of this exclusion so that they do not inadvertently foster its persistence.

Finally, a note on language: all the British Columbian editors and designers consulted on this matter do their best to ensure that new or revised courses on which they work use inclusive language. As suggested at the beginning of this chapter, this is not always a matter of explicit policy. An informal survey of fifty-six post-secondary institutions across Canada, conducted in 1986 by the Association of Colleges and Universities of Canada, asked administrators at the larger insitutions "whether they have a policy of using 'gender-neutral language' in university publications." The findings were that "attempts to make calendars and university publications free from sexist language are informal, and 'very few universities have sensed a need to formalize this practice' " (*Globe and Mail*, December 31, 1986:A9). It is important to apply pressure wherever possible to change this, so that all distance educators have support when working with course authors or consultants who are wedded to what Wendy Martyna has labelled "He-Man" grammar (Rich, 1979:241). As universities seem especially resistant to change in policies, this will need considerable effort.

Students

Programme and course content, and inclusive language, represent one aspect of the university-level institutions' responsibility towards their students. But what of the students themselves, both actual and potential?

Iris Price, as president of the British Open University's Student Association, writes of the attractive flexibility of distance education:

> While I am an Open University student I am much more in control of my own education. Not only have I much more freedom to choose a wide variety of courses, crossing disciplines from year to year, should I choose to, but also determining myself the amount and level at which I study....I am the one who makes the decisions (1985:25).

The flexibility of distance learning described by Price is obviously desirable for the increasing numbers of adult learners with multiple responsibilities, regardless of sex. However, it is particularly important for women, who continue to be more likely than men to experience severe limitations on their personal time and freedom for a significant period of their adult lives.

The popular conception of the sexual division of labour may have changed in the last twenty years, but the reality remains very much the same. Indeed, the underlying joke behind popular movies like *Mr. Mom* or comic strips like *Adam* is that it is ridiculous for a man to be a housekeeper. In a recent article concerning Canadian women in education, Maryann Ayim of the University of Western Ontario writes that "until women are relieved of some responsibilities of child care and housework, it is unrealistic to expect much time or energy to be left for bettering themselves in the job or the profession" (1986:221). She bases her argument on a survey about housework conducted by the Canadian magazine *Homemakers,* using a random selection of 10% out of 2,974 completed questionnaires. She paints a gloomily convincing picture:

The amount of help and support given to married working women by their families is depressing. Whether women worked or not, husbands were reported to spend an average of 1½ hours per day with the children. Working mothers received more help with the household chores from their families, but even here much is left to be desired: "only 6 out of 10 homemakers indicated that their husbands do any specific chores around the house" (p. 36). Among part-time homemakers, two-thirds acknowledged the sharing of some duties by husbands whereas only one-half of the full-time homemakers acknowledged such help. As well, children were expected to share more of the chores of women holding jobs outside the home.

The sample questionnaires also indicated that 41% of the full-time homemakers with children and 30% of the part-time homemakers with children had no alternative arrangements for children (p. 42).

It seems possible that younger women either have been convinced that the traditional sexual division of labour is rapidly disappearing or have not realized the implications of the traditional position for women in education. A recent preliminary survey of women students, conducted in November 1986 by SFU's Centre for Distance Education, ended with the open question "Do you have any general comments on the subject of Women in Distance Education?" Twenty-two percent responded, in effect, that the advantages of distance education were not gender-specific. Interestingly, all of the women who responded in this way were single, and all but one were in the lowest age group (17-27). It is impossible to draw any certain conclusions on such a limited sample, but this preliminary survey would seem to suggest that younger, unmarried women have a different concept of female experience from their elders, although it is also possible that this difference of perception is based on generation rather than age, and that these young women will retain their optimistic view of gender relations into later life.

Enrolment statistics from a variety of sources seem to support the perception of the older women students that women especially find distance education an appropriate solution to their educational problems. The statistics of the Open University Consortium of British Columbia recorded that, in September 1986, 62.8% of students were female; in December 1985, the figure was 65.3%, numbers which correspond fairly closely with proportions reported by other institutions. UVic, for instance, reported that their distance education student population was 60% female (Ruggles *et al.*, 1982:20) and UBC reported that of the 57% of Guided Independent Study students responding to their survey between August 1983 and July 1986, 63.57% were female. These statistics should be seen in the light of statistics recorded by a 1983 survey of general adult education in Canada, which reported that "Women were more likely than men to enrol in adult education. In fact, the majority (56%) of participants were women. Their participation rate was 21% versus 17% for men. This difference held up for every age group, with the greatest gap (9 percentage points) occurring among 17-24 year olds" (Devereaux, 1984:6). Women seem to have a particular need for adult education and more specifically a need for distance education.

Distance learning creates problems as well as solving them; perhaps it would be more accurate in any case to say that it changes problems. The domestic problems caused by family members' studies are well-documented. Indeed, the perception that married bliss and adult studies are not always compatible was in part the basis of Willie Russell's popular play and film, *Educating Rita*. The reason for the use of the impersonal phrase "family member" above is that it is not always the Ritas whose education transforms their adult lives, and that husbands and fathers as well as wives and mothers may suffer from such domestic conflicts.

There is perhaps some validity in the younger students' perception of the benefits of distance education as not gender-specific, insofar as men as well as women will suffer from the conflict between family commitments and their studies. Pauline Kirk, whose original comments on the subject aroused considerable interest in the British popular press, observes that "the practical problems of a married woman student may make study more obviously stressful for her, but my research has suggested that home-based study can cause great personal strain for both sexes" (1977:20). The older women responding to the Centre for Distance Education survey seemed to feel that the "more obviously stressful" implied the more extremely stressful, but it was interesting to see how many of them spoke in positive as well as negative terms about their family situation, commenting on the importance of their husbands' support, or the help given by their children (or even simply the greater age of their children). Of those who commented on the special importance to women of distance education, 23% remarked on the supportive attitude of their families, although some qualified this by referring to other women who had suffered from family opposition to their studies. This supports the perception of Tremaine and Owen that despite popular and well-based fears about family conflicts in very many cases, children, husbands, and boyfriends are extremely proud of the student in the family and boast about her successes. One partner often encourages the other to begin studying as well and some of the most successful students are husband and wife partnerships. Relationships may even improve with shared or broader interests (1984:50).

Studies at Athabasca University would seem to support the belief that women students have greater problems; they indicate that: "women students are more likely than men students a) to feel a lack of self-confidence, b) to be concerned about how to contend with the disruption in their family lives caused by their return to university, and c) to report problems in balancing their multiple responsibilities" (Coulter *et al.,* 1983:12). Certainly this seems to accord closely with the observations of most distance educators: conscientious tutors frequently remark on the importance of fostering adult students' self-confidence in every possible way.

A more detailed study of students of both sexes in SFU's School of Criminology's Distance Education courses was undertaken in 1985, and this section concludes with an overview of some of the findings which relate to women students. One interesting comparison concerns the motivation of Criminology students:

> A large percentage of females (61%) state general interest as their primary reason for enrolling in Criminology, as compared with the males of whom 32% state general interest. The largest group of males (46%) indicate job advancement as their primary reason for study, compared to just 10% of the females (Faith, 1985:26).

However, when students are concerned only with their career goals, the proportions change significantly:

> *Primary Career Goal of Respondents.* A large percentage of males are employed in criminal justice occupations (50%), whereas just one (1.19%) female is in a criminal justice occupation. There is less disparity on the question of career aspiration: 93% of the males desire to remain and advance within, or enter, a criminal justice profession, compared with 67% of the females (of whom less than 10% have had any direct experience in criminal justice).
>
> Females expressed little interest in management careers, only 16% of those planning careers in criminal justice. Forty-six percent of the males expected or hoped to enter management. On the other hand 9% of the males and 19% of the females plan to go to law school after completing an undergraduate degree, and 7% of the females, compared to 2% of the males, intend to work toward a Master's degree. Females also constitute the total 13% of the respondents who desire a career in community services (*ibid.,* p. 28).

An interesting postscript to the survey of distance learners in Criminology is that a small number of the students in this programme are confined to prison. SFU has a well-developed prison education programme through which university courses are taught in prison classrooms. However, given the small numbers of females who are incarcerated, such classes do not exist in female institutions. Instead, women in prison who wish to study at a university level are enrolling in distance education courses. One particularly bright young woman is studying criminology with the goal of entering law school when she is released from her present confinement. Distance education in British Columbia may thus be perceived as serving rehabilitative as well as pedagogic functions.

Working in Distance Education

The numerical approach to this subject offers very few surprises. Nevertheless, this is perhaps the proper place to begin, with an overview of academic staff. SFU, like other B.C. university-level institutions, provides the students in its distance education programmes with a tutor-marker (who gives grades, makes detailed comments on assignments and provides telephone contact). A survey of sex ratios since Summer 1983 shows that sex ratios are well-balanced, sometimes with more men than women and sometimes more women than men serving as tutors.

Table 1
Sex Ratios of Tutor-Markers (percent)

Semester*	Male	Female
Summer '86	44	56
Spring '86	52	48
Fall '85	44	56
Summer '85	43	57
Spring '85	56	44
Fall '84	60	40
Summer '84	62	38
Spring '84	58	42
Fall '83	46	54
Summer '83	64	36

*Note: Despite the prevalent myth, there is NO winter in Canada.

The statistics from OLI show a similar balance; in fact, in the current semester the numbers of university-level tutor markers show a precisely 50:50 sex ratio.

The ratios change noticeably when one moves one rung higher up the ladder of prestige. Tutor-markers can be either faculty members or graduate students, but course supervisors, who are responsible for the courses they supervise as representatives of the faculty, school or department offering the course, are normally, though not invariably, faculty members. Here the preponderance of males varies from 73% to 94%.

Table 2
Sex Ratios of Course Supervisors (percent)

Semester	Male	Female
Summer '86	87.5	12.5
Spring '86	73	27
Fall '85	83	17
Summer '85	81	19
Spring '85	74	26
Fall '84	79	21
Summer '84	94	6
Spring '84	86	14
Fall '83	82	18
Summer '83	79	21

Course supervisors at SFU's Centre for Distance Education are frequently the course authors; the sex ratio of this group is at present 74% male and 26% female. Only within the Faculty of Education are the proportions balanced; exactly 50% of their course authors are female.

This brief overview should not end without some comments on the achievements of some women colleagues working fulltime as distance educators at the university level within B.C., or having some power to steer the future course of distance education in this province. The difficulty here is *embarrass de richesse:* there are so many talented and creative women in this field that omissions are inevitable.

In B.C. in 1986 we were all especially aware of women's contribution to distance education, because we had been honouring Audrey Campbell, a woman whose contribution was particularly generous, on the occasion of her retirement. Audrey worked in distance education at UBC for 17 years as the Head of its Guided Independent Study Program. She is well-known outside B.C., and outside Canada, too, because of her excellent performance as host for UBC of the International Council for Correspondence Education (now

International Council for Distance Education, ICDE) World Conference in 1982, and also because at that conference she played an important role in steering the newly formed ICDE's Women's International Network. Moreover, this year (1986-87), the President of the Canadian Association of Distance Education (CADE) is a British Columbian woman, Arlene Zuckernick of UVic. Another British Columbian woman, Margit Nance of SFU's Office of Continuing Studies, is this year's President of the Canadian Association of University Continuing Education (CAUCE), the parent organization of CADE. CADE's brand-new *Journal of Distance Education (JDE)*, a peer-reviewed international journal based in Canada and intended as a forum for discussion of current theory, research and practice in this field, is edited by Dawn Howard, a member of SFU's Centre for Distance Education's staff. This appointment is important, as the editorial policy of a respected journal (as *JDE* shows every sign of becoming) can help both form and express opinion on all the various aspects of women in distance education, from choice of pronouns to affirmative action.

This section could go on for pages; for example, a significant majority of distance education instructional designers in British Columbia are now women. But the central fact is established: women working in distance education in B.C. have made a contribution of vital importance to the field provincially, nationally and internationally. Even so, the traditional patriarchal power structure is virtually unchanged: there is the usual preponderance of males at the top and females at the bottom of the hierarchy. Though individuals may properly praise themselves, as a society we have little cause for self-congratulation.

Conclusion

University distance education fills an urgent need for many people and will continue to do so at least for the foreseeable future. Therefore, it is necessarily forward-looking in some respects as the various institutions seek to attract and serve students. Nevertheless, we should not forget that educational institutions, like other institutions, are immensely self-protective and conservative about power, and that changes in the sexual balance of power seem particularly threatening to many people. Universities in Canada have not changed radically in the ten years since a statistical survey commented that "in general women in the [academic] profession are concentrated at the lower ranks, are less likely to have the security of a fulltime tenured position, are less well paid at every level than their male counterparts and, with very few exceptions, are absent from the positions and bodies with any influence and power within the universities" (Vickers and Adam, 1976:99). Of the fifty-six universities surveyed by the Association of Colleges and Universities of Canada, only eight claimed to be encouraging or participating in affirmative action programmes, and none of these eight were west of Ontario. It would certainly be desirable for students and professionals in distance education in the western provinces if this association were to reactivate its plans to study in detail the status of women on campus, as this is likely also to affect women off-campus (*Globe and Mail,* December 31, 1986:A9). Meanwhile the essential daily battle continues.

References

Ayim, Maryann. (1986). "Women's Rights: A Seamstress' Analysis." *Canadian Journal of Education, 11*(3), 215-30.

Coulter, Rebecca, Rosalyn Delehanty, and Barbara J. Spronk. (1983). "Distance Education and Women's Studies." Unpublished paper presented to the Annual Meeting of the Canadian Research Institute for the Advancement of Women, Vancouver, B.C.

Devereaux, M.S. (1984). *One in Every Five: A Survey of Adult Education in Canada.* Ottawa: Statistics Canada and Education Support Sector, Secretary of State.

Faith, Karlene. (1985). "The Study of Crime at a Distance." Proceedings of the 13th World Conference of the International Council for Distance Education. Melbourne: La Trobe Micropublishing.

Kirk, Pauline. (1977). "The Tip of the Iceberg: Some Effects of Open University Study on Married Students." *Teaching at a Distance, 10,* 19-27.

Price, Iris. (1985). "The Student Perspective of Distance Education." *International Council of Distance Education, 7,* 25-27.

Rauhala, Ann. (1986). "Low Marks Handed Out for Equality on Campus." *Globe and Mail,* December 31, p. A9.

Rich, Adrienne. (1979). *On Lies, Secrets and Silence.* New York: W.W. Norton.

Ruggles, Robin H., John Anderson, David E. Blackmore, Clay Lafleur, J. Peter Rothe and Terry Taerum. (1982). *Learning at a Distance and the*

New Technology. Vancouver: Educational Research Institute of British Columbia.

Tremaine, Marianne and Judy Owen. (1984). "The Female Majority: Women who Study Extramurally." *Teaching at a Distance, 25,* 45-50.

Vickers, Jill McCalla and June Adam. (1976). *But Can You Type? Canadian Universities and the Status of Women.* Toronto: Clarke Irwin.

GENDER-RELATED PATTERNS IN CHOICE OF MAJOR SUBJECT OR DEGREE COURSE AT FERNUNIVERSITÄT

by

Christine von Prümmer and Ute Rossié

Christine von Prümmer, born in Germany in 1946, graduated from Smith College, U.S.A., in 1969 and received her M.A. in Sociology and Political Science at Konstanz University in 1973. As a research officer she worked in and conducted different research projects in the area of educational biographies and violence against women. In 1978 she joined the academic staff at the FernUniversität as a researcher responsible for course evaluation and studies of different aspects of distance education. Since 1985 she has been concentrating on women in distance education. Together with Ute Rossié she is currently conducting a large-scale research project comparing the situation of women and men studying at a distance.

Ute Rossié, born in Germany in 1951, received her Diploma (M.A.) in Social Sciences from the Ruhr-Universität Bochum in 1978. In 1979 she joined the academic staff at the FernUniversität as a researcher of course evaluation and different aspects of distance education. In 1986 she completed a study on visiting students at the FernUniversität.

Introduction[1]

The West German FernUniversität (Distance University), based in Hagen, was founded in the mid-1970s and admitted its first 1,360 students in the academic year 1975-76. Since then it has expanded, with the total number of students registered ten years later reaching 31,930, of whom 18,334 were studying for a degree. From the beginning, women have been extremely underrepresented among the FernUniversität's student population, both absolutely—less than 25% of the students are women—and relatively, compared to traditional West German universities, where the proportion of women has reached 40%.[2]

Frequently the reason for this low percentage of women students is assumed to be the limited range of subjects available at the FernUniversität and the fact that these subjects are considered more attractive for men than for women. This, however, is not a sufficient explanation since, compared to other West German universities, women are underrepresented within each of the degree programmes. Another attempt to explain the underrepresentation of women is based on the assumption that distance education puts more pressure on women than on men, since they have to take care of their families in addition to studying and often holding down a job. This assumption is contradicted by another one which postulates that distance education is especially suited for women who are housebound, since it does not require a fixed schedule or extended absence from home.[3]

The lack of information about the situation of women at the FernUniversität led us to undertake a major research project. As part of this survey we asked students about their course choices with a view to possible gender-related differences in the reasons why students decide on a particular degree programme.

Some Relevant Characteristics of the FernUniversität and Its Students

Degree Programmes at the FernUniversität

The FernUniversität currently offers six degree programmes at the Master's level (two M.A. programmes and four long-term diploma programmes leading to the "Diplom II") which would take a fulltime student a minimum of four years to complete. In addition, there are four degree programmes on a lower level (short-term diploma or "Diplom I") which require three years of fulltime study. Students can choose between social sciences or education for the M.A., or electrical engineering, computer science, mathematics, or economics for either of the diplomas. In 1985-86 half the degree students at the FernUniversität were registered for a degree in economics, with the preferences of women (52.6%) and men (50.6%) roughly equal. The distribution of students in the other degree courses shows some not totally unexpected differences between women and men.

Table 1: Distribution of Students in Degree Programmes at the FernUniversität 1985-86 (percent)

All degree students major subject	women (n = 4,166)	men (n = 14,168)	sum (n = 18,334)	proportion of women row percent
Diploma programmes				
economics	52.6	50.6	51.1	23.4 (n = 9,360)
computer science	15.8	24.5	22.6	15.9 (n = 4,134)
electrical engineering	1.9	11.3	9.2	4.8 (n = 1,687)
mathematics	4.1	6.3	5.8	16.2 (n = 1,061)
M.A. programmes				
education	20.8	5.3	8.8	53.7 (n = 1,618)
social sciences	4.7	2.0	2.6	41.6 (n = 474)
New degree students major subject	women (n = 1,935)	men (n = 5,718)	sum (n = 7,653)	proportion of women row percent
Diploma programmes				
economics	49.0	46.2	46.9	26.4 (n = 3,589)
computer science	17.6	28.4	25.7	17.3 (n = 1,966)
electrical engineering	2.2	12.5	9.9	5.7 (n = 758)
mathematics	3.6	4.6	4.3	21.2 (n = 330)
M.A. programmes				
education	17.4	3.5	7.0	62.7 (n = 536)
social sciences	10.2	4.8	6.2	41.6 (n = 474)

The distribution of all students and of newly matriculated students in degree programmes in 1985-86 parallels that of the previous academic year.[4] The exception is in the M.A. programmes, where the major in social sciences was newly introduced.

Description of the Sample

This study comprises two sets of students: a complete cohort of female students, and an equally large number of male students in a corresponding sample. The basic characteristics of both groups include the following:

- degree students (fulltime and parttime students, including students registered at other universities but taking part of their degree courses at the FernUniversität);
- students first registered at the FernUniversität for the academic year 1985-86;
- students re-registered for the summer semester 1986.

These basic parameters were chosen because the study is also concerned with the reasons why students register for a given subject area or degree course, and only degree students can reasonably be expected to answer these questions. First-year students were selected because they are still relatively new to the FernUniversität, but by the time they received the questionnaire, they already had some experience with distance education. We decided to include only new students in our survey in the hope of doing a follow-up study, when these students are halfway through their degree course (that is, have taken their preliminary exams) or have discontinued their studies at the FernUniversität.

Because of the comparatively low number of female students, we have included all women who fit the basic sample parameters. Male students were selected as a stratified random sample which aimed to mirror the group of female students in the main characteristics of matriculation status and subject area/degree course. Since the number of women exceeded that of men in education, the sample was made up with men enrolled in electrical engineering. Thus, the total number of men is equal to that of women.

The data reported in this paper have been taken from the survey which forms the main part of our research. We used a mail questionnaire for two reasons: the sample of 2,430 students was too large to allow interviews with all of the students selected, and distance students are accustomed to communicating with their university in writing.

Student Response: Basis of Analysis

At the time we started writing this paper a total of 1,186 students, almost half of the sample population (48.7%), had not only returned their questionnaires but had also provided extensive written comments to the open-ended questions. These were analyzed with the help of a category system which served to reduce the complexity of the answers, to summarize them, and to interpret them.[5] The categories were derived from the material itself and from previous research, including our pilot study. Just under half of the respondents are women (48.5%). The distribution of respondents in the FernUniversität's degree programmes corresponds fairly well to the sample; for women it also corresponds to the total population of newly registered degree students in 1985-86. Because the men were sampled to match the groups of women students, the distribution of the male respondents does not reflect their enrolment patterns among the degree students in general.

Table 2: Distribution of Respondents in Degree Programmes (percent)

Degree students major subject	women (n = 573)	men (n = 609)	sum (n = 1,182)	proportion of women row percent
Diploma programmes				
economics	45.7	46.3	46.0	48.2 (n = 544)
computer science	18.7	22.2	20.5	44.2 (n = 242)
electrical engineering	1.8	2.5	2.1	40.0 (n = 25)
mathematics	3.1	4.4	3.8	40.0 (n = 45)
M.A. programmes				
education	19.7	9.4	14.4	66.5 (n = 170)
social sciences	10.8	14.5	12.7	41.3 (n = 150)

Choosing a Degree Course

The Diploma in Economics

The FernUniversität offers both a short-term and a long-term diploma in economics which can be completed after three or four years of fulltime study. Slightly more women than men are studying for the long-term degree, which corresponds to a Master's degree.

Table 3: Distribution of Students in Long-term and Short-term Diploma Courses in Economics (percent)

	women (n = 262)	men (n = 282)	sum (n = 544)	proportion of women row percent
Degree goals				
long-term diploma	57.3	54.8	56.0	49.3 (n = 304)
short-term diploma	37.4	37.6	37.5	48.0 (n = 204)
no degree wanted	3.1	7.1	5.2	28.6 (n = 28)
other degree	2.3	.7	1.5	75.0 (n = 8)

Economics at the FernUniversität comprises both political economy ("Volkswirtschaftslehre") and business administration ("Betriebswirtschaftslehre"). It is designed as an integrated subject area, and students take introductory courses for both fields during the first four semesters of study. Specialization takes place only after the preliminary examinations, two years into the degree programme.

Since our sample was drawn from newly registered degree students, most of our respondents have not yet selected a specialty area. Some students have had previous study and/or work experience and already know whether they will concentrate on political economy or on business administration. Still others entered the programme with enough credits to start specializing straight away. From information we were given by these students, it seems that those opting for business administration have a direct interest in applying their knowledge or their degree to their jobs and careers. Those students opting for political economy, on the other hand, seem to be more motivated by a wish to comprehend economic developments and political decisions more generally and theoretically.

The reasons our respondents give for choosing economics as their major subject are predominately related to their jobs. They wish to utilize their studies in their present occupation, either as background knowledge or for securing their present positions or improving their chances of occupational advancement:[6]

> I wish to gain more insights relating to my present occupation. In this way I can broaden my knowledge basis and secure my position. This, in turn, will furnish opportunities for promotions and increase my career prospects.

> The degree in economics can be applied to my present job. It is the only degree offered by the FernUniversität which is relevant to my work and helpful for my career.

Others wish to start a career in a totally new field or to become self-employed:

> If I'm successful in getting the degree I could enter an area in health administration where I could utilize my previous work experience as well as my degree: ultimately my goal is a management position in the administration of a large hospital.

> I'm thinking of starting my own business, and if I do economics will be useful for managing it.

Quite often these students wish to leave their jobs as civil servants and start a new career in "free enterprise." Interestingly, this is especially true for tax officers, who study economics because this degree is a prerequisite for self-employed tax advisors. The degree in economics enables them to start a new career in a related field if it does not improve their chances at promotion within the tax office hierarchy. Slightly more men than women specify this as their motive for choosing the subject.

> [I study economics because of] the possibility of improving my promotion chances as a tax officer or, alternatively, of using the

degree to leave the civil service and enter the "free" arena of business.

In addition to these career-oriented students, a number of respondents need the degree in order to find a job in the first place or to re-enter the labour market after a period of interruption or unemployment.

Another reason for studying economics is that it may complement another course of study. These students find it useful to add the distance courses to their course of studies at a traditional institution.

A number of respondents wish to re-enter an interrupted degree course or add the university degree to their previous occupational training. A few of our respondents are marking time at the FernUniversität, studying economics in order to have a head start at another university upon leaving the army. This reason is necessarily mentioned only by men, since women are not in the army.

> After I complete my two years as a soldier I plan to study law at a traditional university. Studying economics now will help me to decide on my area of specialization and provide useful background knowledge.

Some students say that they expect courses in economics to help them prepare for attending a traditional university when their children are older and they don't have to stay at home. This reason is referred to solely by women, which suggests that the traditional division of labour which places childrearing responsibilities on women is still prevalent.

Other external factors enforce students' choice of economics: either they lack the necessary entrance qualifications to study other subjects, or the FernUniversität doesn't offer the subject of their choice. If a preferred subject is mentioned by our respondents, it tends to be law, which is available only as a minor subject.

> Originally I wanted to study law in order to improve my chances of promotion in the tax office. Since I couldn't study law at the FernUniversität, I chose economics in the hope that this subject will also be helpful professionally. I'm thinking in terms of either a career within the tax office hierarchy or a change-over into business.

More often students say that economics was the most interesting of the subjects offered or, conversely, that the other subjects were even less relevant or attractive. It is safe to assume that these students are more motivated to get a university degree as such than to study economics because of their interests in the subject matter itself.

> I'm not interested in mathematics or computer science; education and sociology are too theoretical and offer no future employment opportunities.

Where "interest in the subject" is explicitly mentioned as a reason for choosing economics, it is directed to different aspects of the field. There is a generalized interest which refers more to political and entrepreneurial decision-making and to the understanding of economic and social processes in our society; there is a more specialized interest which refers to applications of the knowledge to students' jobs and/or studies at other universities; and there is an intellectual interest in the subject matter.

Here there are no striking differences between women and men, although women tend to mention a more generalized interest while men are slightly more motivated by career goals. We would have expected these differences to be more pronounced.[7] Our overall impression of the questionnaire results is that there are significant gender-related differences concerning students' motivation for wanting a degree and for studying at a distance.

Female and male respondents differ noticeably in terms of references to their families as factors influencing their choice of subject. Of the few men who referred to relatives in this context, the majority needed the background in economcs in order to enter or head a family business. Some of the women, too, plan on using their economics degree in similar ways. But as illustrated by the following quote, there is a slightly different slant to their motives:

> A degree in economics will help me to be taken seriously when I talk about matters relating to the family business.

One man and five women mention that they decided to study economics because their partners were taking the course or working in a field with a background in economics.

In addition, women need to study a subject which will allow them to enter or re-enter the labour market after having taken time off to have and raise children. Economics is seen as a good basis for better chances in the job market.

> I need a degree in economics since I will have to earn money when my children are old enough. I want to finish my interrupted course

of studies in order to have better opportunities in the labour market when I get ready to enter it.

None of the men gave this reason and, indeed, men don't refer to their children at all when talking about their choice of subjects.

One woman expressed her feelings that a knowledge of economics and a degree in that area are important for her to be accepted as an equal in her profession:

> I took economics for reasons related to my job. I thought I could gain further knowledge in business administration which I could apply to my work. For instance, I want to improve my standing with my male colleagues, all of whom have university degrees. Thus far they really patronize me when I try to contribute to a professional discussion. I want to be able to argue on their level *and* to be taken seriously by them.

None of the answers given by male respondents to this open-ended question suggests that they don't feel accepted by their peers in their profession, although we believe that this is a reason for both men and women to want a university degree in the first place.

The Master of Arts Degree

The M.A. programmes at the FernUniversität entail four years of fulltime study and comprise one major and two minor subjects each. Currently, education and the social sciences are the only two majors students can choose, but a range of minors is available. More than one quarter of all respondents study for an M.A. (27.1%): 170 students take education and 150 students take sociology as their major subject. Women predominate in the former subject, and men in the latter.

Table 4: Distribution of M.A. Students in the Two Major Subjects (percent)

Major subject	women	men	proportion of women
	(n = 175)	(n = 145)	row percent
education	64.6	39.3	66.5 (n = 170)
social sciences	35.4	60.7	41.3 (n = 150)
All M.A. students	100.0	100.0	54.7 (n = 320)

Women and men differ in their choice of minor subjects. In addition, divergent patterns emerge in the combinations of second and third subjects with either the education or the social science majors.

Women in Distance Education

Table 5: Minor Subjects in Order of Preference: M.A. Students in Education (percent)

All students in education	women (n = 112)		men (n = 56)		all respondents (n = 168)	
Second subjects:	psychology	42.0	sociology	39.3	psychology	37.5
	sociology	23.2	psychology	28.6	sociology	28.6
	literature	11.6	literature	10.7	literature	11.3
	philosophy	8.9	philosophy	8.9	philosophy	8.9
	law	7.1	law	5.4	law	6.6
	mathematics	4.5	economics	3.6	mathematics	3.6
	economics	.9	mathematics	1.8	economics	1.8
Third subjects:	psychology	33.0	sociology	37.5	psychology	33.3
	sociology	26.8	psychology	33.9	sociology	30.4
	law	13.4	law	14.3	law	13.7
	philosophy	12.5	philosophy	3.6	philosophy	9.5
	literature	8.9	literature	3.6	literature	7.1
	economics	2.7	mathematics	3.6	economics	1.8
	mathematics	-	economics	-	mathematics	1.2

Table 6: Minor Subjects in Order of Preference: M.A. Students in the Social Sciences (percent)

All students in the social sciences	women (n = 61)		men (n = 87)		all respondents (n = 148)	
Second subjects:	philosophy	27.9	psychology	25.3	philosophy	25.0
	literature	23.0	law	24.1	psychology	23.0
	psychology	19.7	philosophy	23.0	law	21.0
	law	16.4	education	13.8	education	12.8
	mathematics	11.5	literature	5.8	literature	12.8
	education	-	mathematics	2.3	mathematics	1.4
	economics	-	economics	1.2	economics	.7
Third subjects:	psychology	25.0	law	28.6	psychology	22.9
	literature	21.7	psychology	21.4	law	22.9
	law	15.0	education	13.1	literature	14.9
	education	13.3	philosophy	11.9	education	13.2
	philosophy	10.0	literature	9.5	philosophy	11.1
	economics	3.3	economics	7.1	economics	5.6
	mathematics	3.3	mathematics	-	mathematics	1.4

Students who want to earn a degree in education at the Fern-Universität seem generally to be interested in social science subjects. They tend to combine their major subject with either psychology or sociology or both as their minor subjects. Over two-thirds of all students in education chose psychology for their second (33.3%) or third (37.5%) subject, and nearly 60% are taking sociology as one of their minor subjects (30.4% and 28.6% respectively). The most popular combination by far is education as the major subject with psychology and sociology as the minors. Forty-four out of 113 women (38.9%) and 25 out of 57 men (43.9%) have chosen to study this combination. The predominance of these two subjects holds true for both women and men, but women prefer psychology while men prefer social science courses.

The major subject social sciences tends to be combined with a wider range of subjects, notably with psychology, law, philosophy, modern German literature and education, in that order of preference.

Gender-related differences are especially obvious in the areas of modern German literature and law. The former is definitely favoured by the women: nearly a quarter of them (23.0%) chose literature as their second subject, a further 22% as their third subject. However, only 15.3% of the male respondents chose modern German literature as their second or their third subject. To the men, the study of law seems more important: 24.1% decided on this for their second subject, and a further 28.6% as their third subject.

This discrepancy could be a result of the general preference of women for languages and cultural and social sciences which shows in the enrolment statistics of traditional German universities. The same statistics show that men predominate in law courses.[8] As far as the specific situation of distance students is concerned, women, who are less likely to be in paid employment already, may choose to take "general knowledge" subjects for intellectual stimulation. At the same time, if they want to utilize their degrees for entering the labour market, they need to study a subject which can be applied to jobs open to them. Men, on the other hand, might be able to use a knowledge of law in their present jobs even if it does not provide them with a specific law degree.[9]

The reasons students give for choosing the M.A. programme in education or sociology are basically similar to those given by respondents studying economics. Job-related reasons predominate, especially with students who study education as their major subject and with students who combine either of the major subjects with psychology.

> In my present area of work I come across many problems for which a knowledge of education would be relevant and useful.

> I wish to be able to understand—and then solve—conflicts of a psychological or sociological kind which keep coming up in my job.

A number of respondents are studying these subjects because they are working as teachers and want to apply their knowledge of education to their jobs.

> The reason for my choice of subjects is my job as a teacher of religion in a vocational school and in a school for handicapped children.

Some respondents study the combination of sociology, education and psychology out of their interest in human nature, specifically in children, even though they will not be able to use their knowledge or their degree working in a pedagogical field.

> I am very interested in all areas which deal with people, especially with children. I would really have liked to become a primary school teacher, but unfortunately this is not possible because of the labour market situation.

More often, though, it is a more generalized interest which determines the choice of subjects.

> I am generally interested in social processes and structure and in the interaction of people on various levels.

Quite often the emphasis is on the minor subjects rather than the major ones. As with students in economics, the limited range of degree courses leaves students with few options if they want or need a degree through distance studies.

> It wasn't possible to study for a degree in either psychology or law which I would have preferred. Therefore I had to settle for a subject which would build on my previous experience and serve as continuing education.

> Sociology and pedagogics don't interest me. I only chose my major subject as a means to have access to the subjects which really interest me. Later on I plan to enrol at a traditional university and get an M.A. in philosophy, history, and law.

Again, there are gender-related differences in M.A. students' choice of minor subjects. Women—who study modern German literature more often than men do—would have preferred to get a degree in a language, linguistics, or related subjects if they had been available at the FernUniversität.

> Before I enrolled at the FernUniversität I studied French and English literature with a view to becoming a secondary school teacher. This combination of subjects is not offered in a degree course at the FernUniversität. At the same time, my career goals had changed and I wasn't sure I still wanted to be a teacher. Then, too, my interest in education has become stronger because of my son. And lastly, I'm hoping to have better employment opportunities with an M.A. than I would have with a teaching diploma.

In general, women who are "interested in the subject" tend to mention their own children or their experience working with other children more frequently than men do.

> I was really interested in the subject. Also, I already knew something about the field and I had practical experience in bringing up my own children.

Men, by contrast, might mention their wives or friends but not their children. More often than their families they indicate that their political, union or other civic activities are the basis for their interest in the subject.

These differences between women and men may not necessarily reflect a difference in involvement in political and social concerns, since a number of women do mention such activities in other contexts. It is also interesting to note that—unlike computer science, for instance—men don't seem to study education and social science subjects "for fun" or "in order to exercise and expand [their] mind" as well as using it in some more direct way.

The Diploma in Computer Science, Electrical Engineering, and Mathematics

Students wishing to study a mathematical or technical subject at the FernUniversität have a choice of computer science, electrical engineering, or mathematics as their major subject. Degrees conferred are either a short-term diploma ("Diplom I") which takes six semesters of fulltime study, or a long-term diploma ("Diplom II") which takes eight or nine semesters. In theory, this is true for all three degree courses, but in practice students of computer science are strongly encouraged to enrol only in the longer programme or are actively prevented from taking the shorter course. Almost all of the respondents in computer science, therefore, are aiming to get a long-term degree.

Table 7: Distribution of Students in Long-term and Short-term Diploma Courses (percent)

Degree goals Computer science	women (n = 107)	men (n = 135)	sum (n = 242)	proportion of women row percent
long-term diploma	85.0	85.2	85.1	44.2 (n = 206)
short-term diploma	2.8	.7	1.7	75.0 (n = 4)
no degree wanted	12.1	12.6	12.4	43.3 (n = 30)
other degree/no answer	-	1.5	.8	- (n = 2)
Mathematics	women (n = 18)	men (n = 27)	sum (n = 45)	proportion of women row percent
long-term diploma	55.6	48.2	51.1	43.5 (n = 23)
short-term diploma	16.7	14.8	15.6	42.9 (n = 7)
no degree wanted	22.2	37.0	31.1	28.6 (n = 14)
other degree/no answer	5.6	-	2.2	100.0 (n = 1)
Electrical engineering	women (n = 10)	men (n = 15)	sum (n = 25)	proportion of women row percent
long-term diploma	60.0	33.3	44.0	54.5 (n = 11)
short-term diploma	30.0	33.3	32.0	37.5 (n = 8)
no degree wanted	10.0	26.7	20.0	20.0 (n = 5)
other degree/no answer	-	6.7	4.0	- (n = 1)

Table 7 shows slightly more men than women among the respondents, which may be because our sample was slightly slanted to include more male students in these subjects. The proportion of students not aiming for a degree is fairly high in mathematics and in electrical engineering. This is partly because these students study at the FernUniversität in order to supplement their studies at a traditional university. Also, a number of students don't need a degree and study out of interest in the subject matter.

Of those computer science students who have answered the open-ended question as to their choice of subject, about half mentioned their "interest in the subject" as a reason for choosing it. A noticeable difference between women and men is that men tend to explain this interest with the importance computer science has for the future.

The future belongs to computer science.

For years to come computer science will offer good job opportunities and career prospects.

In addition, male respondents mention more often than the women that working with computers is fun and that they want to turn their hobby into a career.

> I had previously been in contact with computers but found that my friends' computer games became boring very quickly. I chose to study computer science because I wanted to gain some background knowledge and insight into the workings of computers.

Women, on the other hand, explain their interest in computer science with reference to their interest in mathematics and science subjects in school or with previous experiences at other universities.

> At present there are good job prospects in computers. My interest in this subject dates back to my first degree course at a traditional university where I took classes in this field.

Unlike respondents in other degree courses, students of technical and mathematical subjects rarely give the limited range of subjects at the FernUniversität as their reason for choosing their field of study. The only group showing an interest in other subjects seem to be mathematicians, four of whom mention that they would have preferred to get a degree in physics or in biology.

At the same time, students enrolled in mathematics are generally more interested in the subject as such than in its immediate usefulness. Men as well as women say that their interest in mathematics dates back to their school days, and for women especially it's been a dream for a long time to study this subject at a university.

On the whole, women in computer science, electrical engineering, or mathematics tend to mention the aspect of further education more frequently than their male colleagues. Our impression from the open-ended questions is that women like to gain previous study or work experience—and therefore confidence—in these subjects before they embark on a degree course.

> Computer science was the natural choice since my work involves programming business computers.

Very few of the men among our respondents give this reason, which suggests that men don't hesitate as much to enter a degree programme in technical and mathematical areas.

As in economics, more women than men say that they are studying a technical or mathematical subject at the FernUniversität in order to finish a previously aborted degree programme.

> I started out studying mathematics but discontinued my course after seven semesters when I started a family. Later I had a job in administration which involved electronic data processing. This coincided with my own interest in the subject and this in turn caused my choice of computer science as my major subject.

Frequently students' decisions to study computer science are job-oriented, with both women and men intending to broaden their knowledge, supplement their work experience, and apply their studies to their present occupation.

> I'm working in the field of data processing and wanted to get background knowledge and more insights into computers.

A change of careers, as was mentioned frequently by students of economics, does not seem to be a factor in the decision to study computer science.

More women than men express their hope that a degree in computer science will improve their employment chances, perhaps because unemployment is especially high in jobs with a high proportion of women, and therefore women must consciously re-orient their career plans before they enter or re-enter the labour market.

> I'm hoping that this subject will open up more occupational opportunities. Since this is an area where teachers are still needed, I might get a permanent contract as a schoolteacher of computer science. Failing that I have a better chance of finding another job in this field and thus avoid being unemployed again.

Other women give the reason that computer science was introduced as a subject in the schools with no emphasis on its occupational relevance.

> On the one hand mathematics has always been my favourite subject; on the other hand I felt that computer science would offer me an intellectual challenge. An additional consideration has been the introduction of computer courses into our schools.

Considering the traditional division of labour which holds mothers responsible for bringing up the children, it is possible that these women want to utilize their knowledge when helping the children with their homework.

Looking at other degree students, we found that few men but a number of women refer to their families as influencing their choice of subject and that none of the men mentions his own children. This pattern is even more extreme in the case of technical and mathematical degree programmes, where it is only women who seem to be influenced in their choice of subject by family-related factors.

Some women felt the need to be more knowledgeable in the subject in order to support their husbands in their work.

> My husband wants to start his own business in the field of electronics. My studies not only provide me with an understanding of what it's all about but also with a basis for actively helping him.

Others hoped to be able to rely on their husbands to help them through difficulties.

> I would really have preferred to study biology which is not available at the FernUniversität. I decided on mathematics because my husband is a mathematician and therefore able to help me in my studies. I also decided on computer science because there was nothing else I could take. Now it has turned out to be so interesting that I'm considering switching over and taking computer science as my major subject.

In addition to these reasons, some of the women and none of the men mention their need to take a subject that would draw on their previous experience as well as give them better chances for re-entering the labour market after raising children.

Women in "Non-Typical" Subjects

Today, when the percentage of women in conventional universities in West Germany has risen to approximately 40%, we still find very few women in courses leading to a degree in science or technology. This is particularly pronounced at the FernUniversität. In order to get some information about the women who do study these subjects and about their motives and problems we included two questions which refer to their choice of a "non-typical" subject. These statements were derived from our pilot study and from previous studies done on women in male-dominated fields.[10]

One question consisted of a set of six statements, and students were asked to rate each of these statements according to how closely it fits their own situation. There were five answer categories, ranging from "1=fits my situation exactly" to "5=is totally different." Table 8 shows the answer patterns of the three groups of women who take computer science, electrical engineering, or mathematics as their major subject for a degree at the FernUniversität.

Looking at Table 8, we find that respondents of all three degree programmes agree most strongly with statement A: "I really enjoy solving mathematical and analytical problems and/or working with theoretical models." Given the small numbers we are dealing with here, we have to be careful in interpreting our findings. Still, it seems that women studying mathematics and electrical engineering find this statement especially suited to describe their own motivations for taking the course.

The numbers are even smaller with respect to statements B: "My partner and I started studying at the same time, and were both interested in this subject," and D: "My partner works in this area and promised to help me with my studies; this encouraged me to try it." Since these two items refer to the relevance of partners in deciding to study a mathematical or technical subject, they could be answered only by those women who actually do have a partner in a steady relationship. If it is possible to see a pattern at all it points in the direction that these items fit the situation of electrical engineers more than that of mathematicians and computer scientists.

Most respondents can't apply item C: "I wanted to prove that a woman can study a mathematical or technical subject as well as any man" to their own situation. On the other hand, item E, "I am technically minded and enjoy working with mechanical things," seems to reflect their own situation quite accurately and points to the fact that women who study these subjects do so out of a genuine interest.

The only significant difference between students in the three degree programmes is found in the agreement or disagreement with statement F: "I'm hoping that a degree in this field will open better opportunities in the labour market." Predictably, it is women in computer science who feel more strongly that their choice of subject will open more opportunities in the job market. About 60% of these women say that the statement fits their own situation "exactly" or "to a great extent." They are clearly oriented toward working in the field of electronics and want to use their degree to improve employment chances and better their career prospects.

Table 8: Agreement and Disagreement with Statements Concerning the Choice of "Non-typical" Subjects (percent)

Women in Computer Science (107 respondents)

	exactly		This statement fits my situation to a great extent		This statement fits my situation to some extent		a little		not at all/is totally different	
	abs.	%	abs.	%	abs.	%	abs.	%	abs.	%
A:	44	41.9	35	33.3	18	17.1	7	6.7	1	.9
B:	4	4.4	2	2.2	5	5.5	2	2.2	77	85.5
C:	8	7.6	7	6.8	16	15.2	23	21.9	51	48.6
D:	6	6.7	6	6.7	5	5.5	5	5.5	68	75.5
E:	22	21.1	35	33.6	26	25.0	13	12.5	8	7.7
F:	31	29.5	33	31.4	20	19.0	9	8.6	12	11.4

Women in Electrical Engineering (10 respondents)

	exactly		This statement fits my situation to a great extent		This statement fits my situation to some extent		a little		not at all/is totally different	
	abs.	%	abs.	%	abs.	%	abs.	%	abs.	%
A:	7	70.0	2	20.0	1	10.0	0	-	0	-
B:	1	12.5	1	12.5	0	-	1	12.5	5	62.5
C:	2	20.0	1	10.0	0	10.0	3	30.0	4	40.0
D:	2	25.0	0	-	1	12.5	0	-	5	62.5
E:	5	50.0	1	10.0	3	30.0	1	10.0	0	-
F:	1	10.0	0	-	3	30.0	2	20.0	4	40.0

Table 8: Agreement and Disagreement with Statements Concerning the Choice of "Non-typical" Subjects (percent)

Women in Mathematics (18 respondents)

	exactly		to a great extent		to some extent		a little		not at all/is totally different	
	abs.	%	abs.	%	abs.	%	abs.	%	abs.	%
A:	13	72.2	1	5.6	3	16.7	1	5.6	0	-
B:	0	-	0	-	0	-	0	-	10	100.0
C:	1	5.6	3	16.7	4	22.2	4	22.2	6	33.3
D:	0	-	1	10.0	0	-	0	-	9	90.0
E:	4	22.2	5	27.8	5	27.8	1	5.6	3	16.7
F:	0	-	5	27.8	7	38.9	1	5.6	5	27.8

The statements were:

A: I really enjoyed solving mathematical and analytical problems and/or working with theoretical models.
B: My partner and I started studying at the same time and were both interested in this subject *(respondents with partners only)*.
C: I wanted to prove that a woman can study a mathematical or technical subject as well as any man.
D: My partner works in this area and promised to help me with my studies; this encouraged me to try it *(respondents with partners only)*.
E: I am technically minded and enjoy working with mechanical things.
F: I'm hoping that a degree in this field will open better opportunities in the labour market.

Women studying mathematics or electrical engineering, on the other hand, don't have much hope that earning a degree will improve their employment opportunities. Their choice of subject is clearly motivated more by their intellectual interests and ability and less by their expectation of utilizing their degree in a job. This might reflect either a certain resignation on their part or that they don't feel the need to study only what is useful in terms of employment.

Apart from the list of statement choices, we asked an open-ended question in which students were asked to comment on their decision to study a "non-typical" subject. The most striking characteristic of the answers was the fact that these women refuse to see themselves—or to be seen by us—as "non-typical" or special. This corresponds to the fact that most of the respondents said that item C: "I wanted to prove that a woman can study a mathematical or technical subject as well as any man" did not reflect their own situation. The answers range from a simple questioning of the assumption that these subjects are "non-typical" for women to detailed explanations of their reasons for rejecting the assumption.

> I never thought of my choice of subject as being untypical. I thought "untypical" are areas such as mechanical engineering which require practical courses. I would not have been strong enough physically to study for this kind of degree.

> As far as I'm concerned the choice was not untypical. The subject is simply the one which suited me best, in terms of being interested as well as being capable of mastering it.

We were quite puzzled at first by this emphasis on not being unusual in studying subjects which in fact have a very low proportion of women students. One possible explanation might be that successful women do not, or will not, recognize the difficulties other women have in their chosen field. Another explanation might be the total rejection of the whole concept of specific roles for women and men. Respondents who don't accept the fact that women and men are assigned different roles in society cannot accept the idea that there are supposed to be subjects more or less suited to the role of women.[11]

> I'm against the traditional role behaviour which has men studying mathematics, women studying social work—if they study at all. After they get their degrees, the men get jobs, the women are unemployed. On top of that, those jobs which are typically female are usually underpaid.

> There is no such thing as a typically male or typically female subject. Everyone studies those courses she or he is interested in. In my case this interest is determined by economic considerations, which in this day and age means getting a mathematical and/or technical degree.

As was the case in the FernUniversität's other degree programmes, a number of women say that their choice of subject has been influenced by their families. Quite often this influence is felt to be positive.

> It was my father who furthered my interest in science, mathematics, and technical subjects and who supported me in my refusal to fit the traditional picture of what a girl or woman should be like.

In other instances, as was to be expected, women were prevented by their families or their environment from studying science, mathematics, or a technical subject.

> At first I was scared off from following my original intention of studying electrical engineering. Instead I let myself be talked into enrolling for the "typically female" Master of Arts programme. During my first semester, though, I became convinced that I actually am capable of academic study, and now I plan to change my major subject and study electrical engineering after all—in spite of being a woman.

It seems that women who develop an interest in science or in a mathematical and technical field do so very early on, usually during their school years.

> Even in school I was more talented in mathematics and science subjects, which meant that I enjoyed them more and was more interested in the subject matter.

The fact that a relatively high number of women refer to school when talking about their choice of a degree course could reflect a need to explain their interest in the chosen subject. This, in turn, suggests that maybe the choice itself was not so matter of fact and "typical" as they would have us believe. This assumption is strengthened by the frequent mention respondents make of their fear to enter a degree programme in a mathematical and technical field, a fear that they only overcame by becoming familiar with the subject either on their job or in a previous course of studies.

> I lost my fear of technology when I was a biology student.

> My reason for choosing computer science was the way my job developed: bank clerk—systems organizer—organizational programmer, which wasn't planned but which I simply grew into.

While these women feel safe in studying a mathematical and technical subject because of their previous experience, others want to meet the challenge they expect their chosen field to pose for them.

> Women, too, can do anything.

> No one has ever been able to mould me according to some preconceived notion of how I should be. I have always been convinced that I can do anything other people—whoever they may be—can do. At the very least I can try to do it.

Concluding Remarks

Apart from the actual distribution of respondents in the different degree programmes, our findings in this phase of the study include impressions gained from open-ended questions rather than statistical analysis. Nevertheless, it is clear that there are gender-related differences in the degree courses students choose to study at the FernUniversität, and we can identify gender-related patterns in the reasons they give for their choices.

The most elementary difference between the women and men studying at the West German FernUniversität is the fact that only one in four students is a woman. The distribution of women and men in the available degree programmes also shows gender-related differences. The proportion of women is highest in the M.A. programmes, especially the M.A. in education where they are the majority of students. This doesn't come as a surprise since education and the social sciences, as well as the M.A. degree, are traditionally courses with a higher proportion of women. The share of women in the FernUniversität's diploma programmes ranges from one in four in economics to one in six in computer science and in mathematics; the proportion is lowest in electrical engineering, where only one in twenty students is a woman. Again, this comes as no surprise as these subjects are traditionally preferred by men.

The questionnaires contained some open-ended questions on students' reasons for enrolling in a particular degree programme. The answers were often quite detailed and complex, but nevertheless some patterns did emerge:

- In all of the degree programmes, *occupational considerations* are very important for both women and men when deciding what courses to take. These considerations range from getting more job satisfaction through consolidating one's position, or getting better promotion prospects in one's present occupation, to preparing for a new career in a totally different field or starting up one's own business. There is a slightly different emphasis on these aspects, but the real dissimilarities in these job-related factors are the fact that women also need their degrees in order to enter the work force in the first place, or to re-enter it after taking a break in order to have and raise children. More women than men study at a distance because they want to complete a degree which they started at another university.

- While both men and women may choose a subject because their *partner* (spouse or friend) is involved in the same or in a similar field, this is a factor much more relevant for women. And, at least in our study, only the women make a connection between their *children* and their major subject. This may be indirect, as in the case of getting a degree to better their chances for re-entering the labour market after an interruption. The connection is more direct in the case of women who study education and/or psychology and explain their interest in the subject with reference to their own children.

- Because of the *limited range of degree programmes* at the Fern-Universität, the chosen course may be only a stop-gap for students who would have preferred to study for a degree in another area. This is especially obvious in economics, which tends to be a substitute for a law degree. The situation is slightly more variegated in the M.A. programmes where the minor subjects often seem more interesting and attractive to students than the majors of education and sociology. Here women might have preferred to study languages or literature, men might again have preferred law, and both groups would have liked the option of getting their degree in psychology. The only students completely happy with their choice of degree programme seem to be the electrical engineers and the computer science students, none of whom would have preferred another course of studies.

- After this it is reassuring to find that a large number of students choose their degree courses because they are *interested in the subject*. When this interest is a generalized interest in the field and in economic, social, and political processes and decisions, which one wants to understand and maybe influence, students are more likely to be motivated to choose economics or the social science programmes. Students in the latter courses also have an interest in human nature and in child development. Mathematicians, on the other hand, tend to have an intellectual interest in the subject matter, while students of computer science and electrical engineering seem to derive their interest in the subject either from their jobs or from their enjoyment of science, mathematics, technology, and working with computers.

In order to go beyond the straightforward division of subjects into "female" and "male," which is suggested by the distribution of students in the degree courses, we included a set of statements and an open-ended question on the reasons women had for choosing electrical engineering, computer science, or mathematics for their major subjects.

- The most striking characteristic of the answers was the vehement *rejection of being labelled "non-typical."* In spite of the fact that the proportion of women in these subjects ranges from 4.8% in electrical engineering to 16.2% in mathematics, these women feel that there is nothing special about their wanting to get a degree in a mathematical or technical field. Often this denial of being "non-typical" is explained in terms of there being no differences in women's and men's roles in society. But most of these women have in fact enrolled in their course only after having overcome various obstacles or gained enough confidence in their ability to complete it. It therefore appears that they either consciously or unconsciously ignore the difficulties women have in entering these fields.

This summary of our results, while reflecting only tentative explorations of our research, represents factors which struck us as being more than just individual motives for a student's choice of degree programme. Rather, the data reveal gender-related patterns of response, which reflect on both women's traditional educational tracking and, relatedly, family responsibilities, and on contemporary challenges to gender roles.

Notes

1. The primary data for this paper were culled from a major research project which we are conducting at the FernUniversität. The larger study is broadly concerned with the compatibility of distance study with family and work commitments. This paper focuses specifically on female students' reasons for selecting particular course subjects or degree programmes. Although definitive conclusions cannot be drawn until the full study is completed, the preliminary findings illuminate the need and value of gender-related research in distance education.

2. See Bock, Braszeit and Schmerl, 1983:44-45, and von Prümmer, 1985:19-20.

3. See "Mentor. Zeitschrift für Erwachsenenstudium" (1980). No. 8, "Frauen im Fernstudium," Hagen. See also Peters, 1976; Peters, 1981; and von Prümmer, 1985:35-38.

4. von Prümmer, 1985:40-41.

5. See Bock *et al.*, 1983:107-8, where a similar approach is used to analyze interviews.

6. The quotes are taken (and translated) directly from answers to open-ended questions.

7. See Swift, 1982. See also Bartels, 1986; this is an empirical study of the FernUniversität's graduates in economics. A comparison between our results and these two studies should prove interesting since there are some fascinating (if subtle) differences in their findings concerning the career orientation of women as compared to men.

8. Bock, *et al.*, 1983:48-53.

9. Swift, 1982, and Bartels, 1986.

10. See C. Erlemann. (1983). "Frauen in Naturwissenschaft und Technik." In Bock, Braszeit and Schmerl, 1983:94-105.

11. These results do not correspond fully with the findings of Erlemann (*ibid.*, 97). Her respondents in male-dominated fields had made a conscious decision to "be something special" in studying science or technology subjects. The discrepancy might be because women in traditional universities see themselves as isolated. Distance students, on the other hand, do not see their presence in these areas as the exception rather than the rule. Nevertheless, both sets of respondents are similar in their rejection of the traditional female role.

Selected Bibliography

Arbeitskreis Wissenschaftlerinnen an den Hochschulen von NW. (Ed.). (1984). *Memorandum II. Privilegiert und doch diskriminiert.* Dortmund.

Bartels, Jörn. (1982). *Absolventen.* Hagen.

Bartels, Jörn. (1982). *Drop-out at the Distance University in the Federal Republic of Germany.* Hagen.

Bartels, Jörn. (1983). *Studienabbrecher.* Hagen.

Bartels, Jörn. (1986). *Die Absolventen des Fachbereichs Wirtschaftswissenschaft: Eine empirische Untersuchung.* Hagen.

Bartels, Jörn, Fritz Helms, Ute Rossié and Jürgen Schormann. (1984). *Studienverhalten von Fernstudenten. Eine vergleichende Untersuchung von Studienabbrechern und Studienfortsetzern.*

Bock, Ulla, Anne Braszeit and Christiane Schmerl. (1983). *Frauen im Wissenschaftsbetrieb. Dokumentation und Unterschung der Situation von Studentinnen und Dozentinnen unter besonderer Berücksichtigung der Situation in Nordrhein-Westfalen.* Weinheim.

Bock, Ulla, Anne Braszeit and Christiane Schmerl. (Eds.) (1983). *Frauen an den Universitäten: Zur Situation von Studentinnen und Hochschullehrerinnen in der männlichen Wissenschaftshierarchie.* Frankfurt.

Bruohl, Günter R. (1981). "Ist das Fernstudium 'frauenfeindlich'? Einige statistische Daten geben interessante Aufschlüsse." *Con-tacte, 1,* 25-28.

Bundesministerin für Bildung und Wissenschaft. (Ed.) (1984). Grund- und Strukturdaten 1984-85.

van Eckevort, Ger. (1983). *Vrouwen in de Open Universiteit: Eeen vraag voor onderzoek en beleid.* Heerlen.

van Eckevort, Ger. (1984). *Vrouwen in de Open Universiteit: Een aanvulling.* Heerlen.

Griffiths, Moira. (1980). "Women in Higher Education: A Case Study of the Open University." In Rosemary Deem (Ed.), *Schooling for Women's Work.* (pp. 126-41). London: Routledge and Kegan.

Körnig, Helga. (1979). *Bildungsexpansion und Fernstudium als bildungs- und gesellschaftspolitische Aufgabe.* München.

Körnig, Helga. (1985). "Distance Education as a Social Chance for Women." Paper given at the 13th ICDE World Conference, La Trobe University.

Peters, Otto. (1976). *Die Fernuniversität: Das erste Jahr. Aufbau—Aufgaben—Ausblicke.* Bericht des Gründungsrektors. Hagen.

Peters, Otto. (1981). *Die Fernuniversität im fünften Jahr: Bildungspolitische und fernstudiendidaktische Aspekte.* Bericht des Gründungsrektors. Hagen.

von Prümmer, Christine. (1983). *Report on a Study Leave Spent at Athabasca University, Edmonton, Canada.* Hagen.

von Prümmer, Christine. (1985). *Women in Distance Education 1: Gender-Related Differences in the Choice of Degree Programs at the FernUniversität Hagen.* Hagen: University Publication (Zentrum für Erwachsenenstudium).

Raehlmann, Irene. (1984) *Arbeitertöchter im Fernstudium: Studieren neben dem Beruf. Ergebnisse einer Voruntersuchung.* Hagen.

Stahr, Ingeborg. (1985). *Projekt: Die Studien- und Arbeitssituation von Frauen an der Hochschule. Projektbericht.* Essen.

Ströhlein, Gerhard, and Hartmut Raiser. (1984). *Exmatrikulationen an der FernUniversität 1979-1984: Bedingungsanalysen und Prognosen im Kontext der Einführung von Studienmaterialgebühren.* Hagen.

Swift, B. (1982). *What Open University Graduates Have Done: A Report, Based on a 1980 Survey of 3,000 Graduates, of the Occupational Outcomes of Studying with the Open University.* London: Milton Keynes.

WOMEN AS DISTANCE LEARNERS IN ISRAEL

by

Yael Enoch

> **Yael Enoch** is a lecturer in Sociology at Everyman's University, Israel's Open University. She received her Ph.D. from Tel Aviv University in 1980. Her main areas of professional interest are sociology of education and sociology of the professions. She previously taught at Tel Aviv University and Beit Berl College in Israel and at the University of Connecticut, U.S.A., and is presently engaged in developing distance education courses in social stratification and sociological theory.

Author's Note: Margalit Ganor and Esther Goder from Everyman's University evaluation department supplied statistical data concerning EU's students and graduates. They also commented on an earlier version of this paper. My sincere thanks to both of them.

From a counsellor's diary: June 15, 1985

Registration for the fall-winter semester is closing in just one week. It's hot. And it's our busiest period. We really ought to be more people sharing this job. I have to advise veteran students as well as talk to scores of prospective new students who are still not certain whether they really want to venture a course at Everyman's University (EU). I have to help some of the students to decide on the last two courses needed for their degree, while trying to help others decide which course to take as their first.

Today I saw around twenty students in about 2 1/2 hours. That makes 6-7 minutes for each on an average. Most of them have "regular" problems like we get every week. They could probably have found the answers to their questions in our printed information material but preferred to come and see a person, rather than consulting the written word. As is often true on counselling days there were a few encounters that impressed themselves on my fatigued mind, cases that made me feel that our job is really worth doing.

In order to talk to a counsellor Ruth has travelled for three hours by four buses from her small village in the Jordan Valley. She is tall, pretty and 32 years old. She studied Chinese language and literature at the Hebrew University in Jerusalem for nearly two years. Then she married, had three children and now lives with her family in a new housing development 1 1/2 hours and two buses away from any city. Her husband works long hours to provide for his family and Ruth has "suddenly" discovered her frustration from not having completed her degree. This time she is determined to succeed despite her heavy work load at home. She is willing to compromise as far as choice of courses are concerned, as EU's distance education programme is the only way a woman in her personal situation can study for a degree. I was impressed by her determination, and together we decided on a sequence of courses in literature and social sciences which, together with the credits she will be able to transfer from her previous studies, will enable her to achieve her goal in two or three years. It will be hard work, but I am sure she'll make it.

Sara and Hanna entered my office together. They are close friends, both teachers in their mid-forties. Despite the 30°C outside, they each wear a long-sleeved dress, stockings, and a scarf tied tightly around the head—the traditional outfit of the ultra-orthodox Jewish woman. To become teachers they studied (twenty years ago) at a special college for young orthodox women. Taking courses at EU will be their first encounter with education in a general secular framework. They both seemed somewhat apprehensive and were probably happy to have each other for moral support. Though it was never stated explicitly, it seemed important to them that EU offers them the opportunity to study at the tertiary level without leaving their families and their close-knit community, where secular studies, especially for women, are still not entirely acceptable. They chose their first course after careful deliberations: an introductory course in social psychology. While studying at EU they will both have to attend to their large families as well as their fulltime teaching jobs. However, in light of their religious and social background, they have shown courage and determination in making their decision to study; these same qualities, I am sure, will make them persistent and successful distance learners.

Jeanette is a veteran student at EU. She has accumulated six out of the eighteen credits needed for the B.A. degree and feels certain she is going to complete. She came to discuss the choice of her first advanced level (seminar) course. Jeanette is a divorcée in her early forties who is bringing up her three children alone and without financial support from her former husband. She was born in Morocco and came to Israel when she was in her teens. She never attended high school. Instead she married young and lived with her husband in a poor development town, where she remained with her children after her husband abandoned the family. Jeanette works as a parttime secretary at the local community centre. I have met her before in my capacity as a member of our scholarship fund committee; without financial aid she would not have been able to continue her studies. I admire this woman. With hardly any previous formal education she embarked on her first academic course and succeeded. This whetted her appetite, and she decided to continue. She is bright and has accumulated a lot of life experience. She is a "natural" at studying, despite her lack of general background knowledge. I would have thought that mathematics or computer-science, which are self-contained subject areas, would have attracted this type of student, but Jeanette wishes to study Jewish history and social sciences. Not an easy task for a person with her background. So far she has succeeded—not brilliantly, but she has passed every course she has attempted. With such a record, there is a good chance she will struggle through.

Israeli Society: A Brief Profile

Israel is a small country of 21,500 square kilometres (8,000 square miles) with approximately four million inhabitants. It has grown and developed rapidly during its thirty-eight years of independence. From 870,000 inhabitants in 1948, it has reached its present size by absorbing immigrants from over a hundred different countries, representing a vast spectrum of languages, traditions and educational backgrounds. As a society in continual growth, it has offered full employment and rapid occupational advancement, even for those who lacked the formal educational credentials which are a *sine qua non* for middle-class occupations in the Western world. This trend has to some extent culminated and today a bachelor's degree is a common entrance requirement, even to junior management or secretarial positions. This change from a situation where you could "prove your worth" on the job to one of strict credentialism has of course mainly affected the newcomers on the job market, among them many women who wished to find employment after having spent many years raising a family.

Equality: Dream or Reality?

Israel is a country that prides itself on offering equal rights and opportunities to all its citizens, regardless of race, religion or sex. The Declaration of Independence, signed May 15, 1948, states:

> [the State of Israel] will ensure complete equality of social and political rights to all its inhabitants irrespective of religion, race or sex.

The declaration notwithstanding, the achievements of Israeli women in all spheres of social activity fall far behind those of men. Let us illustrate this point by a few examples:

- Though women constitute around 50% of Israel's voters, over the years a total of no more than 10% of the members of its parliament (Knesset) have been women.

- The earning power of women is lower than that of men, with the average hourly wage of a man being 21% higher than that of a woman with similar educational qualifications (Ginor, 1983).

- Women as a group, and particularly older women, have had less formal education than men. The median years of schooling is 11.5 years for men and 11.3 years for women (CBS, 1985).

- Of the total number of academically trained persons in Israel, that is, those who have at least a B.A. degree, only 35% are women (CBS, special series, no. 643).

Differences in educational attainment between Israeli men and women can be explained to some extent in terms of the cultural norms prevalent in those countries from which a large proportion of adult Israelis have immigrated. In the Muslim-Arab culture, where approximately one-third of adult Israelis were raised, a boy, who eventually had to work and provide for his family, received more formal education than a girl, who was mainly trained for family and domestic responsibilities. This tradition was also characteristic of the rural areas in eastern and central Europe from where another large proportion of adult Israelis immigrated.

In Israel, compulsory education is provided free of charge for boys and girls alike, and both receive at least ten years of education, from age 5 to 15. Among the graduates of a full high school programme (twelve years of schooling) boys and girls are represented in equal numbers. A majority of the girls take a purely academic programme in high school, whereas many of the boys opt for a vocational-technical track. However, when we look at the proportion out of the relevant age group (20-29 years) who continue to tertiary education at a university, we find a slight underrepresentation of women: 11.6% as compared to 15.1% (CBS, 1985). Many young women choose shorter and less prestigious forms of post-secondary education. Female students, for example, form a vast majority of the student population in teacher training colleges, nursing schools and art colleges.

The dropout rate for women in conventional universities is higher than that for men. Whereas women make up 48-50% of the undergraduate student population in Israel's universities (CBS, 1985), they receive approximately 45% of the bachelor's degrees awarded in any given year, 30% of the master's degrees and 18.4% of the doctorates (CBS, special series, no. 603). Women also form a higher proportion of those graduates who have spent a longer than average time obtaining their degree.

Marriage and the responsibilities for a growing family clearly impede a woman's tertiary education more than a man's. It is an accepted norm in Israeli society that a young woman who marries a fellow student will postpone her studies and seek gainful employment to help her husband finish his degree, while in due time he will reciprocate by working in his acquired profession while she finishes her degree. In many cases, however, these plans are never carried out, and at the age of 30 the woman finds herself with a half-finished degree, a feeling of frustration and failure plus the responsibility for young children. The distance teaching programme at Everyman's University (EU) provides the ideal solution for such women. Older women who wish to re-enter the job market after their children have grown up, or women who wish to improve their chances for career advancement, have also found this programme well-suited to their needs. Why can these women not be accommodated by conventional universities?

Higher Education in Israel

Seven universities function in Israel, but none of them offers off-campus programmes. They all maintain high standards of academic excellence, admitting to some of their schools and departments (law, medicine, computer science, psychology) only one out of ten, twenty or even fifty applicants. Applications from would-be parttime students at the undergraduate level are usually not accepted. Furthermore, candidates who do not possess the full entrance qualification, such as those who lack full high school diploma, have very slim chances of being accepted, even as mature students. This policy is understandable in a situation where the demand for tertiary education far exceeds the supply of university places.

All of Israel's universities are situated in major cities, making them hard to reach for adult students who live and work in outlying areas and who have to depend on public transportation. Finally, tuition fees are very high: annual fees amount to up to two month's net salary for an average Israeli employee.

In the early 1970s, it became evident that there was a need for an alternative form of tertiary education, one which could cater to those adults who wished to acquire an academic degree but who, for a variety of reasons, could not fulfil their ambition within the existing universities. In 1974, it was decided to create Everyman's University, a single mode distance teaching university. EU began operating in 1976, modelled on its "older sister," the Open University in Great Britain.

Women as Students at Everyman's University

Given the gender inequities within Israeli society and the difficulty for mature women in attaining entrance to the conventional universities, one might perhaps expect that EU would have a majority of female students. However, if we consider women as a minority group in the sociological sense (Hacker, 1951), it would be expected that they would have had to yield to the more powerful group (the men) in the "competition" for access to this type of higher education. This is a situation known from other distance teaching universities, most notably the FernUniversität in Germany, where 77% of the students are male (Bartels, 1985).

The following table shows the gender composition of the EU student population for each semester, from the first semester in 1976 up to and including the nineteenth in Winter 1985.

As may be seen from the table, in the first three semesters the majority of students were male. However, from the fifth semester onwards, there is a consistent, though small, majority of female

Everyman's University: Israel

Table 1: Students in Academic Courses at EU by Semester and Sex (percent)

Semester	1	2	3	4	5	6	7	8	9	10
	(1976)									
Sex										
Female	37	38	43	49	52	55	55	55	52	52
Male	63	62	57	51	48	45	45	45	48	48
Total N	100	100	100	100	100	100	100	100	100	100
	(2196)	(3190)	(3888)	(4813)	(6136)	(5869)	(6329)	(7185)	(7459)	(10351)

Semester	11	12	13	14	15	16	17	18	19
									(1985)
Sex									
Female	51	53	51	54	53	51	51	49	52
Male	49	47	49	46	47	49	49	51	48
Total N	100	100	100	100	100	100	100	100	100
	(8525)	(10011)	(7848)	(10768)	(8411)	(9120)	(8052)	(8581)	(7459)

Source: EU's evaluation staff.

students. (In comparison, at Israel's conventional universities there is a small majority of male students at the undergraduate level and a more substantial dominance at the graduate level.) EU is thus neither a male monopoly nor a refuge for bored housewives but rather a university with a student population that consists of men and women in nearly equal numbers.

When we look at the subjects and courses chosen by the students, we find that the traditional differences between the sexes also persist at EU.

Table 2: Regular Students at EU by Sex and Field of Study (percent) Semesters 16–18

Semester	16		17		18	
Sex	F	M	F	M	F	M
Field of Study:						
Humanities	78.4	58.7	80.7	59.3	77.3	57.7
Sciences	21.6	41.3	19.3	40.7	22.7	42.3
Total N	3810	3904	3281	3081	3250	3420

Source: EU's evaluation staff.

Table 2 shows that, in a given semester, around 80% of the women at EU take a course in the humanities or social sciences, whereas only around 60% of the male students are enrolled in these fields.

Since no entrance requirements prevent women from taking introductory level courses in the natural sciences or in mathematics, their preference for subjects which are traditionally "feminine" is likely to be at least partly the result of early childhood socialization (Maccoby and Jacklin, 1974). By the time the adult gets to university, his or her choice of subject must be respected. Equality of opportunity does not necessarily imply that every person (man or woman) has to study the same subjects but rather that each person is free to choose an area of particular interest in which he or she can attempt to excel. To a considerable degree, however, these choices are socially determined on the basis of traditional gender expectations.

Why Do Our Students Choose Everyman's University?

Six to seven thousand students per semester, around half of them women, are registered at Everyman's University.[1] Who are they, what are their social and educational backgrounds, and why did they choose this educational framework?

EU differs from other Israeli universities in two important respects: 1) it operates by distance teaching; and 2) it has a completely open admissions policy—any person can register, and no entrance examination or interview is administered. The question therefore arises as to whether our students, particularly the women amongst them, choose EU mainly because of its liberal admissions policy or rather because this mode of education is compatible with their personal circumstances.

Seventy-two percent of the women who study at EU (compared to 65% of the men) have a high school matriculation certificate, that is, they fulfil the basic formal requirement for acceptance at one of the conventional universities. Among the women who study mathematics and natural sciences the proportion is even higher: 84%. Many of EU's students have had some previous tertiary education: 46% of the women and 37% of the men. In many cases the women have studied for one or two years at a university prior to their marriage; others have completed a two- or three-year course at a teachers training college. Thus, we may conclude that a majority of EU students, and in particular female students, are well-qualified academically to take up studies for a bachelor's degree. Evidently they did not choose EU mainly because of its "open door" policy.

Nine percent of the female students list their occupation as full-time housewives; the rest combine full- or parttime employment with their studies in addition to their responsibilities as wives and mothers (83% of the women are married and a further 12% widowed or divorced). A large proportion of them—27%—are teachers in kindergarten or elementary school, while the rest are engaged in a variety of occupations, including clerical work, nursing, agriculture and industry. Lack of time is presumably the main factor which has prevented most of our students from studying at the conventional universities. This assumption was borne out by a survey questionnaire completed by 2140 students (1081 men and 1059 women) registered for semester 16 (Winter 1984) in which the students were asked about their main reasons for registering at EU.[2] Whereas only one-fifth of the students said they were attracted to EU because of its easy admission policy, around 80% of the women (and around 70% of the men) stated that studying at

EU, unlike conventional universities, permits them to organize their time as they wish. In the case of most of the women, this time flexibility offered the possibility of combining studies and domestic responsibilities. Another important reason for choosing EU, mentioned by a large proportion of students (45% of the women and 39% of the men), was that they could study at EU without having to leave their own community.

In sum, the main attraction of EU for its students, particularly its female students, is the flexibility of its distance education programme. In addition to the majority of students who preferred EU because it teaches at a distance, and to the smaller, though significant, group who were attracted by its lack of entrance requirements, around one-third of the students, slightly more women (32.3%) than men (28%), state as a main reason for seeking out EU the opportunity to choose a multi-disciplinary degree programme, whereas in conventional Israeli universities it is compulsory for students to choose one or two academic majors.

In other words, a majority of students come to EU for *practical reasons* (distance education); around 20% of the students (over one-third of the over-40 age group) saw EU as a *second chance* to obtain an education they would not have been able to obtain elsewhere; and around one-third of the students preferred EU mainly for academic reasons (with most of the students listing more than one reason).

Do They Succeed?

As we have seen, EU offers a realistic opportunity for women who wish to take up academic studies alongside their other responsibilities. How many of the students pass the various hurdles along the route and obtain the coveted degree? And are there any differences in this respect between men and women?

In a typical semester, semester 18 (Winter 1985), around 40% of the students, men and women alike, are newcomers to EU; 24% have six credits or more, the equivalent of one year at a conventional university. Only 8% of the students have accumulated more than eleven credits; in other words, they have completed at least two-thirds of the eighteen credits required for a B.A. degree. The success rate for a single course is 45% of all students registered in the course, male and female. The overall low rate of success can to some extent be explained by the fact that the proportion is calculated out of the total number of students registered for the course, including those who never took an active part in it, that is, who never submitted any of the written assignments.

By its very nature, EU attracts a large number of students, both men and women, who never intended to take a full academic degree. They wish to study a few interesting courses. When registering for their first course, only 44% of the women (and 50% of the men) declare their goal to be an academic degree. The rest pursue a course out of general interest or because a specific course (such as computer science) may help them in their professional activities. It is very likely, however, that some of the students who started studying "out of general interest" or in order to test themselves will eventually become degree-oriented students. Their success in the first one or two courses may whet their appetite. On the other hand, by its very nature this type of educational framework is bound to have a high dropout rate. People with a lot of other responsibilities find it difficult to spend ten to twelve hours every week studying, and some students register without a realistic understanding of the time required. Taking all of these factors into consideration, the issue of success/failure rate is rather more complex than just considering the number of students who receive their final degree.

Everyman's University Graduates

EU started its operation on a very small scale, offering its first two courses in 1976. Until, and including, November 1985, 356 graduates have completed their B.A. at EU, 148 of them women (41.6%), even though women constitute 51-55% of the total student population.[3] Despite the small numbers which preclude far-reaching statistical conclusions, it seems that the dropout rate at EU is higher for women than for men, which is also true at the conventional universities.

The female graduates entered EU with more previous formal education than the males: 65% of the women had a high school matriculation certificate as compared to 53% of the men, and 64% of the women had at least one year of post-secondary education compared to 53% of the men. The female graduates also obtained significantly higher grades than their male counterparts: 63% of the female graduates (as compared to 44% of the male) completed their degree with an average grade of 80 or higher (out of 100).

A majority of all EU students, both men and women, study courses in the humanities and the social sciences. However, as previously discussed, a significantly higher proportion of EU's female students (80%) than of the males (60%) have chosen these fields. However, in the graduate population the differences between the sexes have vanished: 28.4% of female and 25.5% of male graduates obtained a degree in science or mathematics. It appears that those women who chose a "non-traditional" track have a high success rate, whereas some of the men have adapted their initial "traditional" male choice to a more realistic evaluation of their capabilities and fields of interest. One can only speculate on what would have happened if more women had been exposed to at least one introductory course in the science-mathematics field. Would they too (like many of the male graduates) have discovered that their interests and talents lie in a field not traditionally sought out by members of their sex?

Even if EU were to abandon its liberal policy and make one science course a compulsory requirement for all humanities majors (and one humanities course required for all science majors) it is not very likely that a large number of women would "convert" to science. The structure of the science courses, especially the advanced courses, demands participation in a number of lab exercises and field trips, most of which take place only on certain days and at the central EU campus in Tel Aviv. As pointed out earlier, a large proportion (70%) of the women chose EU particularly because it enabled them to study where and when they wished. How can a mother of young children who lives in Elath (400 km south of Tel Aviv) be sure in June, when she is required to register for a course that starts in September, that she will be able to participate in two full-day laboratory sessions at the EU campus in November and December?

Whereas only 44% of the women in the total student population (and 50% of the men) intended to study for an academic degree at the time of registering for their first EU course, these proportions were, as might be expected, much higher among the graduates. Seventy-four percent of the graduating women and 70% of the men intended from the very beginning to obtain a degree. A further 13% started studying to acquire certain skills and thus improve their opportunities for advancement in the job market. Only 13% of the women graduates and 17% of the men took their first course at EU out of a desire for knowledge and general education.

In sum, what characterizes the majority of these first graduates is a good educational background as well as a strong determination. Yet over one-third of the women graduates and close to one-half of the men acquired an academic degree without having graduated from high school. The motivation, determination and self-discipline of these students must indeed have been extremely strong.

Discussion

Everyman's University fills an important gap in the system of higher education in Israel. The question that remains to be answered, especially from the point of view of our female students and graduates, is whether attaining the coveted degree does indeed help graduates to gain promotions or find interesting jobs. And if it does not, does that imply that the project has failed, that it has created hopes and ambitions which can perhaps never be fulfilled? As the number of graduates so far has been too small to warrant a systematic investigation, the following will be a rather impressionistic discussion, based on informal conversations with a small number of graduates.

Some of our graduates pursued their studies to gain knowledge, to develop personally, or to prove to themselves that "they could do it." These graduates are generally happy with their achievement and do not at this stage seek ulterior rewards for their hard work. Graduates of this type have in many cases enrolled in Master's degree programmes at conventional universities. The fact that studies for advanced degrees at these universities require fewer hours of classroom attendance than undergraduate studies make these programmes more accessible to EU graduates. The independent study skills they have acquired during their years as distance students contribute significantly to their success in advanced studies.

Another large group of EU graduates, particularly of the women, already have a profession with which they are essentially satisfied. They wanted their academic degree for personal development and to qualify for higher positions within their professional field. The degree may help them become school principals or head nurses or to advance to management positions in the industrial plants where they are employed. Most of these graduates feel that their effort has been worthwhile and that their degree will indeed help them achieve their goals.

The more problematic group of graduates consists of women (and men) from disadvantaged backgrounds. They are the ones who worked hardest to succeed, overcoming major obstacles to prove to themselves that they are as talented and as motivated, if not more so, than the people who were born in more privileged social circumstances. But they may have developed unrealistic expectations of what a university degree will do for them. Some of them will be disappointed. "Yes," they agree, "I am a different person now, I talk and I think differently, but what use is it all if I still have to live in a near-slum area and work in a low-paying job in an office or factory? I have acquired no marketable skills."

It is hard to deal with this type of criticism. Until now EU has offered only academic courses, but recently more professionally oriented courses have been added: the department of computer science is developing rapidly; a high school teacher's diploma can be added to the B.A. by approximately one further year of study. If EU succeeds in creating more professional programmes, in nursing, social work or dietetics, for example, this will be of particular importance to future female graduates. As relative newcomers to an increasingly credentialized job market, women need well-defined professional skills.

It is not suggested that EU should give up further development of courses in the pure academic fields which are the backbone of any university programme. More courses and especially a larger variety of advanced level courses are needed, especially in the social sciences and the humanities. And hopefully one day in the not too distant future, EU graduates will be able to continue towards their Master's degree by distance education.

In conclusion it seems fair to say that EU offers many women a unique chance to improve their education and skills. The equality of participation, persistence and achievement between men and women is certainly encouraging. However, there still exists in Israel a large untapped pool of potential students for whom present educational structures, including EU, are too demanding and inflexible. This group probably includes many women already combining family and employment responsibilities. Individually tailored studies would of course be an additional burden on the university's administration, but the effort would be worthwhile. Let us hope that as a result of its continuing development EU will be able to accommodate many of those potential students whom it does not reach today.

Notes

1. In addition to these individually registered students, around 4,000 students per semester study EU courses within the framework of other educational institutions, such as at teacher training colleges.

2. They could give as many reasons as they wished.

3. This difference is to some extent explained by the fact that 44% of the women, compared to 50% of the men, intended to study for a degree when registering for their first EU course.

References

Bartels, Jörn. (1985). *The FernUniversität of the Federal Republic of Germany*. Mimeographed paper.

Central Bureau of Statistics (CBS). Special Publication Series, no. 643 and no. 603. Jerusalem.

Central Bureau of Statistics (CBS). Statistical Abstracts of Israel. (1985). Jerusalem.

Ginor, Fanny. (1983). *Socio-Economic Disparities in Israel*. Tel-Aviv: Am Oved Publishers.

Hacker, H.M. (1951). "Women as a Minority Group." *Social Forces, 30*, 60-69.

Maccoby, Eleanor E. and Carol Nagy Jacklin. (1974). *The Psychology of Sex Differences*. Palo Alto, California: Stanford University Press.

Chapter 5

TEACHING ART AT A DISTANCE IN NEW ZEALAND

by

Jeanne Macaskill

> **Jeanne Macaskill**, N.D.D., D.F.A. (Honours), studied painting and sculpture at the Chelsea School of Art in London, where she also taught in the School of Art and the College of Advanced Education. She also taught and exhibited in France. Beginning in 1972 she taught in tertiary institutions in her native New Zealand; there she developed the Advanced Studies for Teachers Unit Art papers, served on the staff of the Wellington Teachers College, and prepared art education materials for children and their teachers. Jeanne Macaskill is a well-known practicing artist, and most recently she has taken a position as visiting fellow at the Brisbane College of Advanced Education in Australia.

Author's Note: The research for this paper was completed with the particular help of Rosemary Stokeil, ASTU Tutor in Art Papers; Maureen Friend, Ann Johnson and Helen Reid, students of the ASTU Art Papers; Rei Henry, Art Advisor and student of ASTU Art Papers; and many other art students located throughout New Zealand. To all these women I extend gratitude.

Introduction

In the mid-1980s, two events brought New Zealand into the international spotlight: first the bombing by French agents of the "Rainbow Warrior," a Greenpeace vessel visiting New Zealand at the time, and then the government's refusal to welcome U.S. warships carrying nuclear arms. Both events caused a great deal of international controversy and aroused interest in this uniquely independent nation. New Zealand has 3.3 million inhabitants, most of whom are of British stock; the indigenous population, the Maoris, form about 14% of the population. New Zealanders are very proud of their socialist-oriented country and their belief in equality and fair opportunity, including racial harmony. In a country that is dedicated to equality, a good fair education for all is the ideal. While the situation is still far from the ideal, and many people are in fact disadvantaged, the New Zealand Education Department gives as much service to as many people as possible.

With a rise in the awareness of the importance of the Arts in the expression of the nation's cultural life, Art became a compulsory subject for all children up to fourteen years of age. It was agreed that art is a useful part of education, that it can join in with other subjects, or can stand on its own, and that it can involve all sorts of people—children, their parents and teachers—with or without specialist training. One way to educate teachers was to establish papers through the Advanced Studies for Teachers Unit, a correspondence programme.

The Advanced Studies for Teachers Unit

New Zealand has a large, rurally based population; people have traditionally earned their main income through the exports of meat, wool and dairy products. With the belief that all people should have equal opportunities, the Education Department established the Correspondence School to enable children in outback areas, children of lighthouse keepers, and so on, to have an education equal to that of any other child in the land. This school grew rapidly and now has about twenty thousand students, both primary and secondary as well as adults getting a "second chance" education. In the 1960s, another section was established, the "Advanced Studies for Teachers Unit" (ASTU). Through this unit teachers working in the classroom were able to train to acquire credentials. Later, the Unit established papers for a Diploma of Teaching—a qualification equal to a university degree that can be taken only by a qualified teacher. The Unit is now run by a Teachers College and offers Higher and Advanced Diplomas.

In the late 1970s, the Secondary Teachers Union persuaded the Education Department to establish papers that unqualified teachers could take through the Unit to qualify them as Art Teachers. Nine papers were prepared and offered to all teachers. These papers cover diverse aspects of Art Education, and they usually attract a wide range of teachers. The Education Department encourages flexibility and a variety of approaches by teachers:

> Teachers work in highly individual ways and vary their approaches to meet different circumstances...teachers need the reassurance that,

while there may be no step-by-step instructions about how to teach, there are available to them a number of tested alternatives. The teacher has a professional role: to determine the most appropriate way of working in a particular circumstance (Department of Education, 1978).

These papers cover a wide range of material for any teacher taking Art lessons at any level, and they are divided into three groups of study:

- the methodology of teaching the practical and creative aspects of Art and Craft; development of perception; Art History and Art Appreciation;
- the history and philosophy of Art Education, and the specialist knowledge needed for teaching in this subject area;
- the development of the personal skills and creativity of the teacher.

The third aspect is based on the New Zealand attitude that to be a good teacher of Art one must also be a practitioner. The work done in this area is unique to New Zealand. All students are expected to do some sort of painting and drawing, without coming to any compulsory workshop. They have no direct help from the tutor, and this causes many problems, including self-doubt and lack of confidence. Special techniques have been developed for tutoring students, with great success.

Students of ASTU Art Papers

A survey taken of a sampling of two hundred and fifty of the students of the Art papers produced some interesting figures. Both men and women are able to take ASTU papers, but the clientele is mainly women (80%). These are the students we will discuss, the great majority of whom are primary teachers. The percentage of women taking papers varied considerably, with only 55% taking a practical paper about strategies for teaching adolescents to 88% taking a paper on the teaching of Art Appreciation. The majority of the teachers in primary schools are women, and the overall percentage that take our papers reflects this fact. The area most popular with women teachers is Art Appreciation, which has been seen as a women's preserve. (Theoretically, the practical doing and making of Art has had more importance for men than for women.) For example, the "Understanding Art" paper allows for tours to Art Galleries, an activity that particularly appeals to women. This appreciation for established artists' work is consistent with the programme's philosophy, as stated in the course syllabus:

> Students need to know about the social context of art, and the significance different cultures and societies give to art works and to art. They need to recognise the variety of responses that are made by people, groups, cultures and organisations to art works, and to recognise that there exist many and varied bases of judgement which give rise to many different sets of values given to art and art works (New Zealand New Draft Syllabus for Art Education, 1986).

Reasons for Enrolling in Art Education ASTU Papers

A survey in the form of a questionnaire to all students has revealed the reasons why women take these papers. Distance education is the only choice for many teachers in the rural areas, whereas teachers living in the cities have the option of face-to-face courses at a local Teachers College. We questioned the students as to why they studied with ASTU rather than attend face-to-face courses at the Teachers College. The following reasons, in order of preference, were given for their choice.

Method of Study

They learned better through distance than in a face-to-face situation: working on their own meant that they "really have to learn" the material before writing it down in the assignments. Some of the students who took ASTU papers tutored by the writer of this article also attended one of her "face-to-face" classes at the Teachers College. Their comments are relevant here: "We did much more work really when we studied by distance but in the end we learnt more" and "we found having the ASTU materials on hand all year helped us to learn more, as we could refer back to it easily for practical purposes and to prepare for the exam at the end of the year." Another said "I preferred the very individual attention I gained from being tutored by the ASTU."

Flexible Learning and Working Times

For many of the women, the fact that the face-to-face classes were held during the late afternoon or early evening period was a problem. Looking after their children and cooking the main family meal of the day meant they were not free to attend college classes at those times. Another reason was plain tiredness. One said, "the thought of sitting down to study at 4:30 p.m. in the afternoon after a heavy day, preceded by a frantic two hours getting the family organized, was just too much. I knew I could well drop off to sleep!! However at nine o'clock at night I seem to get a 'second wind' and I can get in two or sometimes three hours of thorough study before I go to bed."

The Chance for Further Study

This was especially important, it appears, to those in rural areas. It is interesting that this reason was offered more often than the need to gain qualifications. These papers are taken by teachers in their own time, they pay the quite high fees themselves, and voluntarily enrol if they feel the need in some way.

One teacher who had been out of the work force for some time, while starting her family, writes appreciatively. As she had no class to use for her teaching component, she was able to work with her own children. "The course provided a marvellous interim period between parenting and my return to the teaching profession. Being able to include my family was a great bonus."

Female teachers in many primary schools are not elevated to senior positions and as a consequence have less chance of being sent to refresher courses. The Equal Opportunities group is trying to rectify this situation. Meanwhile, many teachers use these courses as the only available way of getting continued upgrading and contact with new ideas.

Qualification

Women in more senior positions put the need for further qualifications high on the list. An Art Advisor who travels in a country region advising and helping teachers take art lessons commented as follows: "Art courses have given me increased confidence, greater knowledge and better qualified me for the position I hold."

To Gain Greater Self-Confidence

Many women find themselves suddenly in the position of taking several classes in Art Education through rearrangement of the responsibilities in the school's programme. *(Men* take the sports, and *Women* the art and music; this is still quite a common division.) Suddenly flung into a new situation, they use the ASTU papers to help them. A typical letter from a student reads, "I am sorry to say I am not an 'arty' person and know very little about art. I am finding this work rather difficult." However, these problems are overcome: "Upon commencing this ASTU paper I felt, like many teachers, very inadequate, but with your encouragement and guidance, and the practical experience and reading, I feel now that I can run a programme in my class that would incorporate a wide range of Art Appreciation. I now feel very confident in this area."

Individual Tuition and Confidentiality
Two great strengths of distance education are the fact that each student is tutored as an individual, in privacy—which appeals to many women in the area of Art. Drawing and painting in front of other adults is often very daunting, and many preferred to experiment at home. "You are the first person I have ever shown my work to" writes one student from a small rural town. "Your helpful and encouraging comments have spurred me on and I have decided to get the small still-life drawing framed."

A Chance to do a Personal Study
Many women use the papers to justify their having some time and space of their own. One paper has an in-depth study in one medium especially designed to give the teacher a chance to develop her personal skills further. One teacher writes, "the opportunity to develop artistically has been of tremendous value and I'm sad that the course is over in this respect. It gave me the chance to develop my photography without anyone in the family saying I was wasting time or money!"

Success Rate for Students of ASTU Art Papers

Many women who had registered found they were unable to start the course, because of changes in family circumstances, jobs, pregnancy or, in one or two instances, lack of confidence in their ability. A much smaller number were forced to withdraw before completing the course, for reasons including personal or family illness or injury. The most demanding reason was sickness of a parent. Male students in similar circumstances more often requested an extension of assignment deadlines and managed to keep going to the end.

Remarkably, of those who started the course, 98% completed it. The Unit encourages success in such subjects and the policy has been not to record marks until the student has completed good work.

Such a strategy requires that work be returned with comments and advice, and the student resubmits it with proper alterations. The year's work of either four or six large assignments, each incorporating several sections, accounts for 60% of the final mark. The other 40% are gained through taking a rigorous exam. Curve marking is not considered appropriate and in over six years as a tutor I have seen only two students fail the exam, which means failure on the paper.

Designing the Papers

In all distance education the most important factor is that clear and well-planned resources are used for instruction. The success or failure of an ASTU paper in Art Education is determined by this criterion. However, in terms of helping individual teachers develop skills and abilities in techniques and approaches to painting, printmaking, drawing or other art forms, care is given to see that the student can succeed. The content of the course must be suitable for adaptation to any classroom situation and to any environment in which students live and work.

Planning of the course includes a pattern of progression so that the first assignment contains material and exercises that give the student a background to the subject. The ASTU provides printed material and slides of Art works, and exercises must be designed in such a way that all students will be capable of achieving some success. The practical exercises in drawing, for example, also allow for expression by a gifted and experienced artist. The major paper with the largest enrolments, "Basic Studies in Art Education," has as its major theme the subject of "Line." All students, from beginners to advanced artists, can work on different exercises, making quite different sorts of line. Students are only required to do simple patterns, and one or two drawings, in line, recording a simple object. As one introduction to a course points out, "you do not have to be a skilled and trained artist to do this course—if you were Leonardo da Vinci you certainly would not have enrolled in it!"

One of the problems in designing the Art courses is trying to give the student an indication of the amount of work required. In assigning a written essay, it is easy enough to require "about so many hundred words," but with a series of practical art exercises it is much harder to define quantitative limits. Some adults like to do many rough sketches before making the completed art work; others start at once on their major work. Suggestions of length of time to be spent on particular sections have a daunting effect. Many students do not feel they have achieved enough with what "could be expected in two hours" and feel guilty if they carry on longer. It seems that some students, uncertain about what is required, work extremely hard not only to do the exercises to an excellent standard but also to present them artistically. Such students don't always manage to keep their standard up all year because they spend too long on the first assignment. The course should contain a section on the amount of effort expected while also strongly cautioning the student against spending *too much time.*

Another problem is the lack of an appropriate, affordable text. Tutors must offer reference suggestions which students must locate for themselves.

Tutoring Students

This discussion relates to the practical component of the Art papers, the student's own drawing, painting, printmaking, or whatever art form is selected. The tutor faces problems in this regard. While each assignment is given a mark, those responsible for tutoring the art papers never see themselves as "markers," as do some other tutors who work for the Unit. The aim is to improve the students' performance throughout the course so that at the end of the year they can succeed in passing at the level required. This requires a great deal of sensitivity and individual consideration for each student. Since the tutor does not necessarily ever meet the student face-to-face, there is usually complete reliance on correspondence. Through letters the tutor must become acquainted with the student, to be able to gauge the level of performance that can be expected.

In setting marks, the tutor has to take into account:

- the required standard of work expected for the paper;
- the standard that would be expected from each individual student, remembering that they come from many varied backgrounds;
- how far the student comes in relation to the first point of assessment, and how to find a way to help the student bridge this gap without losing confidence; and
- allowance for individual creativity and originality.

Confidence Building

The aim of developing the students' self-confidence is very important in this particular subject area. Some adults lose confidence very easily, especially in the Arts. Consequently, a method has been evolved to give the student support while at the same time keeping work "up to standard." The "sandwich method" is a technique involving three simple steps—first praising the good qualities of the student's work (there is always something!), then giving good sound advice and criticism, and finally praising again and ending on a positive note. This works wonders, and tutors in these papers find the women who take them increase their energy, self-confidence, standard of work and output, and they grow considerably in both knowledge and skills.

"Thank you for helping me battle on—I feel much more relaxed with the drawing and am actually beginning to *enjoy* myself," writes one student who had not drawn or painted since she was twelve and who found that putting the initial marks on paper was very intimidating. "I just cannot wait to start the big painting; I never thought I would achieve enough confidence to do anything like this," writes another, a solo mother with several children who in the end gained great pleasure and joy from the Arts papers and from the practical exercises in particular.

Allowing for Individual Differences

Certain exercises are expected to be carried through in a careful, detailed manner that requires thought and consciousness rather than developed skills and talent. At the beginning, a wide range of work arrives, and it soon becomes apparent that the students' work reflects their own attitudes. For example, students who have acquired art skills and qualifications prior to entering our course often send in work that is obviously quickly done. On the other hand students who are diffident often send in work that is extremely careful and thoughtful, even though they may never have drawn or painted before.

The criteria for marking such work includes:

- understanding and completion of all the required exercises;
- awareness of the significance of the particular area studied;
- care and sensitivity shown in doing the particular exercises;
- presentation and attitude towards caring about the work done;

- amount of work done;
- originality of ideas and a creative and imaginative use of materials;
- conventional considerations when judging any art work, such as use of colour, design, and so on. These, however, are not the dominant criteria, as would be true in a conventional circumstance where performance in art is being appraised.

The students learn what is required and develop surprisingly well as the course progresses. However, it is always a challenge to the tutor to give really good constructive advice which will facilitate the student's progress. The student will not grow without criticism; praise alone is not enough. Well-supported and confident students who are given encouragement to grow and think for themselves will develop as individuals who exhibit originality and sensitivity in their work. Through the tutorial system, and the design of the course, the personal style of each student develops noticeably.

Setting Standards

The standard for results comes in two ways. One is how the tutor handles marking and advising the student on her work. The second is the student herself. *She* has an idea in *her* head of the requirements of such a paper at university standard and believes that her work must attain the highest level. Many send in work that exceeds the requirements of the assignment. Indeed, the standard of work submitted by students in the Art papers is in many cases the highest of all the students in ASTU. Even the amount and quality of the written work that accompanies the assignment is in many cases higher than work required in other areas. As a result, the demands of packeting, responding to and marking Art papers is a very heavy workload for tutors, who are compensated for the extra amount of work in their tutoring allocations.

Some students have to be counselled not to work too hard, as many can burn themselves out early in the year. The final review of the whole year's work shows an enormous amount of material drawn, painted, printed, and so on by the student. Since the students are teachers, much of the work they have done can be useful as resource material for their own courses.

While standards are closely monitored by the tutors, some students' work is not marked until they reach the desired level of achievement, which they manage to do in nearly every case. In effect, the students set their own standards, and ultimately their expectations are well in line with the requirements of the course.

Conclusion

One might think that studying at a distance is disadvantageous to art students, especially, as is the case in New Zealand, where students have no face-to-face contact with their tutor. However, comparisons of practical art work reveal that the distant student succeeds as well as any student in face-to-face classes at the Teachers College. Even more interesting is that the retention and success rate of students in these papers is comparable with students in other subject areas in ASTU, despite complaints that the Art Papers are the "hardest and most demanding papers to take." As one student said:

> I could not believe the amount of work that was required of me when I began! It was a real battle to get up enough courage to send in the first assignment—I kept trying to do it better each time. Now that I have completed this paper there is a real gap in my life, because I have never learnt so much or become involved to such a degree. I feel I may really manage to become an artist one day!! Anyway, I know I am a much better Art teacher as a result of this study and will not drop my newfound interest in a hurry!

Herbert Read quotes William Godwin who, in 1797, said: "The true object of education, like that of every other moral process, is the generation of happiness" (1966:1). While this may not be our only aim, it is surely one of them, and it describes the outcome for the women who take ASTU Art papers in New Zealand.

References

Department of Education. (1978). "Art in Schools, The New Zealand Experience." Wellington, New Zealand.

New Zealand New Draft Syllabus for Art Education J1 to F7 (1986).

Read, Herbert. (1966). *The Redemption of the Robot: My Encounter with Education Through Art.* New York: Trident Press.

SAMPLES OF STUDENTS' ART WORK, NEW ZEALAND

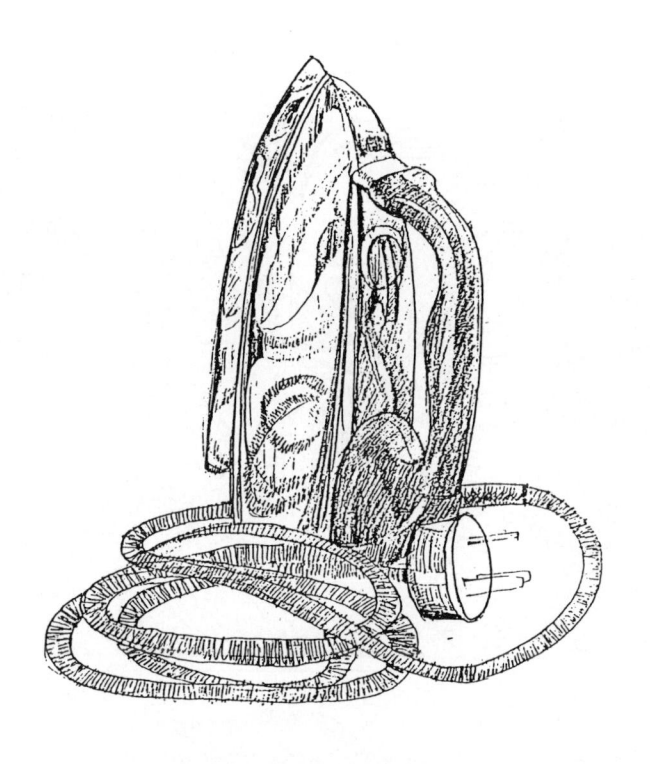

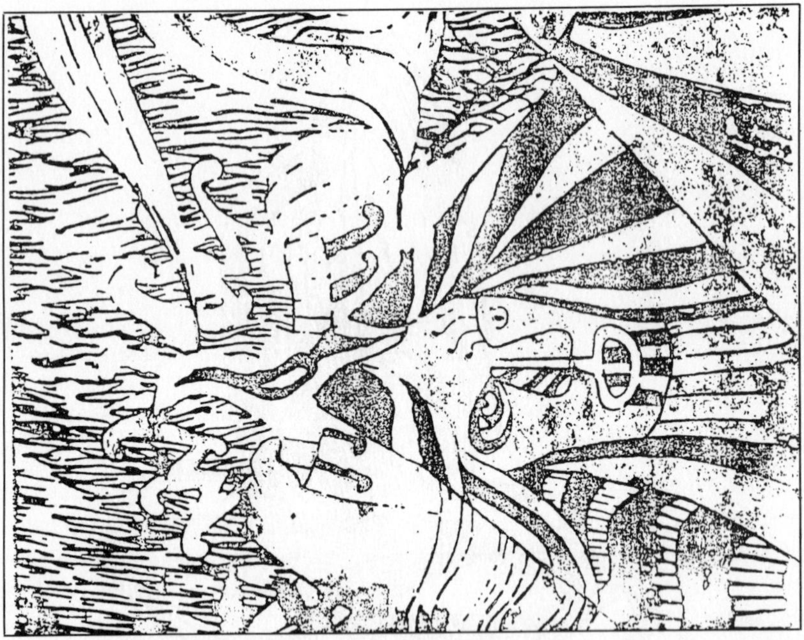

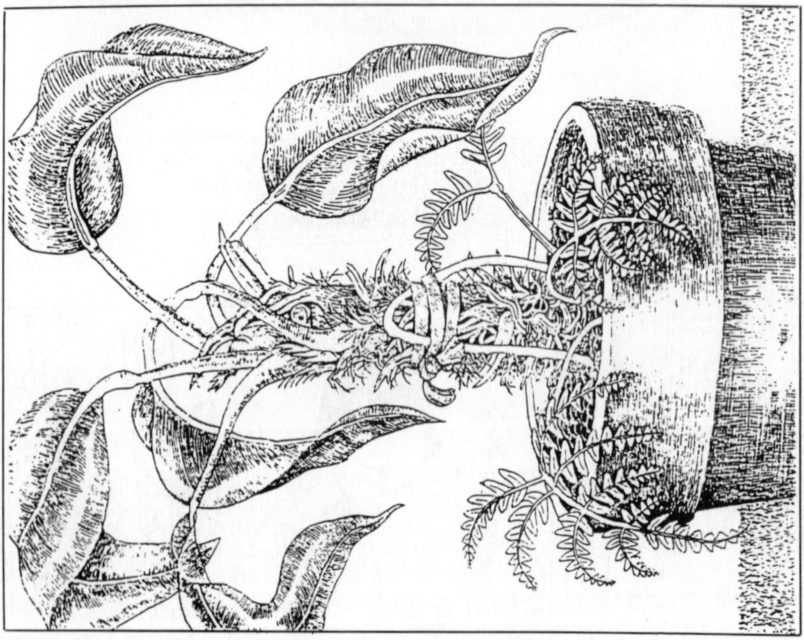

DISTANCE EDUCATION AS A MEANS OF ENHANCING SELF-ESTEEM AMONG ADULT FEMALE STUDENTS IN SWEDEN

by

Birgitta Willén

> **Birgitta Willén** combines the role of teaching at a distance (adult education at Lund University) with her research work in distance education (Uppsala University). Her doctoral thesis (1981) evaluated distance education in Swedish universities, and she is currently with a research project investigating university distance education in Australia, West Germany, Canada and the Nordic countries. She has also done research for the National Board of Universities and Colleges.

Introduction

An important educational goal in Sweden has been to increase access to higher education for adults whose study opportunities have been limited because of residential distance from university towns, fulltime employment, or family responsibilities. More flexible entrance requirements have been gradually introduced at universities, evening classes have been expanded, and distance education programmes have been implemented (Dahllöf, Kim and Willén, 1978). As a consequence, the student population at Swedish universities now includes a great many parttime students, a significant portion of whom are studying at home. Distance education is especially important for women who are unable to attend classes either during the day or in the evening because of childcare responsibilities.

During the planning of reforms in the area of adult education little attention has been given to the fact that women and men have different life situations and different motives for studying. One of the purposes of this paper is to underscore the importance of those differences in the context of distance education in Swedish universities (Willén, 1981, 1983, 1984). To this end, I have recently surveyed a population of distance learners and identified certain salient characteristics of this group. For example, distance learners are older than traditional students, most of them over age 35. Their motivations for studying are related to occupational goals as well as self-improvement through general education. Women in particular tend to indicate a desire for general education as their motive for entering or returning to university. Two-thirds of these students would be unable to study if distance education had not been initiated, and it is primarily women who are dependent on this alternative mode.

The Life Situation of the Distance Student

As confirmed by the findings of my investigation, women between the ages of 25 and 40 were employed outside the home far less often than men, because they often stay at home to take care of their children; a marked increase in the professional activity of women occurs after the age of 45. Among employed students, almost all the men worked fulltime, and 25% of the women worked parttime. A large portion of employed women worked as teachers whose scheduled working hours are fewer than those of most fully employed people. Overall, women in all age groups spend much more time at home; nevertheless, fewer women than men are able to study without interruption, which is consistent with my hypothesis that the social role of women as family caretakers impedes their goals outside the domestic arena.

It appears that both men and women were strongly supported in their educational strivings by people in their environment, and women under age 45 received even more support than men from their parents. Nevertheless, men over 25 demonstrated far more self-confidence than women. Only 36% of female students between 35 and 44 believed they could succeed in their studies, even though 65% of this group had in fact completed their studies successfully after three terms, with no differences in this regard between women and men. (See Table 1.)

What Distance Education Has Meant to the Students

Four years after completion of their studies, the students were asked the following open question: "What has distance education meant to you?". Eighty-two percent of the group (N=454)

Table 1: The Students' Life Situation in Relation to Sex and Age (percent)

Situation	-24 M	-24 F	25-34 M	25-34 F	35-44 M	35-44 F	45+ M	45+ F	Total M	Total F
Married or cohabiting	9	33	73	78	89	84	88	73	78	78
Have children who need looking after	5	17	55	58	79	84	53	33	69	60
Parents positive to studies	82	100	63	74	49	57	33	16	46	53
Husband/wife positive to studies	23	67	72	75	77	76	79	72	65	69
Employed										
Full time	55	50	86	57	98	62	92	74	89	63
Part time	83	67	96	75	95	75	96	67	95	73
Housewife/man	–	–	1	25	1	25	2	24	5	27
	–	17	1	28	–	24	–	10	–	22
Anticipate succeeding with studies	50	67	60	42	56	36	47	40	56	40
Plan to study more than 10 hours/week	55	67	46	49	47	55	50	65	47	53
Actually studies 10 hours/week	24	–	26	32	33	46	43	56	55	41
Have studied without a break	20	–	18	9	25	12	30	16	23	11
Have no parallel studies	71	67	70	72	72	71	69	65	63	59
Time spent on work in the home 5 hours or more/week	–	67	11	58	5	53	–	29	6	50
Time spent on work in the home 9 hours or more/week	–	–	1	20	–	13	–	–	–	13
N	22	6	187	149	151	114	88	78	448	347

Source: Willén, 1981:106.

answered the question and one-third of the respondents stressed the importance to them of distance education as a mode of study. A smaller percentage of the answers (19%) implied that distance studies had been of significance for occupational reasons. Over 50% emphasized that distance studies had resulted in greater self-esteem, increased general knowledge, good relations with teachers and other students, and greater insight into the implications of university education. This category, in contrast to the other two categories, stressed the psychological and social effects of distance education. Only 5% of the answers took up negative factors. The question as to the value of distance education in retrospect has been answered in different ways by men and women, with women responding more openly and emotionally than men and providing longer answers. Since the answers were assigned to more than one category of response, Table 2 shows a larger number of answers than the number of people who replied to the question.

Table 2: The Value of Distance Education in Retrospect, in Relation to Sex (percent)

	Male	Female	Total
Negative experience	6	3	5
Study form important	31	36	33
Occupational reasons	17	22	19
Self-realization	53	60	56
Other	7	2	5
Total	114	123	118
N	246	208	454

Source: Willén, 1981: 191.

As shown in Table 3, students were queried as to the value of distance education according to previous educational background. Fulltime workers commonly mentioned that distance education was the only alternative, because they had no possibility of taking leave of absence in order to move to a university town, or because distance education did not require attendance at lectures. As one female student expressed it:

> I feel extremely positive toward distance education and the opportunities it provides for those who live far from a university town, or for those who, like me, have small children. I have read several subjects at university before and I think distance education is planned in such a way that it can easily compete with the regular university courses.

Table 3: What Distance Education has Meant to the Students in Relation to Educational Background (percent)

Answer	Previous university education		No previous university education			
			Teachers		Others	
	M	F	M	F	M	F
Negative experience	6	2	–	18	6	3
Positive opinions						
Study form	32	46	33	35	28	21
Occupational situation	15	20	13	12	20	27
Self-realization	47	51	67	71	67	71
Other	8	3	–	–	7	1
Total	108	122	113	136	128	123
N	146	114	15	17	85	77

Source: Willén, 1981: 193.

Men frequently reported that the distance course had contributed towards a change in occupation and, in some cases, a better job. Women who had not been previously employed credited the course with enabling them to find work, and other women were able to advance from parttime to fulltime employment.

There were interesting differences between those with previous experience of academic studies and those without such experience. The former group, especially the women, drew attention to the fact that this was a positive study form, a result which is fascinating considering that this group had a basis for comparing distance education with conventional classroom study. Those without previous academic experience, on the other hand, were more likely to stress that the distance course had been of importance for their occupational situation and their self-esteem. Respondents with prior experience in higher education may have already acquired a certain amount of self-esteem in this regard.

When the answers were distributed according to age, it was, above all, the two younger groups of women who valued the distance education mode of study, probably because many of them are caring for family and children. Their answers often referred to these responsibilities, unlike the answers given by the male students (see Haukaa, 1976; Brock-Utne and Haukaa, 1980).

Below are three examples of how female students have answered this question:

> I think the course was splendid. It made it possible for me to study despite [responsibility for] small children and a lack of babysitters. It suited me perfectly. It also meant that the family got used to me studying and I have continued to do so. Now the children are older and after one more term I shall have my B.A. If it had not been for the distance course, I might not have started studying at all. As it was, I had some experience when I started the next course.
>
> It was an easy way of making the transition to fulltime studies. It would have meant a minor revolution for me and my family if I had gone over to fulltime studies from the very start. Distance education gave both me and my family a year to adjust to the idea without venturing [into it] all at once. Women's studies and careers are so often interrupted when they have a family. This was so in my case. Without distance education, I might never have taken up studies again.
>
> [My studies were] extremely stimulating. Married women with small children are often tied to their husband's work [location]....[Distance Education allows us a chance to enter] a field of our own....The children demand a lot of attention and some stimulation from the outside world is necessary. I am more stimulated by my distance studies than by my parttime job, in spite of agreeable colleagues.

The occupational situation of those under the age of 44, especially female students, more often changed for the better. On the other hand, older students more often valued their distance learning because their studies increased their self-esteem. Seventy-nine percent of the female students over age 45 stated that the distance course had been extremely positive in this sense.

When the answers were distributed according to motives for studying, only very slight differences between the groups materialized. One difference was interesting. Male students who began a distance course with the intention of changing their occupational situation answered that the distance course had had a positive effect on their occupational situation twice as often as other male students.

Increased Self-Esteem as a Result of Studies

A most interesting and somewhat unexpected finding of the survey was that many students credit distance study as having had a positive effect on their feelings of self-esteem. The reasons for this effect included increased general knowledge, good relations with teachers and other students, and greater insight into the overall implications of a university education.

It could be said that one of the goals of all education is to further the self-esteem of the individual. This aim has probably been most emphasized in connection with adult education; although it is not defined as a specific goal, it constitutes part of other goals—such as increased equality, social justice and cultural consciousness. However, these goals are on a macro-societal level, and in this project we are most interested in students' goals on an individual level wherein self-evaluation is difficult and complex.

In one of the most frequently used Swedish educational reference books, self-esteem is defined as: "the value one attaches to one's own personality" (Egidius, 1977). This definition may appear simple, but the concept of self-esteem has fascinated researchers from many disciplines. The most usual approach to the measure of self-esteem is a psychological one, where self-esteem is regarded as an important explanatory variable. The work done by Sjöstrand (1974) is well worth mentioning in this connection. Sjöstrand shows that the majority of researchers in this field consider self-esteem to be learned through social interaction:

> The common view among [researchers] is that we learn our worth...
> by observing how other individuals react to us, praise us and blame
> us (p. 26).

Relations to dependents—parents, close friends and teachers—are of importance in this regard. Another significant factor is social status, i.e., "the higher the social status that an individual enjoys, the more likely he [or she] is to evaluate himself [or herself] positively" (*ibid.*, p. 33). Different occupations are associated with varying social status. High-status professions are often those which require long and arduous theoretical training (Björck, 1967; Herloff, 1967). A number of investigations have shown that pupils who choose theoretical subjects at school are likely to evaluate themselves more highly than those who choose practical subjects (Johannesson, 1967; Willén, 1973).

Sjöstrand defined certain conditions which increase the likelihood of positive self-esteem. Accepting parents are a prerequisite, and the personality characteristics of an individual should coincide with those rated highly by the social environment. The level of aspiration should also be in agreement with the individual's actual ability and achievement, and he or she must possess a strong defence against criticism (Sjöstrand, 1974:64). Sjöstrand also points out some important consequences of low self-esteem:

- such individuals feel unhappy and anxious;
- such individuals have little faith in their own ability to improve their lives by achievement or social contacts;
- these individuals are characterized by social incompetence; they do not function satisfactorily in a social context, living in the shadow of society and showing qualities which make it difficult for them to cooperate with others;
- the behaviour and personality characteristics which seem to have the effect of low self-esteem are not those which are rewarded by the social environment *(ibid.,* p. 78).

Self-esteem, therefore, is a complex concept which is difficult to measure and to relate to other variables. For our purposes the most important part of Sjöstrand's analysis is her discussion of self-esteem as a variable which both explains and is explained by behaviour and experience:

> The relation of self-esteem to other variables is best described as a circle where the effects of self-esteem at the same time tend to be the determinants of self-esteem *(ibid.,* p. 83).

Zetterberg has studied the same type of problem in another context, namely, that of the individual's situation at work and implication of lifestyle in this connection. Zetterberg contends that an individual's self-esteem has two sources, an inner one and an outer one. The inner source is judged to be more stable and reliable than the outer one, which is of a more temporary nature and, at times, even non-existent. Zetterberg says that the inner source depends on whether or not we succeed through our actions in matching our intentions, and whether we are competent, enterprising and capable in this regard (1979:34). The outer source, on the other hand, depends on how others evaluate us, especially those to whom we are closest, such as our parents.

Hypothetically, a distance course can increase self-esteem in relation to work, family and friends. In our investigation we were most interested in students' motives for study and to what factors they attributed their increased self-esteem. We selected students who, in one way or another, had explicitly mentioned self-esteem in their answers to the open question concerning what distance education had meant to them, which included 60% of the female respondents and 53% of the male respondents.

Seventeen percent of the 454 students who answered the question stated that their self-esteem had increased as a result of studies. A considerably larger proportion of women than men (25% compared with 11%) emphasized that this was an important result of their distance education.

In Table 4, the distribution of male and female students who mentioned the concept of self-esteem is presented according to the categories which emerged when the material was analyzed. Over a third of the women said that their self-esteem increased because they had succeeded in doing what they set out to do. It was clear from many of the answers that the respondents were unsure at first of their study capacity, especially women without previous experience of university studies. This explanation was most often given by women in the youngest and oldest age groups.

Table 4: Increased Self-Esteem as a Result of Distance Education, in Relation to Sex (percent)

	Male	Female	Total
Increased self-esteem	11	25	17
N	246	208	454
Reason			
Succeeded with studies	23	38	33
General or unspecified	31	25	27
Increased knowledge	15	25	22
Positive effect on work	23	8	13
Social	8	6	6
Total	100	100	100
N	26	53	79

Source: Willén, 1981: 199.

We pointed out earlier that there were qualitative differences in the answers to this question, and that these were related to the sex of the student. Female students seemed to find it easier, or perhaps felt the need, to express themselves more explicitly and in a more varied manner than male students. Increased self-esteem as a result of increased knowledge was mentioned by 25% of the female students and 15% of the male students. We considered that the two categories "succeeded with studies" and "increased knowledge" were so close to each other that increased self-esteem in these respects could be said to be related to factors within the individual.

It is worth noting that women, more often than men (63% as opposed to 38%), attributed their increased self-esteem to what we chose to define as inner factors. Almost 25% of the male students as opposed to 8% of the female students answered that their self-esteem had increased in relation to work. This can be accounted for by the fact that more women than men were not gainfully employed.

The difference between men and women also may partly depend on their different attitudes at the very beginning of their studies and, indeed, we know from the results of the evaluation that male students were considerably more often confident that they would succeed. There were slightly more women than men who planned to spend at least ten hours a week on their studies, and men, more often than women, thought that their employer took a positive attitude toward their studies.

In their investigation of adult students, Johansson and Ekerwald drew attention to the fact that many students manifested an anxiety in relation to studies which was directly related to self-esteem, and which female students were more likely to verbalize. The students were also of the opinion that lack of self-esteem is one of the reasons why people do not study. The authors, however, formulate a seemingly opposite hypothesis:

> Lack of self-esteem is one of the reasons why certain adults study. Several of the students, among other reasons, seem to study in order to strengthen unstable self-esteem or in order to discover themselves. They often believe that other people are afraid of studying and interpret this behaviour in terms of self-esteem because this is the very problem which is of current interest for themselves. Those who do not study more often seem to have come to terms with themselves and have a more stable notion of what they can and cannot do (1976:158).

In our study, increased self-esteem was more frequently cited as a benefit of distance learning by students, especially females, who had no previous experience of university studies, as shown in Table 5. The older the student when she/he began distance studies, the more her/his self-esteem increased (Table 6). The distribution of answers according to motive for studying revealed no differences.

Increased self-esteem was clearly related to previous experiences and levels of aspiration of different students or groups of students.

Table 5: Increased Self-Esteem as a Result of Distance Education, in Relation to Educational Background and Sex (percent)

Answer	Previous university studies M	Previous university studies F	No previous university studies M	No previous university studies F
Increased self-esteem	5	15	18	38
N	146	114	100	94
Reason				
Succeeded with studies	25	29	22	42
General or unspecified	–	29	44	22
Increased knowledge	38	29	6	22
Positive effect on work	25	6	22	8
Social	13	6	6	6
Total	100	100	100	100
N	8	7	18	36

Source: Willén, 1981:201.

Table 6: Increased Self-Esteem as a Result of Distance Education, in Relation to Age and Sex (percent)

Answer	25-34 M	25-34 F	35-44 M	35-44 F	45– M	45– F
Increased self-esteem	8	20	11	32	13	26
N	102	88	82	73	62	47
Reason						
Succeeded with studies	22	50	33	26	13	42
General or unspecified	33	28	33	22	25	25
Increased knowledge	33	17	–	39	13	8
Positive effect on work	11	–	11	9	38	17
Social	–	6	22	4	13	8
Total	100	100	100	100	100	100
N	9	18	9	23	8	12

Source: Willén, 1981:202.

In this connection, we must also pay attention to the values prevalent in society, in this case primarily those concerning education, but even those concerning professional roles versus, for example, the role of the housewife (see Holter, 1973; Wernersson, 1980). Different professions are clearly associated with differences in social status, and status differentials influence an individual's self-evaluation.

In Swedish society, education has been an important political question during recent decades, employed to effect changes in society or, at least, to increase the possibility of change. Thus, education in itself represents something of social importance to the individual, and failure in studies may have a negative effect. The interaction between the life situation, past experiences of the individual, and participation or non-participation in education is complex. However, considering how much money and effort is being invested in education in many parts of the world, we must refine our knowledge of the effects of education both on individual levels of self-esteem and benefits to society as a whole.

Conclusion

We realize from our study that women and men often have totally different life situations, and women generally have the responsibility for upkeep of the home and the care of children. We also know that more men than women have fulltime jobs, and that men have a better educational background which in part determines their employment advantages. Relatedly, the effects of higher education are often different for women and men. Women more often than men increase their self-esteem when succeeding in education, whereas men evaluate their studies in relation to their jobs. When working with adult education we must take these facts into consideration, and in this context, distance education has given evidence of being an especially effective mode for women.

References

Björck, A. (1967). *En studie av hur elever i årskurs 12³ uppfattar yrkens status samt en orientering om dessa elevers yrkesönskningar.* Göteborg: Pedagogiska Institutionen, Göteborgs Universitet. Mimeo.

Brock-Utne, B. and R. Haukaa. (1980). *Kunskap uten makt: Kvinner som larere og elever.* Oslo: Universitetsforlaget.

Dahllöf, U., L. Kim and B. Willén. (1978). "Strategies for a Broader Enrollment in Swedish Higher Education." In R.S. Pike, N.E.S. McIntosh and U. Dahllöf. (Eds.). *Innovation in Access to Higher Education,* (pp. 247-327). New York: International Council for Educational Development.

Egidius, H. (1977). *Psykologi, pedagogik, psykoterapi-termlexikon.* Lund: Berlings.

Haukaa, R. (1976). *Kvinner og voksenopplaering: Ärsaker til den selektive rekruttering.* Oslo: Rapport froan Psykologisk Institutt, Universitetet i Oslo.

Herloff, B. (1967). *Västsvenska gymnasisters uppfattning om olika yrkens status. Ett försök att konstruera ett mått på status-påverkan vid intressemarkering.* Göteborg: Pedagogiska Institutionen. Mimeo.

Holter, H. (1973). *Könsroller och samhällsstruktur.* Stockholm: Prisma.

Johannesson, I. (1967). *Tonåringar i skolan. Delrapport III. Självvärdering och kamratvärdering.* Stockholm: Pedagogik-psykologiska Institutionen, Lärarhögskolan i Stockholm. Mimeo.

Johansson, L., and M. Ekerwald. (1976). *Vuxenstudier och livssituation.* Stockholm: Prisma.

Sjöstrand, Ch. (1974). *Grundskolemiljö och tonårselevers självvärdering.* Licentiatavhandling. Göteborg: Pedagogiska Institutionen, Göteborgs Universitet. Mimeo.

Wernersson, I. (1980). "Klasskillnader i konsekvensen av könstillhörighet." *Rapport från Pedagogiska Institutionen, Göteborgs Universitet, 7.*

Willén, B. (1973). *Attityder, värderingar och fritidssysselsättningar hos 14-och 16-åringar i Göteborg, samt en skolsystemsjämförelse.* Licentiatavhandling. Göteborg: Pedagogiska Institutionen, Göteborgs Universitet.

Willén, B. (1981). *Distance Education at Swedish Universities: An Evaluation of the Experimental Programme and a Follow-up Study.* Uppsala Studies in Education 16. Uppsala: Almqvist and Wiksell International.

Willén, B. (1983). *Conditions for Distance Education at the University Level in Sweden and the Other Nordic Countries.* Paper presented to a seminar at Lathis, Finland, September 1983. Pedagogiska Institutionen, Uppsala Universitet.

Willén, B. (1984). *Strategies for Strengthening Student-Teacher Contact in Distance Education: Results of an Evaluation of Distance Education in Swedish Universities.* Derg Papers 9. Distance Education Research Group: Milton Keynes: The Open University.

Zetterberg, P. (1979). *Arbete, livsstil och motivation.* Stockholm: Svenska Arbetsgivareföreningen, SAF: s förlagssektion.

Chapter 7

ATLANTIC CANADA PERSPECTIVES
by
Diana R. Carl, Erin M. Keough, Lorraine Y. Bourque

Diana R. Carl, Ed.D., is an assistant professor in the Education Department at Mount Saint Vincent University, Halifax, Nova Scotia (Canada), where she pioneered the Distance University Education via Television (DUET) service. She received her doctorate from Indiana University in Instructional Systems Technology, and she has worked in distance education for over ten years as both an instructional designer and administrator. She has worked in distance and continuing education in a variety of organizations, including Memorial University of Newfoundland, the University of Mid-America and Indiana University, and as a consultant to hospitals and medical organizations. A founding member of CADE (Canadian Association for Distance Education), Dr. Carl has researched and published on instructional design and advanced technologies.

Erin M. Keough graduated from the University of Toronto in Chemistry (B.Sc.) and came to the Teleconferencing field via a circuitous research route. Contact with the communications and distance education field began in 1976 through programme evaluation of then current projects. She has worked since that time with the Telemedicine Centre, at Memorial University of Newfoundland, in various capacities on a variety of communications projects. Currently Ms. Keough manages all Telemedicine projects for Memorial, including a 95-site province-wide audioteleconferencing network, offering some 15 hours a day of health and education programmes to a variety of professionals.

Lorraine Y. Bourque, Ph.D., is a professor at the Université de Moncton, New Brunswick, Canada, where she just completed a five-year term as Director General of Education permanente. During that period, her interest in distance education led to the implementation of teleconferenced and televised courses at Université de Moncton for francophone adults. She is now serving as Head of the department of Fondements et Ressources Humaines en Éducation with the Faculté des sciences de l'éducation. She has been an active member of a number of committees, including: the Atlantic Association University's Advisory Committee on Technology and Communication; executive committee of the UNESCO subcommission on the status of women; and executive of the Atlantic Provinces Association of Continuing University Education (APACUE).

Editor's Note: The sections which follow describe the distance education programmes of three universities in Atlantic Canada: Mount Saint Vincent University, Memorial University of Newfoundland and Université de Moncton. Each author describes services available to women as distant learners, course content for a primarily female learner population, and their own perspectives as women filling key roles in university distance education.

Mount Saint Vincent University
by
Diana R. Carl, Ed.D.

Mount Saint Vincent University was the first women's university in Canada and in the Commonwealth. As such, it has always had a tradition of service to women. As stated in the university calendar, "The Mount considers the educational needs of women to be a priority, and, therefore, remains particularly sensitive to the changing needs of women in society. Further, it believes there is a place for a university aimed primarily at the higher education of women" (Mount Saint Vincent University, 1986:11). To this date, consistently two-thirds of the student population have been female.

Women figure prominently not only in the population served by the university but in the roots of service as well. In 1873, the Sisters of Charity founded an academy for girls which eventually became Mount Saint Vincent University. In 1914, the Mount became an affiliate of Dalhousie University to meet the needs for the higher education of women, with degrees awarded by Dalhousie University. In 1925, the Mount was chartered as a college and gained the right to grant its own degrees. In 1966, the charter was amended to make the college a university, and in 1971 men were admitted to the university.

During the late 1970s and early 1980s, Mount Saint Vincent University became a Canadian leader in feminist education. An open organizational structure was introduced as an alternative to traditional "male" management structures. The Institute for the Study of Women was founded, and publication of a scholarly journal in feminist research, *Atlantis,* was undertaken. The first federally funded Chair in Women's Studies in a university was given to Mount Saint Vincent University.

The university has been active in outreach programmes since 1920, when off-campus, evening, and summer courses were first offered to mature female students to increase women's access to higher education. The present Director of Continuing Education was hired specifically to address the continuing education needs of women. In 1972 the Mount was the first university in Atlantic Canada to implement a liberal entrance policy targeted at mature female students. In sum, the tradition of making education accessible to women has been a strong factor in the development of the Mount's programmes and services. The step into distance education, then, was logical and based on an articulated need emanating from a female student population.

The Skill Development Leave Taskforce (1983) has called attention to the double burden of employed women who have family commitments. Further, working women commonly have difficulty obtaining promotions, in part because they lack higher education, job-related education, and training associated with new technologies (Menzies, 1982). Devereaux (1984) noted that women attend fewer workshops and courses than their male counterparts, and participation in these programmes is linked to promotion. Working, caring for a family, and commuting to the university compound the burden. With such women in mind, Mount administrators looked at alternative access mechanisms. Distance education was a logical choice.

Distance University Education via Television

Distance University Education via Television (DUET) began in 1982, transmitted to students via cable television service through the Atlantic Satellite Network, a commercial broadcast system distributed over the Anik C3 satellite.

DUET uses one-way videoconferencing to deliver university courses to distant students. One-way full-motion videoconferencing is the combination of a live television signal sent to students at distant locations coupled with a return telephone link to the studio classroom. DUET courses "piggyback" on existing university courses offered on campus, and professors teach simultaneously to the students in the classroom and to the distant students. Distant students participate in the class by means of a telephone connected to a teleconferencing bridge, enabling them to talk with the professor, students in the studio classroom, and students at other locations. They complete the same requirements as do on-campus students and work to the same schedule and deadlines.

One-way full-motion videoconferencing was selected by Mount Saint Vincent University because it enabled the university to reach a distant student population without investing in a separate course structure or various other costly technologies. Using a standard university classroom modified for videoconferencing, and relying on existing course and administrative structures, the university can deliver distance education economically and with existing resources. The ultimate intention is to enable distance education to occur as easily as on-campus education.

Individual professors are responsible for teaching in the classroom, and the university wanted the same delineation of responsibility and autonomy in distance education. Depending on the effect of the videoconferencing medium on the presentations, and on the ability of the distant students to respond using the technologies, the on-campus course is adapted to ensure that distant students can 1) clearly see and hear the presentation, 2) interact with the professor and other students, and 3) complete course requirements in ways defined as important to the intent of the course.

One of the main concerns of those who provide distance education in a broadcast form is that it should not reinforce the ghettoization of women confined to the home. In the design of educational curriculum via DUET, an important consideration is to ensure that students accomplish some of the coursework outside of the home, preferably in the company of others who are either taking the same course or who are interested in the content. Women are encouraged to learn in groups, either in homes or in workplaces, and to support each other; course assignments require students to access resources within the community. The community, then, is viewed as a resource for continuing education.

Courses have now been offered in a variety of subjects, such as accounting, gerontology, marketing and sociology, and at a variety of levels, and the first year of university studies may be completed through DUET. In addition, courses for professional advancement are routinely offered to enable working women to gain needed credentials for promotion.

Enrolments in DUET reflect the intention to reach a predominantly female student population. Consistently, over four years of service, female enrolments in DUET courses account for 90% of the total. All can be classified as mature students (age 25 or older). Most are married and have children between the ages of 10 and 21. Over 90% of these women work outside the home at least parttime and for many the DUET course is their initiation to university. These students clearly want a university education, but many initially express low levels of confidence.

Evaluations have been conducted each semester DUET has been in operation to measure academic achievement on assignments and tests, satisfaction with DUET presentations, interactivity, and adequacy of student supports. The effect of the DUET format on the on-campus student population is also measured through a questionnaire examining course components. Academic achievement in DUET courses has been either on par with or better than achievement in the classroom; comparison of performance of the work of distant students (all of whom are mature) with that produced by on-campus mature students reveals no difference. Satisfaction with the format varies with each course: between 68% and 90% indicate the format is acceptable; 88% indicate they would enrol in another DUET course; and 83% would recommend the course to a friend. Overall, the data gathered for evaluation purposes supports the impression that DUET is achieving its objective of providing an acceptable higher education experience to interested women in Atlantic Canada.

Women's Studies on DUET

Of particular interest is the offering of courses in the Women's Studies Programme offered by Mount Saint Vincent University. These courses were considered controversial for distribution over open-broadcast television because of content and format. Some of the content was questionable, in terms of prevailing community standards, for use over open-broadcast television; such as: a critical analysis of existing institutions such as marriage, the legal system, and the church, or discussions of lesbianism and its relationship to feminism. The format was subject to intense discussion on-campus because of the degree of personal involvement of students with the concepts being discussed. Because the course was open-broadcast, student views, which had normally been confined to a single classroom, were now heard in homes across Atlantic Canada. In putting the course over DUET, we uncovered students who felt a strong need for catharsis, which the broadcast classroom inhibited. The question arose as to whether we could adequately meet the needs of students in the classroom while bringing the content to distance students.

The offering of introductory and second level Women's Studies courses yielded only a handful of registrants but received an exuberant response from a large casual viewer population. Information from the Bureau of Broadcast Measurement indicated that the introductory course was the most-watched programme in its time slot during the Fall 1984 sampling. The "fan mail" received for these courses was significantly greater than for other courses. Letters of praise, as well as criticism, were received regularly, and women called to express their opinions. In one instance a group of female casual viewers called and asked for details on how to form their own study group at work.

Women's Studies over DUET actively involved the community in the educational process and dialogue. While the immediate tangible return to the university was not great, the influence of this content on the community seems to have long-term ramifications for the university which merit further study. One of the primary goals of the university is to further the cause of women in the community, and it appears that by offering this content over television, Mount Saint Vincent University is creating more dialogue on issues of importance to women and showing women in prominent, articulate and inquisitive roles as professors and students, providing positive role models for the community at large.

DUET is Run by Women

Administrative positions in distance education systems tend to be dominated by males; it is they who generally make policy decisions. Mount Saint Vincent University may have been unique in that the DUET system was entirely run by women, from the president to the production technicians. Harding (1986) has stated that there may be a link between the ways in which women think and act and their ability to be more responsive to the needs of other women. While it is difficult to judge whether this female-dominated administrative system has been more responsive, we feel we have tried to listen to and sympathize with the learners and to be immediately supportive in formulating solutions to problems.

The common carrier systems employed, such as the telephone company and the broadcast television facility, were dominated by males with engineering backgrounds. It was a normal part of the course delivery process for the DUET staff to communicate with employees of common carriers and to troubleshoot problems regularly. The interface between the women working on the technical aspects of DUET and these men was characterized by some "interesting" scenarios. For example, although the coordinator possessed expertise in television systems setup and equipment decisions, there was a tendency in meetings for participants who had limited knowledge of the field to accept the recommendations of men who possessed much less expertise. Apparently more justification was required from women presenting a case than from men. Problems of this nature are familiar to all women entering professional arenas from which we have been previously excluded. They will persist until the kind of effort being made by Mount Saint Vincent University is a universal goal: balancing the educational and professional scales.

Epilogue

We do not know if DUET would have been any different if run by men. Since the resignation of the first coordinator, this position has been occupied by a man; however he is the only man in the DUET responsibility area. Would DUET have been any different if it were not influenced by the service tradition of the Sisters of Charity and by the unique position of Mount Saint Vincent University as the first women's university in the Commonwealth? These are perhaps unanswerable questions, but the Mount's unique character as a women's university has had a differential effect. As a unique case, DUET and Mount Saint Vincent University merit examination in the ways in which women serve and are served.

References

Devereaux, M.S. (1984). *One in Every Five*. Ottawa, Ontario: Statistics Canada and Education Support Sector, Department of Secretary of State.

Harding, S. (October 1986). "Women and Knowledge." Address given at Mount Saint Vincent University in conjunction with the Institute for the Study of Women.

Menzies, H. (1982). *Women and the Chip.* Montreal, Quebec: The Institute for Research on Public Policy.

Mount Saint Vincent University. (1986). *Calendar 1986-87.* Halifax, Nova Scotia: Mount Saint Vincent University.

Skill Development Leave Taskforce. (1983). *Learning a Living in Canada.* Volume 1. Ottawa, Ontario: Ministry of Supply and Services Canada.

Memorial University at Newfoundland
by
Erin M. Keough

Memorial University College, established to honour Newfoundlanders who had died in the First World War, held its initial lectures in 1925 in the provincial capital—St. John's. Recognizing the need and value of post-secondary education, one of the priorities of the first post-Confederation provincial government was to elevate the college to university status. In 1949, the bill creating Memorial University of Newfoundland was given royal assent. Then, as now, Memorial was the province's only university. In 1975, a second campus was established in Corner Brook on the west coast of the island, where students can complete their first two years in arts and science programmes.

The province of Newfoundland and Labrador occupies 150,000 square miles and has some 550,000 people living in communities scattered over two land masses. One-fifth of the population resides in St. John's, the capital city. The creation of programmes to address provincial needs, and the provision of outreach programmes to make the university's resources more available to all the people of the province, are integral to Memorial's mandate. Historically, then, the university has endeavoured to provide appropriate types of programmes (credit and non-credit; mediated and non-mediated) to as many provincial centres as is feasible. To broaden its outreach capacity, the university has created a number of special divisions—including Extension, Credit Studies, and Educational Technology—and has fostered the activities of centres such as Telemedicine. Benefiting from this positive attitude toward distance education at the administrative level, these divisions have acquired considerable expertise in their respective fields.

The term "distance education" is increasingly interpreted as mediated instruction at the post-secondary credit or certificate level. To explore the role of women in distance education in the context of Memorial's commitment, I have taken the broader definition of the term: that is, teaching at a distance. In keeping, with the orientation of this book, however, I have limited myself to activities directed through university departments and divisions.

In addition to providing more structured certificate courses, the Division of Extension has been a leader in the field of community development since its inception in 1959, using non-formal educational processes. The division rarely designs programmes targeted specifically at women; however, the division's first and current female director recognizes that females require particular encouragement to participate in post-education opportunities and to assume community leadership roles. The division provides this support through its field staff, who form the main link with the community.

In some instances, the division has worked directly with women and women's groups to increase their awareness of their socio-economic potential. For example, in one programme, the division's field staff worked in informal settings with a group of women to assist with developing skills required to participate in their local development associations; this resulted in an initiative known as the Women's Involvement Committee. In a second example, a videotape *Women in Oil* is being produced by the Divisions of Extension and Educational Technology to serve as the principal working tool of an awareness and education programme that focuses on women's concerns related to the development of the petroleum industry in the region. Topics include female employment in that field and the effect of development on family and lifestyles. A third example is the Rural Women's Learning Project, an effort to assess rural women's needs in several targeted regions and to respond accordingly.

During the 1960s, to enable residents of rural communities to view art works often available only in urban galleries, Extension Services assembled works, reproductions, biographies and audiotapes by and about provincial artists, and circulated them through numerous rural communities in a programme dubbed "Travelling Trunks." The organizer of this programme, who continues to play a prominent role in the Canadian arts scene, subsequently became the first female curator of the university's provincial art gallery in 1972. The gallery, which operates within the Division of Extension, regularly circulates collections through five public galleries outside St. John's as well as providing exhibitions to schools and other locations.

Memorial's Telemedicine Centre has developed an interactive audio-based teleconferencing system that is managed by women. It maintains installations in all the provincial hospitals, vocational schools and university campuses, and in a variety of other health and education agencies. Although Telemedicine was originally planned to serve health professionals and support staff working in isolated areas, its user consortium has broadened to include education agencies and some government departments. The network provides a delivery vehicle for: 1) continuing education courses for all health professionals; 2) post-secondary credit and non-credit courses; 3) related administrative meetings; 4) patient care activities. The network operates some fifteen hours of programmes a day Monday to Friday, which include approximately 20–25 university credit courses per academic term as well as a small number of non-credit Extension courses.

A network of this nature, which reaches fifty-four provincial communities, provides an excellent opportunity for women who cannot relinquish their responsibilities for extended periods to begin or continue post-secondary education. It makes continuing education programming more accessible to members of health groups whose budgets are limited or whose members work as isolated professionals in small hospitals or nursing stations. In both cases, there is little opportunity to travel for professional development. Many groups with a predominantly female population, such as nurses, physiotherapists, food service workers and dieticians, fit into one of these two categories. Their associations attempt to hold meetings as well as education programmes on the network to decrease the sense of isolation frequently experienced by people working in these situations. Beyond its provincial mandate, the Telemedicine Centre plays a developmental role in the applications of various technologies for narrowband networks. It also has an expanding interest in the delivery of distance education to groups in developing countries.

In the various agencies concerned with distance education at Memorial, women are integrated at numerous levels in the development and delivery of both informal and formal education—as directors, researchers, producers, assistant directors, managers, field workers and coordinators. Integration at all levels will make the system more sensitive to issues for women. As distance educators we can be aware of women's needs, and we can raise important issues that might otherwise be overlooked or not developed. To serve women's needs in distance education best, it is important that women are represented at all administrative, design, delivery and instructional levels.

Université de Moncton
by
Lorraine Y. Bourque, Ph.D.

Université de Moncton is a French university founded in 1963 as a result of a Royal Commission on Higher Education in New Brunswick. Although relatively recent, this institution has roots that can be traced up to a century earlier with the founding of three other French universities in New Brunswick. In 1963, these universities suspended their charters and became affiliated colleges to the new university. Since the new university was open to students of both sexes, the four women's colleges in the province, one after the other, opted to close their doors. As it is presently constituted, Université de Moncton no longer has any affiliated colleges; rather it has three university campuses situated in the three main francophone regions of the province.

When Université de Moncton opened its doors, the fulltime students, the professors and the administration were almost exclusively men. With the new policy of admitting women, the situation gradually changed. Presently, approximately 35% of all professors are female, with relatively few women in administration. Approximately 51% of all fulltime students are female, as has been the case for the last few years. Parttime students have always been predominantly female, usuallly at least 70%. From 1981 to 1985, females from both fulltime and parttime programmes accounted for 59.4% of the total number of graduates; this has varied from 54.4% to 64%. In 1977, the Education permanente, Université de Moncton, created the *Institut d'études et apprentissage féminins* in order to facilitate the entry of women to university. Programmes such as *Nouveau Départ* (New Start) were set up to give information to women and to make it easier for those who wished to resume their studies.

The French universities of New Brunswick have been offering services to parttime students since 1938. They first organized these services for teachers, who were mostly women, and later expanded to include courses leading to degrees in, for example, business administration, nursing, liberal arts, social services and gerontology. Both women and men benefit from these courses, although there is usually a larger proportion of women in parttime programmes. These courses have usually been offered on the university campuses; however, to respond to specific needs where the subject matter did not require students to be on campus, some courses were offered at a distance to francophones in different areas of New Brunswick and Prince Edward Island. With developments in the technology of communications, these new media were employed to serve parttime students with limited access to university.

Women were key figures in the establishment of distance education at Université de Moncton, working in planning, decision-making, grant-seeking, curriculum development, and evaluation of courses and of students' responses. The development in the mid-1980s of distance courses through teleconferencing and television involved determination, cooperation at different levels, creativity, hard work, and a willingness by those involved to tread unexplored paths. The Director General of Education permanente supported the use of communications technology for distance education. She recognized the difficulties encountered by adults, and especially women, in gaining access to university, so she gave a high priority to this project.

The collaboration provided by the distance education team and Claudette Beaulieu, the Director of Education permanente for the Centre Universitaire de Moncton, has been fruitful. Teleconference and television courses are now part of the regular programme offered by Education permanente. A larger number of professors now show interest in these courses, and the number of students taking such courses is increasing. Although the long-term financing of distance education is uncertain, Marielle Préfontaine, the Assistant Academic Vice-President, and current Director General of Education permanente, now has overall responsibility for the project and has taken steps to guarantee on-going financing. All in all, the prospects for the project are good.

The women who have directed the project have been well-supported by the professors who accepted the challenge of teaching at a distance and by the members of the distance education team, both men and women. This team was set up to provide support to the students, professors and administrators involved in distance education and to establish links between the university and potential students who can benefit from the new services; it has been valuable in getting students and professors to maximize the value of distance education.

The number of women in distance courses has varied each semester between 55% and 75%. There are many more women, however, who could benefit from continuing education. We need to offer courses which respond to expressed needs, and we need to contact those who hesitate. A continuation of the services of the distance education team should make it possible to reach a larger proportion of women who are seeking a new orientation to their lives and who are ready to try university courses.

Université de Moncton has also worked cooperatively with other universities to develop distance education courses, such as nursing or social services programmes, targeted at specific groups, often mostly women. These are usually areas where course demand exceeds the individual university's capacity to deliver, and collaborative distance education is used as one solution. However, for such services to expand, administrative mechanisms will have to take this collaboration into account. This may mean finding new approaches to funding distance education and recognizing that distance education requires having not only a good professor but also an effective support system.

Distance education has definitely strengthened its position in the universities of Atlantic Canada since 1980. A number of women have helped this happen, and their presence has meant that women's viewpoints have had a better chance of consideration. This does not mean, however, that distance education should be a women's ghetto, any more than it should it be a man's. There should be room for collaboration and for making sure that the best quality courses possible be offered with consideration for all students. The clientele is in large part female, and women will probably remain visible as driving forces, shaping the future of university distance education.

References

Bourque, L.Y. (1986). *L'Education des adultes à l'Université de Moncton. Réflexions et considérations*. Moncton, Nouveau-Brunswick: Université de Moncton.

Bureau des communications en éducation de l'Association des universités de l'Atlantique. (1986). *Groupe de travail sur les consortiums des communications en éducation. Rapport final*. Halifax, Nouvelle-Ecosse.

Université de Moncton. (1985). *Rapport du recteur. 1980-1985*. Moncton, Nouveau-Brunswick: Université de Moncton.

Université de Moncton. (1986). *Rapport d'évaluation des cours offerts à l'automne 1985 par l'enseignement à distance de l'Education permanente de l'Université de Moncton*. Moncton, Nouveau-Brunswick: Université de Moncton.

Université de Moncton. (1986). *Rapport d'évaluation des cours offerts à l'hiver 1986 par l'enseignement à distance de l'Education permanente de l'Université de Moncton*. Moncton, Nouveau-Brunswick: Université de Moncton.

ISSUES OF EQUITY

Editor's Introduction

As a stage of claiming independence, colonized peoples — whether as a nation, a minority group within a nation (including native/indigenous/aboriginal peoples), or universally as females — have commonly rejected the colonizers' education. Renewed value is placed on traditional ways of teaching and learning which reflect cultural pride. Simultaneous with this global twentieth-century movement toward educational self-determination, the dominant societies have become increasingly utilitarian in educational planning, with great emphasis on applied science and technology. This generates a cultural bind for minority groups which are dependent on the economy of the dominant class. Circuitously, as a result of the need for skills that increase opportunities for employment, women and other political minorities remain dependent on mainstream institutions. A number of chapters in this section address the issues that arise when multi-cultural factors enter the educational process and when traditions collide with pragmatic imperatives.

Since 1975, upon gaining national independence from Australia, Papua New Guinea (PNG) has been engaged in the arduous struggle toward self-reliance. The objective of social and political equality for all citizens has been emphasized in official planning documents, and one of the primary aims of national development is to offer equal opportunity to women in all educational, economic and social activity.

The challenge posed by this principle of gender equality is fraught with complications. PNG society, with a population of approximately three million people, is divided by major geographic and communication barriers, with over seven hundred distinct languages. Moreover, females in PNG as elsewhere have been traditionally subordinate to male authority in all spheres of life. Until recently, girls were denied access to even a primary education; at the university level, females comprised only about 15% of total enrolments. Women in PNG have organized national and provincial councils and regional associations, to address their needs and visions for the future. Within these forums it is agreed that further education and desired social change are conjoined objectives, and this is the issue on which Angela Mandie-Filer focuses in Chapter 8. As one of a number of women at the University of PNG who has invested professional effort toward securing greater opportunities for female students, Mandie-Filer identifies the severe obstacles women face in advancing their education. She advocates the use of distance education to reach women who would otherwise be unable to enrol in a study programme, and she discusses reasons why distance education could be preferable for women even when classroom attendance is a choice.

In Chapter 9, Barbara Matiru and Debbie Gachuhi consider the goal of gender equity in the context of Kenya, with a critical examination of distance education course content to determine the extent to which both male and female interests are represented. In this evaluation, they discovered that sex-stereotyping pervades all subject areas and that females are significantly underrepresented even in those courses, such as Home Science, which have been designed primarily or exclusively for females. Consistently and dramatically, males are presented as having more social prominence, by the sole virtue of being male, and as being engaged in more important or interesting activities. The question again arises as to what social benefits are to be gained by equalizing male/female enrolments if the education received is reinforcing traditional assumptions of biologically determined male superiority/female inferiority. Matiru and Gachuhi call on course designers and curriculum planners to become more sensitive to the ways that instructional materials affect students' self-images and to rectify gender imagery imbalances with more positive and realistic portrayals of females.

To many of us in the international distance education community, the University of the South Pacific (USP) represents an enviable working environment. Neither cyclones, economic uncertainties nor governmental upheavals can dissuade us from thinking that life would be far sweeter if, through our office windows, we could see palm trees swaying in the breeze and feel the waters of the Pacific on our campus shore. In an apparently idyllic setting, this university serves eleven island nations through its Extension Services. As an equal opportunity employer this division has done very well—as the collectively written Chaper 10 attests. Marjorie Crocombe, the director, and six of her female colleagues present descriptive and studied perspectives of their work as a unit, with each contributor offering detail that pertains to her own area of expertise and responsibility. The issues they cover include course development, "motivation, persistence and success" among female distance learners, the challenge of teaching science at a distance, and results of a readability survey of USP extension course materials, with a compendium of programmes offered and women involved in continuing education activity. As stated by Crocombe, "women have been in the forefront in this programme as students, teachers, course writers and developers and administrators." For those concerned with questions of gender equity, here is yet one more reason why the University of the South Pacific holds such great appeal.

Since achieving independence in 1947, the people of India have been engaged in an ambitious endeavor to implement democratic policies and institutions in place of the traditional systems of caste and gender subordination. Despite overwhelming mass poverty, illiteracy, disease and colonial legacies of disparity, remarkable achievements have been gained within the educational system. Distance education is one of the primary means by which India is seeking to develop greater equity among its citizens. Many thousands of women are enrolled in home study through twenty-four universities, including one Women's University, and numerous institutes. Nevertheless, women in India continue to be exceptionally disadvantaged in terms of access to education, appropriateness of course choice and content, and prospects for translating education into social or economic benefits.

In Chapter 11, Gomathi Mani of the University of Madras offers data pertaining to female learners and describes programmes that have been developed in India with the use of correspondence materials, radio and television. She illuminates both the challenges faced by distance educators in India and the principles of equity which guide their work. Jyoti H. Trivedi and Kamalini H. Bhansali describe the work of the SNDT Women's University, which offers courses both in the classroom and through correspondence. This women's university is struggling to overcome the daunting problems of expensive facilities, geographical barriers, and the subordinate role of women to raise the literacy rate of India's women above its present 25%. Finally, Dr. Mani presents the comments made by women distance learners about their education as gleaned from her work at the University of Madras. Although there is not yet a basis for celebrating women's progress in India, there is certainly reason to believe that as education becomes increasingly valued as a path toward liberation so will women in larger numbers begin to assume a more equitable share in educational decision-making.

Notable among the innovative initiatives described in this book is the work of Paulene Heiler and Wendy Richards who, in Chapter 12, discuss a unique vocational training programme for isolated mature-age women in Australia. With a focus on the building and construction trades, this programme addresses the importance of training for women in occupations from which females have been traditionally excluded. The authors stress the need in such programmes for support services which will bridge the psychological as well as the physical distances for women entering pioneer territory. The gaining of motivation and self-confidence is understood to be as important as, and directly related to, the acquisition of technical skills. Heiler and Richards describe and critique this programme with insightful observations concerning the unrealistic expectations and demands that educators often place on their students. Taking a student-centred approach, the authors evaluate the programme with considered recommendations for further enhancing the experiential quality as well as the quantifiable success of this unique endeavor.

In the Muslim world, Turkey was the first nation—under Atatürk's leadership early in this century—to include women's rights in development planning. Education was perceived as an essential first step toward alleviating major social problems and it was intended that female citizens, no less than male, would avail themselves of opportunities to overcome widespread illiteracy.

This goal has not yet been realized, as discussed by Ülkü S. Köymen in Chapter 13, and the reasons are deeply embedded in religious traditions which relegate women to positions of domestic subservience. For every gain on women's behalf, new setbacks have occurred. And whereas increased literacy and an expansion of primary and secondary schooling have resulted in a greater demand for higher education, only women from privileged socio-economic circumstances have been granted this opportunity without a struggle. The Open University in Turkey was established in 1982 as an economical means of advancing the nation's educational goals, and Köymen considers the extent to which open learning may directly benefit women.

Native people in Canada now comprise only 2% of the total population, with the heaviest representation in the prairies and in the north. Most of the ten provinces have developed Native education programmes, both in public schools and on the reserves—where 60% of the Native population reside (1981 census data). In Chapter 14, Barbara Spronk and Donna Radtke describe a programme in operation at Athabasca University in Alberta which, through trial and error, is seeking effective approaches to responding to the educational needs of Native men and women. In their discussion of the need to create appropriate modes of course delivery to their primarily female rural students, Spronk and Radtke identify a number of problems these women experience as they attempt to straddle Native and Anglo cultures in attempts to gain a university education. Combining students' comments with their own analysis and detailed descriptions of the programme's development and changes, Spronk and Radtke offer useful perspectives on the ways by which educators must be cognizant not only of individual students' needs but also of the cultural interests of the larger community which those students represent.

The Anangu Teacher Education Program (ANTEP) in Central Australia is the subject of Chapter 15, by Loene Furler and Carol Scott. The students in the programme are primarily Aboriginal adult women who live in traditional communities, many of whom have worked as aides in school programmes for Aboriginal children. In their analysis of the preponderance of female enrolments, Furler and Scott consider the effects of colonization which result in young people dropping out of school at a relatively early age.

This applies to boys, especially, whose Aboriginal initiation rites confirm their cultural identity and result in a rejection of colonizing institutions. Since teaching was considered "women's work" it has been females who have been encouraged to continue with schooling. Aboriginal women have served their families as economic providers and they have maintained separate and independent ceremonial customs; as a consequence, they have not perceived their dominance in education as extraordinary. Their first concern is to liberate their culture from white, western, institutionalized hegemony, but they recognize a need for western skills if their culture is to survive. They also recognize that children will learn with greater acuity and consciousness if their teachers share their own language and cultural values.

As detailed by Furler and Scott, the Anangu project curriculum was based on Aboriginal content and context, including Aboriginal analysis of the effects of white Australian society on Aboriginal life. This ongoing attention to the integrity of the programme is rewarded with the support of the people it is designed to serve, an endorsement that is not a statement of assimilation but rather a step toward a peaceful truce. As white educators gain an appreciation for the cultures their forefathers nearly eradicated, so do they take initiatives to support the preservation of those cultures. The Anangu project is a respectful and model approach to education as a medium of cultural reciprocity. — *K. F.*

WOMEN IN PAPUA NEW GUINEA: DISTANCE EDUCATION AS A MEANS FOR EDUCATIONAL ADVANCEMENT

by

Angela Mandie-Filer

Angela Mandie-Filer received her Bachelor of Education degree (in science) from the University of Papua New Guinea in 1980; she is currently completing an M.A. in education at Macquarie University and a graduate diploma in distance education, by distance courses, from South Australian College of Advanced Education. Since 1980, Mandie-Filer has been coordinator of the University of PNG's extension studies. She is particularly interested in the potential of distance education for the educational advancement of adult learners, especially women. She is married and has one son.

Introduction

In Papua New Guinea (PNG), over the years before and after Independence in 1975, the lack of opportunity for women to achieve educational advancement has been a recurrent issue of debate amongst politicians, educationists and intellectuals. In this modern-day and changing PNG society, education is the key to successful and competitive living for everyone—including women. Within the conventional and traditional modes of formal education, however, women in PNG have generally missed out. This paper is written as a contribution to the search for alternative means of enabling women in PNG to gain educational advancement, and it argues the benefits of distance education as one of those alternatives. The political, social, economic and cultural settings of Papua New Guinea, and their influence on women's exclusion from traditional modes of education, are also discussed. It is argued that distance education, if employed meaningfully, can be an effective alternative for women because this mode is not bound to the rigid restrictions which characterize conventional and traditional approaches to education.

Obstacles to Education for Women

Most women in PNG live in rural areas and receive little, if any, formal education. Women who live in urban areas live as dependents for the most part, whether they have been educated or not. The cultural, social and political systems of PNG, as in other countries, impose expectations that women will get married, have children and look after the home and family. In this context, women are simply not perceived as needing an education. However, as urbanization and development occur, women increasingly have this need. At the same time, there is widespread belief in PNG society, held by both men and women, that women should not sacrifice family responsibility and family welfare for education. At all times, women are expected to be producing food and other resources for the welfare of the family and the upkeep of the home. If a woman were to attend formal schooling through the conventional face-to-face mode, she would have to spend time away from home, and this would be considered wasteful. Many people do not recognize the long-term positive effects of women's ability to contribute more because of knowledge and skills gained through education.

Women are seen as needing special protection. As a result, parents, brothers and husbands are not willing to send females far away from home to urban centres where educational institutions are located. Given the lack of knowledge in rural areas about the social conditions of city life, and the pervasive fear of criminal activities in the city as routinely reported in the media, it is not surprising that rural families don't want to send the women away from home. Even well-intentioned parents, who may respect their daughter's interest in education, will refuse to let her go to the city where, as they perceive it, there are serious law and order problems and a lack of social control or protection.

Since face-to-face educational institutions are situated so far from most areas of the country, and given the geographic realities which limit transportation to expensive air travel, there is little or no contact if a family member does move to the city. The fear of communication breakdown, and the fear of losing a daughter, compound the resistance to letting girls go off to school. When girls or women do go away from home, they suffer distrust from husbands, parents and other relatives. There is fear that a young girl will get pregnant and/or marry someone from outside the village and never be seen again. Parents also fear that without brothers or other males in the family to protect their daughters, the women may be victims of violence and abuse.

Husbands are timid about allowing their wives to attend face-to-face education not so much for safety reasons but more often because of insecurity, jealousy and fear that the wife might become too educated. Some husbands, especially those in urban centres, use their wife's lack of education as a means of keeping her under control. They fear that the wife will meet with other women who may influence her, enabling her to know about life outside the sphere of her husband's world. Husbands, in particular, whether or not they are educated themselves, use traditional cultural and social beliefs to prevent women from progressing—including men who have themselves moved away from traditional controls.[1]

The problems for women are abundant. For example, if a husband and wife, or a brother and sister, are competing for money and other resources required to gain an education, the male will almost certainly be given the opportunity. "In PNG we support and expect *boys* to go to school and get jobs," said a teacher in a public gathering during a debate over the issue of education in PNG. Girls are pressured, in effect, to do badly and to drop out before completion even if they overcome the other problems and actually get to the classroom. Although there are many living examples of women who are the primary support of the family, society still holds the view that men are and should be the breadwinners.

For a woman who is the only source of income for a family, unpaid study leave is out of the question. Some employers are reluctant to release female employees from their duties with pay, to enable them to upgrade their skills, even if they have displayed potential for achieving educational advancement. Employers are additionally timid about allowing or making it possible for a married women to gain educational advancement because they do not want to answer to disapproving husbands. If a wife does seek an education with the help of the employer and the husband feels threatened by this, he will act against the employer. The wife might then have to leave her job for the sake of the marriage, or keep the job and suffer at home with the husband. Also, while the wife is away, there is no guarantee that the husband will look after the children. The lack of childcare is a great hindrance to the education of women who are mothers. Although childcare is not the sole responsibility of the mother, she is always blamed if anything happens to the child.

Women in PNG who are trying to gain educational advancement also experience negative pressure from other women. If one is seen attending classes, she will often be rejected by her peer group and friends, especially if they are uneducated and not interested in studying. In an isolated situation, away from friends and family, the woman will most likely give up studying in order to retain her friends. I have often heard such comments as "why is that old woman going to school when the money should be used to look after her children and educating them?," or "she is trying to be like her husband," or "she is trying to be a man by going to school."

Overcoming the Obstacles

Obviously women in PNG face severe problems in achieving educational advancement through the conventional face-to-face mode of teaching and learning. An alternative means for women to achieve educational advancement is through distance education. The traditional face-to-face mode of education is by definition rigid and restricted. For example, if a woman cannot meet deadlines for assessments or tests, because of difficulties or circumstances as described, she is most likely to be graded fail (F). If she cannot attend meetings, or misses class, she has no chance or way of catching up: in most face-to-face teaching the lecture is not written or recorded. In distance education, by contrast, all of the course content and study materials are readily accessible to the student at any time, and students are rarely subjected to inflexible timetables. Thus, distance education offers women a unique opportunity to develop their potential. This is relevant not just for individual women but for the nation's future. Women in PNG cannot be expected to participate equally in the social, political and economic developments of the country, as stipulated in the national constitution, without the appropriate education.

For some women, distance education can be a means to prove their abilities and hence to compete with men for national scholarships for further studies. For example, if a woman left conventional schooling some time ago with only grade 10 qualification, she can now complete Matriculation (that is, grades 11–12) through the distance education programme offered by the University of PNG in Port Moresby. After completing Matriculation the woman is able to compete with others for National Scholarships for further studies. For conventional modes of study, just getting a scholarship is not enough, because scholarships do not take care of dependents. For this reason, and others previously cited, women with dependents cannot leave home to pursue educational advancement through the conventional mode. The question of dependents also seems to be the major constraint on women with degrees who have to go overseas to gain further educational advancement through the conventional mode. Distance education will provide opportunity to those women who want to study during what one can call "spare" time, that is, nighttime. The flexible nature of distance education allows for possible negotiation to fit study in with daily living chores and responsibilities. Distance education can serve the populations of rural areas, where the majority of women live; in their home environments, parents will be pleased to support their interests, and there are more people around to help mind the children.

Ideally, even women with a university degree could do postgraduate studies through distance education. We all know of the need to keep up-to-date with the rapid developments in every profession. This cannot be done easily through conventional modes where one has to be physically present at the institution. Most women seeking an education tend to get married after receiving their first degree, or even before getting their first degree. Since they cannot leave home and family to go overseas for a year or more, women find it virtually impossible to gain specialist knowledge in their respective fields.

My own case is a good example of how distance education has provided the opportunity for further studies without leaving home to go overseas. While in fulltime employment, and being united with my family, I am able to study for the Graduate Diploma in Distance Education by distance, offered by the South Australian College of Advanced Education. With a new baby it would have been impossible for me to study this course through the conventional mode, which could also have been more expensive: I would have had to get to Australia, find and pay for a place to stay and for childcare, and leave my husband behind in PNG where he needs to be because of his own job. This opportunity to study at a distance has enabled me to gain more specialized knowledge about distance education, my own professional field of interest.

In a good distance education operation, the course material should be self-instructional, whatever the delivery system, so a student can study when it is convenient, without missing out on information because of scheduling and other time conflicts and constraints. Women such as myself can study at night when we are free from family and household duties. We may have to sacrifice some sleep, but at least the choice is there for us. Even during the day at home a woman can study if she can generate some free time. Women may tackle three to four tasks simultaneously, as I have done myself. For example, while waiting for the laundry to get washed or dried, the woman would have the pot on the stove or fire—cooking lunch while she is feeding her child. At the same time she would be making a bilum (string bag) or making a necklace or bracelet. If she is studying, she would replace the bilum-making task with reading course materials.

For some women in urban centres, technology has helped to reduce housework and other tasks, and the time saved can be utilized to achieve educational advancement through distance education. For example, in the city water doesn't have to be collected three or four kilometres from home; many women will have an electric or gas stove and a washing machine.

Women in PNG are quiet learners and thinkers who dislike open competition, especially with men; indeed, the competitiveness of face-to-face education is discouraging to women. Women may gain more through distance education precisely because it allows them to study as quiet learners. In home study, there is no visible domination by male students, as is the case in face-to-face learning situations. A woman returning to the face-to-face mode of education, after years away from it, with twenty to thirty classmates who are mostly male teenagers, will be too intimidated to speak or participate in class. Such women would gain more by reading printed study materials or listening to a recorded lecture, sending feedback comments to the teacher and receiving individual help. In fact, most women in PNG would learn more through distance education than through traditional modes.

Distance education requires students to have some self-discipline and requires hard work without supervision. Women in PNG are already disciplined and hard-working by custom; they also adapt to situations and change faster than men when there is need.[2]

In the urban sector, women move around a lot either individually or with husbands. When women follow their husbands they often sacrifice their own jobs, education and friends—and experience a loss each time they move. If they are enrolled in distance education, however, at least their studies need not be interrupted by a move. When women move to a new place with their husbands there is not much for them to do socially until they become acquainted. Husbands meet new people at work, but unemployed wives have no immediate peer group. This adjustment period can be useful for the woman as a time to gain some education.

Women in the rural areas of PNG can use distance education to upgrade their qualifications. As in Canada and elsewhere, vocational or on-the-job training courses can be taught through distance education. Women in low-paid jobs can use distance education to gain specialist training and advancement. For example, if the nursing course were taught through distance education, many more women would do the course or upgrade their previous training. In Papua New Guinea, keyboard operators, typists and secretaries are females, and a large portion of working women are in these jobs. These women would never have a chance to upgrade their education since they are so low in their job classification. The mistaken idea and belief that these women don't need educational advancement to do their job and live comfortably is strong even to this day, but the problem could be addressed through distance education. Keyboard operators (who are all women at present) can improve on reading and writing and other communication skills through distance education, thus enhancing their promotional opportunities. In some instances, I have observed that younger women with higher formal qualifications have been taken in to replace women with experience and less formal education qualifications. These experienced women would have no chance of keeping up with the changes that take place in their profession, including technological developments, if conventional modes of education were their only options. As adults, these women have less chance of getting national scholarships for formal studies, since younger people competing for national scholarships have higher and better educational achievements.

Distance education provides opportunities for women to engage in educating, besides being educated themselves. Many women who are trained as teachers are not teaching, for various reasons, but are either doing jobs for which they are not trained or are not working at all. These unemployed teachers could do marking and provide tutorial assistance to external students; women can be employed as teachers without having to leave home.

Conclusion

Distance education is certainly the alternative means by which women in PNG can achieve educational advancement. It will enable the introduction of vocational subjects to women with little or no formal schooling as well as enabling those women who have some education to advance further. When employees are required to gain new skills, the flexibility and adaptability of distance education are key conditions for learning. While women are meaningfully employed, and carrying out daily living responsibilities, distance education is a practical and worthwhile mode of education in which these women can be engaged.

Distance education is able to accommodate the many situations and factors that make it difficult for women in Papua New Guinea to achieve educational advancement through the conventional, face-to-face mode. Now is the time in Papua New Guinea for us to promote distance education for the general advancement of women in our society.

Notes

1. For further reading on this subject, see A. Mandie, "Institutional and Ideological Control of Gender in a Transitional Society," in P. King, W. Lee and V. Warakae (Eds.), (1985). *From Rhetoric to Reality? Papua New Guinea's Eight Point Plan and National Goals After a Decade* (pp. 166–71). Port Moresby: University of Papua New Guinea Press.

2. See *ibid*.

Chapter 9

FEMALE IMAGERY IN COURSE MATERIALS: KENYA

by

I. Barbara Matiru and Debbie Gachuhi

> **I. Barbara Matiru** and **Debbie Gachuhi** have been lecturers with the College of Adult and Distance Education (CADE) at the University of Nairobi since 1975 and 1977 respectively. Both have written as well as edited a number of units for the Inservice Primary Teachers Course and the Adult Education Teachers Course. They have also served as coordinators and facilitators for a series of Writers Workshops on Designing and Writing Basic Education Materials. Both firmly believe that distance education is one of the most effective ways of providing an opportunity for people who might not have had a chance otherwise to acquire an education. Working on this premise they have trained distance educators not only in Kenya but also in Tanzania, Uganda, Somalia, Zambia, Botswana, and Mauritius.

Introduction

There is a growing interest in sex differentiation with regard to educational access, wastage and achievements, as well as in school-related factors that may produce these differences, such as curriculum, the design and provision of instructional materials, and the selection of teaching methods. However, until the mid-1980s, these issues have been ignored as they relate to distance education materials, especially in developing countries.

During the second decade of African Independence, there has been renewed emphasis on the promotion of scientific and technological education. In a study carried out in Kenya (Eshiwani, 1982) the author notes that women are poorly represented in the "quantitative" careers. He further observes that women are underrepresented in the science-based faculties of the University of Nairobi, and he points out that if women are to make their contribution to the development of African society they must participate in the more prestigious and better remunerated careers, alongside men. Even in the teaching profession and among salaried directors, where women occupy 34% of the work force, the percentage of women holding senior posts is less than 15%. It seems reasonable that educators would be interested in identifying and addressing the causes of these pervasive male-female imbalances, including those causes contained within school curriculum.

This chapter documents images of women and girls relative to the images of men and boys as portrayed in three different courses being offered by the School of Distance Studies (SDS) of the College of Adult and Distance Education (CADE). We were concerned to know whether there are any discernible factors to explain female underachievement in school. Both quantitative and qualitative methods of analysis were used to examine female images in these three courses.

The Courses

For this study, we focused on the three major courses offered by the SDS:

- Inservice Course for Untrained Primary School Teachers;
- The Adult Education Teachers Course;
- Kenya Certificate of Education Secondary School Course.

The Inservice Course for Primary School Teachers is being studied by 4,500 teachers in primary schools, none of whom has had any teacher training. The course consists of fifteen subjects with six units in each subject. Four of these units were analyzed in this study: English (51 pages); Home Science (37); Professional Studies (63); and Music (22), a total of 173 pages.

The Adult Education Teachers Course is being studied by 3,000 fulltime adult education teachers who are teaching adult literacy classes all over the Republic. This course has eight subjects with six units in each subject. Again, four of these units were used in this study, for a total of 109 pages: Psychology of Adult Education (21 pages); Methods of Teaching Adults (38); Policy and Philosophy of Adult Education (24); and Human Relations (26).

The Kenya Certificate of Education Secondary School Course (KCE) is being studied by 1,200 young people and adults who wish to acquire a secondary school education. At present this course offers seven subjects and each subject has three study guides, one for each academic term. Four of these study guides were analyzed: History (66 pages); Geography (151); English (162); and Mathematics (102), a total of 481 pages. Table 1 shows the scope of this study.

Table 1: The Number of Pages in Each Course

Course	Pages
Inservice Course	173
Foundations Course	109
KCE Course	481
Total	763

Illustrations

All the illustrations in the units were line drawings. Apart from those illustrations that were non-representational, such as maps, animals, mathematical symbols, and crossword puzzles, there were a total of 271 drawings of people analyzed in this study; of these, 179 (66%) were of boys or men while 50 (19%) were of girls or women. There were 42 (15%) which showed a mixed group of people, including boys, girls, men and women. Table 2 gives the breakdown by subject in the Inservice Course.

Table 2: The Number of Times Men, Women, Boys, and Girls are Illustrated in the Inservice Course

Units	Men	Women	Boys	Girls
English	14	1	4	3
Home Science	8	2	2	0
Professional Studies	22	3	9	5
Music	12	0	2	0
Total	56	6	17	8

Men and boys are featured in illustrations 73 times whereas women and girls are only illustrated 14 times. This means men and boys appear five times more often than women and girls. Even in subjects such as Home Science and English, traditionally studied by women and girls, females are hardly illustrated at all.

Almost without exception, the illustrations of boys and men show them involved in activities such as:

fishing	playing football
fighting	milking
herding	driving
studying	praying
conducting	judging
dancing	shouting
playing musical instruments	

Boys herding and milking, conducting, sitting for an examination.

On the other hand, the illustrations of women and girls mainly show them involved in domestic chores such as:

cooking	shopping
carrying water	visiting neighbours

Girls typing, cooking, and carrying water.

These illustrations suggest that women and girls are limited to traditional roles and gender-based assumptions regarding "appropriate" female activity.

As shown in Table 3, the Adult Education Teacher Course similarly presents relatively few female images:

Table 3: The Number of Times Men, Women, Boys and Girls are Illustrated in the Adult Education Teachers Course

Units	Men	Women	Boys	Girls
Psychology	24	7	5	0
Methods	8	2	1	0
Policy and Philosophy	10	3	0	0
Human Relations	1	3	0	0
Total	43	15	6	0

As can be seen from this table, girls are not illustrated at all in these units. Men and boys appear more than three times as often as women. Even in a subject like Psychology, where a more balanced representation would have been expected, men and boys appear four times more often than women. Of all the units studied in this course, Psychology was the most biased. As might be expected, men are everywhere: they are on the way to the market, they are on the farm, on the plains, in adult classes, and in a smithy, busily digging, instructing, herding, attacking, studying and making weapons. As also might be expected, women are again carrying water, cooking and doing domestic chores. Only one woman is doing something different. She is reading!

One group of illustrations in particular reflect how negatively women are portrayed.

Small minds talk about things.

Mediocre minds talk about people.

Greater minds talk about ideas.

In the Kenya Certificate of Education (KCE) Course, the pattern concerning illustrations is repeated, as shown here in Table 4.

Table 4: The Number of Times Men, Women, Boys, and Girls are Illustrated in the KCE Course

Units	Men	Women	Boys	Girls
History	15	4	0	0
Geography	0	0	0	0
English	36	16	2	1
Mathematics	1	0	3	0
Total	52	20	5	1

In these subjects, men and boys are illustrated almost three times as often as women and girls. It is certainly clear that females are not expected to be studying mathematics, where they are not illustrated at all! Men and boys are depicted as being even more active in the KCE course than in the others; they are shown:

exploring	hunting
sailing	in love with girls
carrying a gun	drinking
fishing	driving
teaching	reading
expounding	working as a policeman

On the other hand women and girls are:

giggling	smiling
serving drinks in a bar	writing a letter

In only one illustration is a woman in a valued social role, as a chieftainess.

In sum, girls and women are indirectly taught to develop negative feelings about themselves through the way they are portrayed in illustrations. They are either invisible or portrayed as capable of only domestic and service chores. This is consistent with women's actual position in society, where there are few role models. Girls and women simply are not involved in the exciting activities in which men and boys are engaged. Moreover, they are almost always found in and around the home. These injunctions are reinforced by the illustrations of the study materials, even though females who enrol in a course are by definition defying traditional gender-roles.

Prominence of Characters

The relative prominence given to a male or female in a course signifies the importance attached to each character. This prominence was measured in several ways:

- the number of characters of each sex;
- the number of references to the persons of each sex;
- the centrality of each character;
- the pronouns used to describe them.

Each time a character was mentioned it was counted. However, animals and characters whose sex was not specified were not counted. In all, a total of 174 characters were counted in the three courses. Of these, 101 (58%) were men; 24 (14%) women; 32 (18%) boys; and 17 (10%) girls. This means that male characters constitute over 75% of the total characters in all the courses. Looking at each course in turn reveals how little prominence female characters are given.

The first course which was examined was the Inservice Course. Table 5 gives a character count.

Table 5: The Number of Times Characters are Mentioned in the Inservice Course Units

Units	Men	Women	Boys	Girls
English	20	3	2	3
Home Science	2	8	6	0
Professional Studies	16	3	7	5
Music	0	0	0	0
Total	38	14	15	8

It is evident from this table that boys and men are mentioned much more often than girls and women. In English it is 22:6 and in Professional Studies it is 23:8. In Home Science, where it would be expected that female characters predominate, this is not the case, the ratio being 8:8.

In addition to the number of times characters were mentioned, a count was made to determine which of the characters was mentioned first and in relation to whom. In this course, 43 male characters, 51% of the total characters in the course, were mentioned first. Of these 31 were men and 12 were boys. On the other hand, only 12 female characters (11 women and 1 girl, 16%) were mentioned first. It is even more disconcerting that in a subject like Professional Studies, no female character is central or mentioned first. When women are mentioned, it is usually in relation to husbands and babies. When girls are mentioned it is only in relation to their mothers. By contrast, men are mentioned in relation to the government, the church, the education system, the president, or their clients. Boys are mentioned in relation to their fathers. This seems to indicate that women and girls are mentioned only in relation to the home, while men are busy with worldly affairs.

In terms of pronouns, "he" featured most prominently: 84 times in this course. "Him" and "himself" were used 24 times. The word "she" was used only 47 times, or about one and a half times less often than "he." The words "her" and "herself" were used 43 times. It is interesting to note that "hers," which suggests ownership, was only used once, while "his" appeared 55 times. Men therefore seem to own just about everything.

Although there are fewer characters in the Adult Education Teachers Course, the trend as shown in Table 6 is the same.

In this course, men are mentioned six times more often than women. Neither woman is a central character, nor is she mentioned in relation to anyone. The man who is mentioned in relation to someone is a son inheriting his father's wealth.

Table 6: The Number of Times Characters are Mentioned in the Adult Education Teachers Course Units

Units	Men	Women	Boys	Girls
Psychology	1	1	0	0
Methods	7	1	0	0
Policy and Philosophy	4	0	0	0
Human Relations	0	0	0	0
Total	12	2	0	0

In this course "he" is featured 61 times, compared to "she" which appeared only four times. "Him" and "himself" were mentioned 18 times while "her" and "herself" were mentioned only twice. As expected, the females own nothing since "hers" is never mentioned. However, "his" is mentioned 33 times.

This trend repeats itself once again in the KCE Course as shown in Table 7.

Table 7: The Number of Times Characters are Mentioned in the KCE Course

Units	Men	Women	Boys	Girls
History	21	0	0	0
Geography	0	0	0	0
English	28	8	7	9
Mathematics	2	0	0	0
Total	51	8	7	9

It can be seen from this table that boys and men once again are mentioned much more often than girls and women. In History, it is 21:0, in English it is 35:17, and in Mathematics it is 2:0. In this course, 66 male characters are mentioned first, while only 9 female characters are mentioned first. In the entire course there is no single female character who is central.

In terms of pronouns, "he" is featured 195 times in comparison to "she" which is featured just 36 times. "Him" and "himself" were mentioned 73 times while "her" and "herself" were mentioned 47 times. When it comes to "his" and "hers" the situation is quite revealing: "hers" is mentioned just once and "his" is mentioned 103 times!

Roles of Characters

Predictably, male characters in these courses are portrayed as fearless, strong, brave, hardworking, influential, wealthy, bold, clever and wise. The female characters are described as fearful, doubtful, embarrassed, stupid, pretty, emotional and well-behaved. This tends to confirm the stereotyped gender characteristics. Men and boys, much more often than women and girls, are seen outside the home in the real world where they are adventurous, alert and determined as they travel, farm, explore and navigate. We see them in the classroom, in the wilderness, crossing a river or a desert, on the plains, on the soccer pitch or basketball court and in the king's palace. They are winners and are usually able to hide their fear.

This trend continues when boys grow up and become busy, experienced, organized and wealthy men. They have jobs as engineers, policemen, hunters, camel caravan leaders, athletes, scientists, mathematicians, university lecturers, spacemen, firemen, deep sea divers and businessmen. Moreover, they inherit and pass on their wealth, mostly to their sons.

On the other hand, girls have no roles at all, apart from being sisters or daughters. When they grow up, as women, they become wives and mothers, nuns and nurses, farmers, carriers of wood, or drawers of water. These roles confine them mainly to the home environment and are often not economically rewarding. We find them in and outside the house, at the market, in a banana plantation, on the shore of a river or lake and on the farm. Those few women who venture outside the home have very limited roles; they are either market women, teachers, office workers or nurses, roles typically expected of women.

Women are seen as unreliable and as followers. More often, they are sad and tired. In addition, females are more often clumsy and punished because they are foolish; they lose and break things and don't follow advice. In all cases, females support and assist but never lead or create.

An examination of each course in detail reveals how true these observations are. Here is a list of some of the most frequently mentioned roles and activities performed by male and female characters in the Inservice Course.

Male Roles	
leader	carpenter
father	minister
superintendent	blacksmith
mayor	professor
judge	missionary
inspector	author
chairman	king
president	explorer
civil servant	weaver
	farmer
Female Roles	
mother	widow
midwife	wife
nurse	daughter
nun	granddaughter
	grandmother

Male Activities	Female Activities
leading	looking after baby
setting up committees	doing housework
administering	visiting the clinic
winning an award	labouring
evangelizing	breastfeeding
singing	shopping
telling stories	being ill
learning how to fight	listening
learning Morse code	obeying husband
being circumcised	fetching water
bullying	carrying pots
fighting	fainting
travelling	helping mother
writing books	making pots
discussing finances	grinding
drinking beer	picking lice
slaughtering	learning to show respect

The following adjectives are used to describe these roles and activities:

Male	Female
hardworking	frightened
determined	clever
famous	surprised
heroic	speechless
strong	envious
clever	beautiful
warlike	quarrelsome
proud	sulky
responsible	sweet
wealthy	kind
opportunistic	well-behaved
great	bitchy
dishonest	stupid
immoral	bitter
rough	ugly
cruel	immoral

Depictions of the ways that other people treat male and female characters also contribute to their images. Male characters undergo hardship and suffering, are taught and circumcised. Female characters are warned (by men!), stopped from travelling, ordered to cook, shamefully defeated, put in chains, abandoned by their husbands and laughed at. Images of this kind can only serve to reinforce gender stereotypes.

To illustrate further how men and women are portrayed in this course, here are three examples of text from the units.

- When a man says yes, his personal god (Chi) says yes also...To show his manliness and strength, Okonkwo ruled his family with a heavy hand as seen by the beating of his wife during a sacred week.
- Mourn the warlike men who had become soft like women.
- The girl was told to be agreeable to other wives, not to steal food from other plots, but to work hard on her own, to listen to her husband, obey him, and treat him and his relatives with great respect.

The situation concerning roles and activities is no different in the Adult Education Teachers Course.

Male Roles	Male Activities
blacksmith	learning
settler	leading
government officer	organizing
religious leader	demonstrating
lecturer	driving
teacher	teaching
agitator	acting
potter	arresting rioters
chief	agitating for freedom
elder	caring for the community
modern farmer	caring for animals
policeman	
adult learner	
Female Roles	Female Activities
mother	washing
wife	cooking
grandmother	giving birth
	being unable to inherit

Kenya: Female Imagery in Course Materials

In the KCE course the males and females are shown in the following roles and activities.

Male Roles	Male Activities
headmaster	building schools
clerk	ruling
king	navigating
carpenter	beating wife
game warden	climbing a mountain
fisherman	pitching tents
professor	poaching
doctor	buying a dress
navigator	for daughter
chief	going on a journey
captain	tracking a lion
viceroy	shooting crocodiles
explorer	debating
ruler	digging canals
soldier	getting out of danger
policeman	successfully
driver	paying wife's taxes
missionary settler	choosing a wife
colonizer	
Female Roles	**Female Activities**
nurse	remaining silent
daughter	staying in bed
	sitting on chief's lap
	being afraid of parent
	being lucky to get
	an opportunity
	laughing

In this course there were a number of adjectives which were used to describe male characters. Some of these were:

outstanding	brave
fearless	influential
ruthless	wealthy
wise	impatient

Women, on the other hand, were hardly described at all. The six adjectives used in the entire 481 pages of KCE text were:

unreliable	doubtful
follower	embarrassed
fearful	unwell

The following two quotes from the KCE courses help to point out what the authors think about women.

- Believing strongly that women should get the same pay as men for the same work, I visited the manager of a local factory who has equally strong beliefs to the contrary. After hearing his point of view, I must admit that some of his arguments are sound and need consideration.

  He agreed with me that women are as efficient at their work as men are and even admitted that in some cases they could work quicker, but he was opposed to equal pay as, in his experience, women were not so reliable as men and could not be counted on to stay in one job as long as men did. He pointed out that a firm's working force needed to be stable as continuity was essential and it cost a lot to train a new employee and he had discovered from practical experience that a woman did not stay in any job very long. He attributed this to various reasons; the principal ones being that when a woman had children, she had to give up her job to look after them and that if her husband got a job elsewhere she accompanied him.

  He also held the theory that the nature and temperament of women prevented them from staying in a job for very long as they were ready to leave for trivial reasons such as criticism by a superior or a quarrel with a fellow worker. He pointed out that a man who had a family to support could not leave a job for trivial reasons whereas a single woman with no dependents or a married woman working to buy extras did not feel the need to stay in a job she disliked. As a result, he believed that men deserved higher pay not for their greater efficiency but for their reliability.

- Miriam went to a dance last Saturday, but she did not enjoy it at all, because the young man she went with behaved so badly. He made her pay for her own ticket, danced extremely badly and quarrelled about the price of the food and drink. Poor Miriam had never been so embarrassed in her life.

The Significance of the Study

Although only three courses and twelve units were surveyed in this study, they are representative of the three biggest and most important courses being studied in Kenya by distance education students. The pertinence of the findings is of no less importance. The intention of the study was to discover a trend, either positive or negative, regarding the images of men, women, boys and girls in distance education courses. The courses certainly do not portray girls and women as positively as male characters. Females have been relegated to their traditional roles in society—that of being subordinate, housebound, passive and inferior. Therefore, girls and women who study these courses cannot identify easily with the images portrayed in them.

The researchers believe that balanced social development is desirable. That is, we strive toward a cooperative climate in which girls and boys, and men and women, work together for the betterment of society as a whole. To this end it is essential to ensure that positive images of all individuals are promoted by instructional materials. One way to do this is to sensitize curriculum developers to the importance of these images when designing distance education courses, in order to move more consciously in the direction of the stated goals of education in Kenya. The institutions which are responsible for the production of such materials should be aware of the need to make their designers, editors and illustrators conscious of the images of women and girls that are currently being portrayed in order to deliberately reverse this regrettable trend.

Reference

Eshiwani, G. (1982). "Women's Access to Educational Opportunities." Bureau of Educational Research: A Working Paper.

──────── Chapter 10 ────────

WOMEN IN DISTANCE EDUCATION AT THE UNIVERSITY OF THE SOUTH PACIFIC

by

Marjorie Crocombe, Joan Teaiwa, Arlene Griffen,
Ruby Va'a, Eileen Tuimaleali'ifano, Penelope Schoeffel,
Adi Davila Toganivalu

> **Marjorie Crocombe** is Director, USP Extension Services. She is a Cook Islander who has worked with the University of the South Pacific since 1975, first as Centre Director, in Fiji, then as Coordinator of Continuing Education for the USP region and as Director since 1983. She is responsible for a staff of eighty in ten countries, and she coordinates the administration of the various offices with the assistance of satellite communications via INTELSAT. She is also a writer, editor, and historian; she and her husband, a professor of Pacific Studies at USP, have four children.

> **Joan Teaiwa** is an American married to a Fiji citizen from Rabi Island. She is a graduate of the University of Hawaii and is currently studying for a Diploma on Distance Education from the United Kingdom. Joan is currently a Course Developer for USP Extension Services and a valuable member of the Extension Services Course Development team.

> **Arlene Griffen** is a Fiji citizen. She studied at universities in Australia and England, and she has travelled widely in North America, Europe and the South Pacific. Arlene joined the staff of the University of the South Pacific in 1979; currently she teaches English to both campus and extension students, and she writes and revises Extension courses. Her research interests include women in distance education and feminist literary criticism, particularly of literatures of the Third World. She is currently preparing for publication a feminist critique of selected works from the new literature in English from the South Pacific and a series of interviews with indigenous Pacific women writers.

University of the South Pacific

> **Ruby Va'a** is a Samoan; she worked in the Science Faculty of the University of the South Pacific before joining the Extension Services Course Development team. She is currently conducting research into intervention counselling. Ruby has four children.

> **Eileen Tuimaleali'ifano** is a Fiji citizen who has been working for many years with the University of the South Pacific. She is currently completing her Master's thesis on the readability of extension courses, which will be a major contribution to distance education in the Pacific. Eileen is married to a member of a chiefly family from Western Samoa, and they have four children. She is a Course Developer with USP Extension Services.

> **Penelope Schoeffel** is a sociologist by training. She is Head, USP Continuing Education. Penelope has taught sociology both in Australia and at the University of the South Pacific, and she has travelled widely in Fiji. She and her husband, an historian at USP, have four children.

> **Adi Davila Toganivalu** is a member of one of the prominent families in Fiji; she is the sister of Ratu Sir Kamisese Mara, a former Prime Minister of Fiji. Adi Davila is actively involved in preschool education, and she and her husband, until recently an active politician, have three young children. She is now developing tremendous background experience in the area of early childhood in the Pacific. She works at the USP Extension Services office as the Coordinator of Preschool Programmes.

Introduction
by
Marjorie Crocombe

The University of the South Pacific (USP) is a regional university which serves eleven Pacific states. The region encompasses over a million kilometres of the Pacific Ocean. Islands are small with populations ranging in size from 2,500, in Niue, to 650,000, in Fiji. There are many cultures, languages, educational and political systems—all of which make this university unique. The smallness of the island states, the vast distances between islands and the consequent communications difficulties would have been insurmountable for the USP's distance education programme but for its use of the NASA satellite ATS-1 from 1972 to 1985. In September 1986 USP was allowed to gain access to INTELSAT, which we now use for communicating with our University Centres in most of the countries which belong to the region served by the University of the South Pacific.

The USP's distance education programme was established in 1971 and is basic to the efforts of the University to make its presence felt in the eleven countries of the region. Enrolments have continued to increase year by year as more of the course offerings are made available to students who otherwise cannot have access to higher education. Women have been in the forefront in this programme as students, teachers, course writers and developers and administrators.

USP has two campuses: one in Fiji for general undergraduate and post-graduate teaching, and one in Western Samoa for agricultural students. The distance education programme which is managed by Extension Services is located at the main campus in Fiji. There is little involvement in teaching at a distance at the agricultural campus in Western Samoa at this stage of its development. The University also has nine institutes which specialize in areas which are not part of the normal teaching programmes—research, publishing and consultancies in education, natural and marine science, Pacific Studies, agriculture, rural development, atolls development, language and legal studies. These units also provide programmes for women in development. Complementing the work of the Schools and Institutes is a network of University Centres in ten of the eleven countries. A good communications system is an absolute necessity for the University to serve the region effectively.

This is the first time a coordinated effort has been made to encourage women in distance education to become involved in research and to facilitate publication of their work. The following presents the various aspects of distance education at the University of the South Pacific in which women are involved.

Course Developers at the USP
by
Joan Teaiwa

Of the four academic staff officially designated as course developers in USP's Extension Services, three are women. A course developer must aspire to be an expert in distance education, a student-centred educator, a change-agent, a communicator, a surrogate student, and an academic. Above all a course developer must try to be a good team member who works well with other people—the Coordinator of Course Development, other course developers, colleagues in Extension Services and the regional Centres, writers and tutors in the Schools and other sections of the University. The work requires a high level of competence in English, as instruction is mostly in print. Also, course developers need some background in education (preferably curriculum development and instructional design) and teaching experience. Finally, course developers need tact and diplomacy and must be willing and able to adapt and learn quickly.

A course developer is also expected to improve his/her professional qualifications in addition to carrying a normal work load. Three of the present course developers have studied for Master's degrees parttime and have worked on their theses during study leave or alongside fulltime work schedules. The fourth is developing her skills and qualifications through external studies; she has enrolled in the first course of the Diploma in Correspondence Education offered by the Association of European Correspondence Schools. For this course developer, studying by extension is both an opportunity to improve her skills and understanding of distance education and a chance to know what it's like to be an extension student. While independent study is both an ideal and a rewarding experience, it still needs as much support as possible. Thus, the course developer has been encouraged by the helpful prodding of her coordinator, the understanding of her colleagues, and especially the friendly comments of her tutor.

Mention should be made here of the typists (word processing operators) and secretary in the Course Development section. These six women cope admirably with the demanding work involved in processing and producing 120 courses in a year. They have a close, professional relationship with the course developers, and their efficiency, reliability and dedication are vital to the success of the course development process. Like the course developers, they have acquired their particular skills of course material production on the job, and they represent a type of expertise which is unique at the USP.

Motivation, Persistence and Success Among Female Distance Education Learners of Pre-Degree English Courses
by
Arlene Griffen

Women distance educators and learners at the University of the South Pacific face the same basic problem: too much to do and too little time to do it well. This is true in my own case, for example. Unlike most other tertiary institutions, USP does not recruit separate staff for its Campus and Extension teaching operations but requires staff to teach in both modes. Thus, since 1979, while teaching English courses to students on the Laucala Campus in Suva, Fiji, I have also been a tutor/marker of Extension English courses for our regional students. In addition, I have coordinated our Extension English programme, I write and revise Extension English courses to parallel courses taught on campus, I conduct Extension tutorials through our satellite network and I visit distant learners in their own countries. This multi-faceted teaching role accounts for most of the frustrations and the fulfillments I experience in my job.

The woman distance learner seems to hold the same sort of love/hate attitude towards her education in this mode. I arrived at this conclusion, and others, through a questionnaire/interview survey of women in five USP countries who enrolled in the four pre-degree English courses offered for credit in Semester 1, 1986. I chose countries with the highest enrolments in these courses: Solomon Islands, Vanuatu, Fiji, Western Samoa and Tonga. The four courses were: Preliminary English A; Preliminary English B; Communication and Study Skills I; and Introduction to English Literature. The first two courses are roughly equivalent to English courses offered in the final year of secondary education in the region; the last two courses are equivalent to the Foundation English courses taken on campus by USP students before they begin degree studies.

Table 1: Enrolment figures for Four Pre-degree English Courses
Semester 1, 1986

Country	Female	Male
Solomon Islands	5	84
Vanuatu	32	48
Fiji	27	55
Western Samoa	19	49
Tonga	25	61
TOTAL	108	297

Note: From these figures it is clear that Pacific women are *not highly represented (27%)* in distance education, contrary to the situation in other parts of the world. Extension Studies enrolment statistics for Semester 2, 1985 (50 courses) show a total of 35% for female enrolment. Also see *Note* for Table 2.

The Questionnaire

A forty-question survey was sent to each of the 108 women who enrolled in the four courses, and 16 women were interviewed. The questions were phrased in simple English because most USP students know English as a second or third language and not as their mother tongue. The questionnaire was divided into four sections: Background Information (7 questions); Reading & Learning (9); Tutoring (5); Other Factors Affecting Your Extension Study (19).

Results

From the sample of 108 students, 46 (43%) responses were received. Taped interviews were conducted with 16 of these 46 respondents and took the form of the respondents answering the questions and elaborating on some of them.

Background Information: About two-thirds of the respondents were from urban areas while one-third lived in rural areas; two-thirds were aged 15–30 while one-third was aged 31–40. Nearly all had completed primary school and most of secondary school. The most popular course was Communications and Study Skills I (58%), followed by Preliminary English A (28%). Most respondents enrolled in the classes to continue their education (41%), while 39% enrolled to improve their job performance.

Reading and Learning: Over half the respondents (56%) said they found English an easy language to read and write and they finished all the course assignments. Just under three-quarters (71%) sat the final examination.

Tutoring: Only a quarter (26%) of the respondents said they never needed to seek help with their assignments. Just over one-third (39%) said they always got the help they needed from their tutor either face-to-face or by written comment.

Other Factors Affecting Extension Study: Nearly three-quarters of the respondents (71%) were in fulltime employment. Eighty-two percent did the work for the course at home and nearly all (92%) had enough room and light to work in. Just over two-thirds (67%) of the respondents were unmarried but still had home duties which took time away from their studies. Married respondents all had family duties that took time away from their studies. Both married and unmarried respondents had community/social interests and responsibilities which reduced their study time. Sixty percent of the married respondents had home help from their husbands to free them for their course work.

Table 2: Official Course Results for the Four Pre-Degree English Courses, Semester 1, 1986 (women only)

Country	No. Enrolled	Pass	Fail
Solomon Islands	5	1	4
Vanuatu	32	7	25
Fiji	17	8	9
Western Samoa	19	11	8
Tonga	25	13	12
TOTAL	98	40	58
	(100%)	(46%)	(54%)

Note: The Vanuatu figures include 16 enrolments from Francophone New Caledonian Kanaks attempting to further their education outside their French colonial system. For various reasons, these students were unable to submit most of their coursework or to take the examinations for their courses. They did not return questionnaires.

Table 3 looks at course results in terms of residence of respondents. Urban students clearly have the advantage over rural students because they have easier access to the resources of the USP Extension Centre in their country. At the urban centre, they may attend tutorials with local or visiting tutors. They may take part in satellite tutorials with tutors based at the Laucala Campus in Suva. They may also use the USP Centre library resources.

Rural students, by contrast, are lucky if they can find a good secondary school library in their area or a fellow student to work with on an Extension Course. On the rare occasions when rural areas are visited by local or Fiji-based course tutors, rural students may get help from the tutorials offered during these short visits.

The *Don't Know* column in Table 3 refers to those respondents who did not know whether they had passed or failed the course at the time of response (mid-Semester 2, 1986). There are several reasons for this lack of information: sometimes official results are withheld from students because they have failed to pay all course fees, and sometimes there are delays in processing results because examinations take time to reach tutors/markers in Fiji. No matter how valid the reasons, these delays in receiving course results have negative effects on Extension students.

Table 3: Course Results (urban/rural) Based on Questionnaire Responses, Semester 1, 1986

Residential	No. Enrolled	Passed	Failed	Don't Know
Urban	30	16	4	10
Rural	16	4	6	6
TOTAL	46	20	10	16

Conclusion

The diverse nature of the USP distance education system argues against quick and easy conclusions. However, this survey indicates some factors that seem to apply beyond the English pre-degree courses and their distance learners. While enrolment figures for women are generally considerably lower than those for men, the figures for Vanuatu and Solomon Islands are more extreme than those for Tonga and Western Samoa, with Fiji falling somewhere between the two. Rural distance learners, particularly on outer islands, are much more disadvantaged than their urban sisters. Unmarried as well as married women have considerable family and community duties and responsibilities that take time from their personal pursuits. Though there are individual instances of husbands supporting their wives in their studies, Pacific cultures generally put male interests and power first. The Solomon Islands poet, July Sipolo, sums it all up (check the enrolment figures for her country!):

A Man's World
My brother can sit on the table
I mustn't
He can say what he likes whenever he likes
I must keep quiet
He can order me around like a slave
I must not back-chat
He gives me his dirty clothes to wash
I wish he could wash mine!
If he sits on the front steps
I must go round the back door
If the house is full
I must crawl on my hands and knees
I must walk behind him not in front
Watch my speech when he is in the house
Don't say 'face' but say 'front'
Not 'teeth' but 'stone'
Carry out my love affairs behind his back
Custom allows him to thrash both of us if caught
But he can carry on in front of me
That's his privilege
I must pay compensation
If I'm to get married
Or pregnant without a hubby
A brother can make a living out of his sisters!

Add to her voice these other comments on motivation, persistence and success and we get a better idea of the South Pacific Island distance learner as a woman and as a person:

> It's a good way for working people to get an education. (Samoa)

> I'd like to achieve a higher level of education...which would mean more income for a big family. (Tonga)

> In our culture girls have their jobs and boys have theirs. (rural Samoa)

> In order to maintain the peace in our relationship I have to get his agreement for everything I do. (Tonga)

> He said I was too old to learn. (Samoa)

> One assignment I did in bed at 2:00 a.m.! (Fiji)

> I resigned from all committees, organizations, etc., because of problems at home...that almost succeeded in breaking up our marriage. I was always reminded that the home and family came first—sometimes I was told I was just wasting my time. (Indo-Fijian)

> It was the tightness of life...commitments I have in the family, church and community work. Also my personal life—looking for a husband! (rural Samoa)

It is good; it restores my confidence. (Tonga)

I feel like a big person internally. (Tonga)

I feel braver to take more courses. (Fiji)

It stimulates and refreshes my mind and is very helpful with my work. It helps me to help my children with their English homework. I feel and believe that to educate a woman is to educate a family. (rural Fiji)

Teaching Science by Distance Education
by
Ruby Va'a

Matters such as nuclear winter, space travel, head transplants, or a youth formula are far out of reach of the average South Pacific woman. Just as science is groping for answers, science educators in the Pacific are reaching out to find the best approach to the successful teaching of science.

Currently, science education is very much an underdeveloped, undernourished part of the overall education system for the average Pacific school pupil. It has been even less accessible for the average Pacific woman in the 20–60 age range.

World trends in the teaching of science follow the belief that science is best taught as inquiry-oriented experiences—to develop a questioning-critical attitude through the inquiry/discovery approach which simulates the process of science itself. A recent study in one South Pacific country by this writer has determined that in a rural school, classroom interaction tended to foster conforming behaviour on the part of the pupils, while in an urban school, classroom interaction was more conducive to forming a questioning-critical behaviour. Classroom interaction in science lessons in face-to-face teaching must be replaced by the interactions we try to incorporate into our course materials. Thus, a consideration of such interaction is vital to the development of science courses by distance education.

Science by distance education is yet to be developed fully at the University of the South Pacific. At present, a very limited number of science courses are offered through the distance learning mode. These are at the preliminary (Form 6), Foundation (Form 7) and the first year degree levels. One main difficulty has been how to include practical work with the course materials; this must be resolved before extensive development of science by distance education can go ahead.

But what has this to do with women?

In the Pacific, science is still largely male-dominated. Consider the statistics about the staff of the School of Pure and Applied Sciences at the University of the South Pacific campus in Suva: 8 of the 41 academic staff are women, while 6 of the 10 technical staff are women. Other science-linked departments are similarly male-dominated. For example, in the School of Agriculture in Western Samoa, there are 2 women to 18 men on the academic staff. A similar ratio exists for the technical staff. On the student side, enrolment numbers show that the female:male ratio in the science courses is as follows:

On campus: Year (1986 Sem. 1)	Females	Males	Total
Foundation	79	190	269
Degree (undergrad)	87	232	319
Total	166	422	588

Off campus, our Extension Studies figures reveal the following breakdown:

Year (1985 Sem. 1 & 2)	Females	Males	Total
Foundation	72	209	281
100 Level	–	13	13
Total	72	222	294

By comparison, the enrolment numbers for social science show these courses to be more attractive to women.

On campus: Year (1986 Sem. 1)	Females	Males	Total
Foundation	81	84	165
Degree	300	545	845
Total	381	629	1010
Off campus: Year (Sem. 1 & 2)	Females	Males	Total
Foundation	216	551	767
Degree	1131	1938	3069
Total	1347	2489	3836

This data shows the imbalance in the female:male ratio in the science courses to be greater than in the social science courses.

Extensive development of science by distance education is beginning to take place at the University of the South Pacific, and more science courses are being requested from the countries of the university region. The course development section is trying to meet this request, and moves to establish laboratory facilities around the region have been initiated.

Development in the science courses should make more opportunities available to the women of the USP region, particularly for those employed in a science-oriented job. An increasing number of women enter previously male-dominated fields, and the availability of our Extension Studies courses in technology (mechanics, carpentry, industrial arts), technical laboratory work, computer science and general science should encourage this trend.

A Readability Survey of Extension Course Materials
by
Eileen Tuimaleali'ifano

Background

Since the early years of Extension Services, staff and students involved with Extension courses and studying by extension have speculated that one of the reasons for the high withdrawal and failure rates of USP extension students was the high reading difficulty level of USP extension course materials. This was a reasonable speculation: Extension courses were being written in English by first language expatriate staff for second language regional students. In 1984, data was gathered, using the Cloze readability procedure, on the readability levels of the study materials of six USP extension courses. The primary aim of this study was to conduct an exploratory investigation into whether or not a readability problem did exist and, if so, the extent and nature of the problem.

The Study

The six courses[1] for this study were selected to represent the social sciences and technical subjects: Education and Society; English Foundation A; Accounting Information: Applications; Introduc-

Table 4: Study Results

Courses	No. of Centres	No. of Students M	No. of Students F	No. of Students Total	Mean M	Mean F	Mean O/All	40% and Over M	40% and Over F
English Foundation	3	7	3	10	6.97	6.85	6.91	3	1
Project Planning	4	39	17	56	3.57	4.16	3.86		3
Stats and Soc. Analysis	3	7	4	11	8.19	9.31	8.22*	4	1
Education and Society	3	18	25	43	2.08	4.82	4.75		
Intro to Constitutional and Legal Systems	2	10	7	17	5.05	4.75	5.12	1	1
Accounting Information	2	30	5	35	4.72	6.23	5.47	1	
TOTAL:		111	61	172				9	6

Note: These results include six students from Tonga who sat the test nine weeks into the semester and who therefore may have read the materials from which the tests were compiled.

tion to Constitutional and Legal Systems; Project Planning and Statistics and Social Analysis. Four passages for Cloze testing were randomly selected from study booklets containing the core materials of the courses. The Cloze tests were prepared on the basis of twenty deletions, and each set of tests per course was to be of no more than an hour's duration in all.

One hundred and seventy-two students enrolled in the six courses sat the tests in four USP Centres (Fiji, Tonga, Western Samoa and Solomon Islands) under test conditions.

The results of the test were interpreted according to the criteria of researchers cited by Harrison (1980) and Pennock (1972-73). There is a general agreement through comparison with the results of multiple choice comprehension tests that a score of 55% and more indicates readability at the independence level and a score of 40% and more readability at the instructional level. Distance education materials must be written at the independent level of understanding for students to derive maximum benefit. Below 40%, a student is reading at the frustration level.

Results

Table 4 summarizes the overall results of the study.

Analysis of the Data

From the results of the survey presented above, two features appear to stand out:

- Mean scores indicated that of the six extension courses tested, only one course, Statistics and Social Analysis, was within the reading instruction level of the students, with a mean score of 8.22 over 20. However, 6 of these students were in the Tonga group who sat the test in Week 9 of the semester, and who may have read the materials prior to being tested, increasing their results.

- Of the 172 students who sat the test, only 15 scored an average mark of 40% and over in their respective course tests. Again, 4 of these were Tongan students.

The female students who participated in the survey apparently fared better than their fellow male students in terms of mean scores per course, and also in terms of the over 40% category.

In four of the six extension courses tested for readability, the female students achieved mean scores higher than the overall mean scores: Project Planning; Statistics and Social Analysis; Education and Society; and Accounting Information. When this difference is compared with that of the courses where the male score is higher than the course mean, English Foundation and Introduction to Constitutional and Legal Systems, the differences achieved by the female students are much more significant.

Although only six female students achieved a "50% and over" score compared to the nine males in the same category, in terms of proportion to the total number of participants, this would yield percentages of 9.8 females and 8.1 males scoring over 40% in the Cloze tests. Again, the results achieved by the female students in the survey are higher than those achieved by their male counterparts.

The data collected for this survey unfortunately lacked information on the breakdown of total enrolments in the six courses by gender, so that no conclusion can be reached about whether or not the sex representation in the survey corresponds with the overall proportions. Survey participation, however, suggests that, apart from Education and Society, there is a higher proportion of male students enrolled in extension courses. The fact that the majority of these tests were taken during tutorial times, and the students had no previous knowledge of them, rules out the possibility that the students were not present because of domestic and usual female commitments at the end of the work day, as they would definitely have scheduled their tutorial times into their week's commitments.

Although the sample contains almost twice as many males as females, in comparative terms the results of the survey speak highly of the calibre of the women as extension students. Future USP surveys of this nature might clarify whether fewer females than males are able to commit themselves to extension study, what kind of circumstances inhibit or encourage participation by women, and what characteristics in female students would prepare them for higher readability achievements. If USP is to improve its distance education programme and the readability levels of its course materials, it would certainly benefit from answers to some of these questions.

Note

1. In 1986, one of these courses changed its title: English Foundation A became Communications and Study Skills 1.

References

Harrison, C. (1980). *Readability in the Classroom.* Cambridge: Cambridge University Press.

Pennock, C. (1972-73). "The Cloze Test for Assessing Readability." *English Quarterly,* 5(4).

Women in Continuing Education
by
Penelope Schoeffel and Adi Davila Toganivalu

The Continuing Education section of the Extension Services at the University of the South Pacific has engaged in a variety of activities for and by women since the section was first established by Marjorie Crocombe, now the Director, in 1975. The foundations of this work were established by Marjorie and covered activities such as the Pacific Pre-School Programme and creative writing workshops for Pacific Islands women, which led to the discovery of a number of talented women writers in the region and the publication of their work.

All the staff of the Continuing Education section are women. The present head, Penelope Schoeffel, has an academic background in Anthropology and Sociology with a special interest in women and development. She is Australian but has lived and worked in the Pacific Islands since 1963. Her husband is from Western Samoa. In 1983-84, while her husband was on study leave from USP, she served as National Programme Coordinator for the Women and Development Network of Australia. The Pre-School Coordinator is Adi Davila Toganivalu, who is Fijian and comes from Lakeba in the Lau group of islands. She trained as a kindergarten teacher in Melbourne, Australia. On returning to Fiji, she taught in the YWCA kindergartens for three years and became supervisor of Kindergartens for the YWCA. She is the President of the Pacific Pre-School Council which links pre-school activities in all the USP member countries. The secretary in Extension Services is Mrs. Kesaia Matanimeke who comes from Bua province in Vanua Levu, Fiji's second largest island. She combines her secretarial work with a keen interest in continuing education and has become an expert in the organization of regional continuing education workshops.

The Continuing Education section facilitates the various Continuing Education programmes of the ten USP Centres in the region. These vary from country to country and cover subjects such as foreign and Pacific languages, Pacific arts, crafts and culture, computer awareness and computer applications, use of the mass media, creative writing and special skills training courses. The section works in cooperation with the Pacific regional YWCA office, the South Pacific Commission's Women's Bureau, and a number of governmental and NGO women's projects and programmes in the region.

An example of such cooperation is a current special project of the Continuing Education section which was initiated by Pacific women at a regional workshop held by the South Pacific Commission's Women's Bureau in Rarotonga in January 1985. This project is developing training modules on community health and nutrition with special relevance to the situation in Pacific Island communities. The modules will be used to offer short courses through the USP Centres and may be adapted for distance education courses along the lines of the Pacific Pre-School Teachers Programme. In 1982, two workshops were held for Pacific islanders serving in the region as nutritionists and health educators to outline the contents and orientation of the modules. Further writing workshops are planned for 1987. Seminar sessions are held fortnightly for health educators and nutritionists in the region using the USPNET on the INTELSAT satellite system.

The Continuing Education section also conducts a monthly seminar programme via satellite for women's programme staff working on government and NGO programmes and projects. The Pacific Regional Women's Training and Education Information Exchange deals with exchange of information on educational and training programmes offered to women from the Pacific at the regional, national and international levels.

The Pacific Pre-School Teachers Programme
The Pacific Pre-School Teachers Programme, an achievement by and for Pacific Islands women, is a sequence of three courses offered by distance education leading to the Pacific Pre-School

Teacher's Certificate, awarded jointly by the Pacific Pre-School Council, USP Extension Services and the USP Institute of Education. It is based in the Continuing Education section of USP Extension Services.

The idea for the programme was conceived at a workshop conducted by Diane Goodwillie, a Canadian project officer with the YWCA South Pacific regional office. The workshop was initiated by the YWCA in collaboration with the Continuing Education Section of USP Extension Services and the USP Institute of Education, and involved women working in early childhood programmes in thirteen Pacific states and territories. They came together to discuss their needs and aspirations in relation to the development of pre-schools in the Pacific region. It was funded by the Netherlands Kindergarten Association (Nederlands Comite voor Kinderpostzegals—N.C.K.) and the Australian Council of Churches.

Women from the Cook Islands, Fiji, Kiribati, Niue, Papua New Guinea, Ponape, Western Samoa, Solomon Islands, Tonga, Tuvalu, Vanuatu, Australia and New Zealand took part in the workshop. The consultant was Dr. Jane Ritchie, a psychologist with special interest in cross-cultural child socialization and development patterns, who is Reader in Psychology at the University of Waikato in New Zealand. Other resource persons were drawn from the University of the South Pacific, the South Pacific Commission, the Pacific Theological College, the YWCA, the Western Samoa Pre-School Association and the Fiji Ministry of Education.

The workshop resulted in the formation of the Pacific Pre-School Council which was asked to implement seven recommendations:

1. To bring together people interested in pre-schools, to share programmes, information and problems.

2. To learn more about child development patterns in the South Pacific.

3. To encourage use of local, inexpensive teaching materials and to learn how to make use of them.

4. To share and create written materials for Pacific Island pre-school teachers.

5. To encourage the writing of children's books in local languages and with a local background.
6. To set up and develop a Regional Pre-School Council.
7. To establish a Pacific Pre-School Teacher's Training Course.

Items six and seven were given the top priorities. The newly formed council nominated a number of pre-school teachers from the region, who volunteered to write pre-school teacher's training materials. Pre-school teachers who were unable to take part in writing the materials and who were from countries not represented among the writers volunteered to read the materials produced and provide input relevant to their countries. In August 1981, a workshop was held for the writers to review the materials they had been working on. Dr. Ritchie was in attendance as resource person, and Mrs. Gwen Deverell volunteered to do the final editing and proofreading.

It was decided to offer the programme through Continuing Education—at the non-academic level—to enable women to enrol who did not have advanced secondary education. Admission requirements are a minimum of two years' secondary education and work experience in a pre-school, kindergarten or playgroup. Mrs. Iole Tagoilelagi from Western Samoa became the first coordinator of the pre-school course, and she was succeeded by Mrs. Gwen Deverell, Mrs. Salote Fukofuka (in 1984) and Adi Davila Tognivalu (in 1986).

Course I, "Growing up in a Pacific Society," was first offered in the first semester, 1981; Course II, "Planning Your Pre-school Programme," in the second semester; and Course III, "Pre-School, Family and Community," in the first semester 1983—through Extension Services of the University of the South Pacific. Since then all three courses have been offered every semester. By late 1986, 224 Pacific Islands pre-school teachers had completed all three courses and attained their Certificate.

Funding was sought in 1982 through the Women and Development Network of Australia, who assisted in writing up the project proposal and seeking a sponsoring agency. This search received assistance from the Australian Development Assistance Bureau's Committee for Development Cooperation, and Australian aid funds were made available in 1984 through the sponsorship of the UNICEF Committee of Australia.

Simon Fraser University Distance Education Staff & Friends

Top: Carol Lane, Colin Yerbury, Dawn Howard, Leila Hargreaves, Teresa Book, June Sturrock, Barbara Lange. Bottom: Kay Uno, Catherine Porter, Karlene Faith, Laura Coles, Elizabeth Carefoot, Ellen Sangster, Lesley

Debbie Sentance, Hannah Hadikein, Christine Dempster, Deanne Mackie, Mindy Ferrier

Liz Burge and twin-engined Otter aircraft in the beauty of winter-time northern Ontario. Real distances here!

Barbara Matiru and Debbie Gachuhi in Kenya with course writers in training

Student orientation at Dutch Open Universiteit

Dutch Open Universiteit Study Centre tutorial

USP course developers, Joan Teaiwa, Ruby Va'a, and Eileen Tuimaleali'ifano

June Sturrock | Christine von Prümmer  | Üte Rossié

Jeanne Macaskill | Birgitta Willén  | Diana Carl

Lorraine Bourque | Angela Mandie-Filer 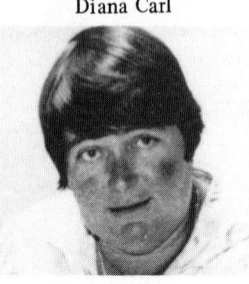 | Barbara Matiru

Debbie Gachuhi | Marjorie Crocombe  | Ruby Va'a

Joan Teaiwa  | Eileen Tuimaleali'ifano 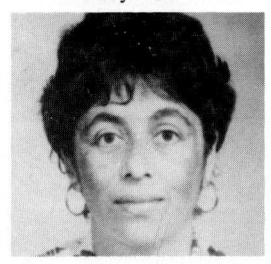 | Arlene Griffen

Adi Davila Toganivalu   Penelope Schoeffel   Gomathi Mani

Kamalini Bhansali   Jyoti Trivedi   Wendy Richards

Paulene Heiler   Ülkü Köymen   Barbara Spronk

Donna Radtke   Loene Furler   Carol Scott

Shelagh Cox   Bev James   Gill Kirkup

Erin Keough with students at Memorial University, Newfoundland

University of the South Pacific: Solomon Islands Centre

Open University, Netherlands

SNDT Women's University, Bombay

Diana Carl (centre) with colleagues Christine Shelton and Bruce Densmore at Mount Saint Vincent University, Halifax, Nova Scotia

Marjorie Crocombe with USP Vice Chancellor and Minister of Communications: Opening of USPNETwork on Intelsat

Debbie Gachuhi with Distance Educators in Kenya

Performance by Fijian students

The courses made use of the USPNET satellite communication network; initially on ATS-1 "PEACESAT" and from September 1986 on the new INTELSAT system. Tutorials and discussions are held fortnightly.

A pilot training attachment scheme began in 1984 to enable small groups of students who had completed the course to observe in a pre-school either in Western Samoa or Fiji as part of their training. Teachers from Kiribati, Solomon Islands, Vanautu and Tuvalu took part in the scheme.

In May 1985, a second Pacific Pre-School workshop was held at Extension Services headquarters in Suva. The workshop discussed the aims and role of the Council and carried out a detailed review and evaluation of course materials. The workshop recommended that the course materials be adapted and translated into Pacific languages so that less formally educated, rural pre-school teachers could be trained.

In 1986 an external assessor, Mrs. Pamela Scraton, was appointed by the Council in consultation with Extension Services and the Institute of Education. She conducted an evaluation and review of the course materials and made detailed recommendations for revising the course. These recommendations, along with those of the 1985 workshop, will be the basis of new developments of the pre-school programme in 1987.

THE INDIAN EXPERIENCE

by

Gomathi Mani, Kamalini H. Bhansali,
Jyoti H. Trivedi

Gomathi Mani, M.A., M.Ed., Ph.D., holds the position of Lecturer with the Department of Adult and Continuing Education at the University of Madras, India and has done so since 1978. She has previously worked as an Assistant Professor in a College of Education for five years. She has been associated with distance education as an instructor, lesson writer, paper setter, valuator, radio and TV script writer and presenter for most of the Indian Universities. Her Ph.D. is on "Evaluation of Distance Education." She has published widely in the areas of adult, non-formal and distance education in national and internation professional journals. She has attended a number of national seminars, workshops and conferences as well as the Thirteenth International Conference of ICDE in Melbourne, Australia in 1985. Dr. Mani is the regional representative of WIN (ICDE) for India and a life member of DAET, SITU and CADE. She is currently involved in research in the area of distance education and women's issues.

Kamalini H. Bhansali received her Bachelor's and Master's degrees at the University of Bombay in Arts and Education. She is currently Vice-Chancellor and a professor emeritus in Non-Formal Education at SNDT Women's University. Mrs. Bhansali has published several works on education in general and the education of women in particular, and she has travelled extensively, teaching at conferences and seminars from London and West Germany to Canada. She is a member of many organizations, including the Committee on Population Education for the Government of Maharashtra, the Commonwealth Association for the Education of Adults, and the Standing Conference on University and Research in the Education of Adults.

> **Jyoti H. Trivedi** has been associated with the SNDT Women's University for over two decades and was the Vice-Chancellor from 1981 to 1986. She comes from a family of pioneers in industry, social reform and education; she is married to an eminent intellectual who was inducted into the Union Ministry as a technocrat. Trained as a gynecologist, Dr. Trivedi takes a keen interest in women's education, especially professional and vocational. In keeping with this commitment, she has developed courses in electronics, computer science and other vocational subjects. At present, Dr. Trivedi is a member of the planning board of the Indira Gandhi National Open University and on the Academic Council of Banasthali Vidyapith University. She is also a member of the standing committee of Women's Research Centres, on the executive council of the Indian Association for Women's Studies, and chair of the Sadhana Educational Complex and Science Committee of SNDT University and of the Association of Medical Women in Bombay.

Editor's Note: In the sections which follow, Dr. Mani describes distance education in India and the development of media systems; Mrs. Bhansali and Dr. Trivedi discuss the activities of the SNDT Women's University, which offers both classroom and distance education programmes; then Dr. Mani comments on the experiences and perceptions of women distance learners in India.

Distance Education in India
by
Gomathi Mani

India is the seventh largest and the second most populous country in the world, with 684 million people, over a sixth of the world's population. About three-quarters of the population live in villages; their main occupation is agriculture. India achieved independence in 1947 and has adopted a parliamentary form of government based on universal adult franchise and a mixed economy. India has made notable advances in agriculture, industry and science and technology and is self-reliant in many sophisticated areas of industry with substantial progress toward the exploration of space.

In spite of all these advances, India is still a developing country, and the per capita annual income is only about US$189, one of the lowest in the world. Mass poverty and illiteracy still defy solutions. Over the last four decades, enormous expansion of educational facilities has taken place, and yet, according to the 1981 census, the literacy rate is only 36%, including those who can only sign their names. According to one estimate, the effective literacy rate—that is, the ability to read newspapers and other written materials with ease—is 20% at most. The overall female literacy is only 24.8%, almost half the male literacy rate of 46.9%. Literacy is significantly less common in rural areas (40.8% male and 18% female) than in urban areas (65.8% and 47.8% respectively). Meeting the national problem of illiteracy is a top priority for all educational systems—formal, non-formal and distance education.

Distance Education

Distance education in India has a history of nearly three decades. Persistent efforts have been made by both government and voluntary organizations to achieve universal literacy and expand opportunities for female education. Advances notwithstanding, India could not cater to the increasing social demands for education, a result of the twin explosions of population and knowledge. As the demand far exceeded the available resources and infrastructure in the formal system, India had to identify an alternative and economical mode of education. Correspondence education was then a primary learning method for certain classes of working adults, for the homebound, for the remotely isolated rural population and for countless others who for reasons of their situations, job requirements or personal preferences seek to further their general education or update their skills by distant learning methods. For the distant learner in a developing country like India, correspondence study was and is the primary learning method.

Development of Correspondence/Distance Education in Indian Universities

Higher education through correspondence first received serious attention in India in 1961, when the Ministry of Education appointed an Expert Committee on Correspondence Education, with the purpose of examining the feasibility of such a system of education in Indian Universities. In pursuance of the recommendations of this committee, the University of Delhi established the Directorate of Correspondence Education in the year 1962-63 and offered B.A. courses through correspondence as a pilot project. Subsequent evaluation of correspondence courses identified the need for flexibility in applying the system to the varying conditions in the country. The experiences of other countries using distance education methods, such as Australia, UK, USSR, and the USA, were examined. Distance education programmes developed rapidly, and the response to the B.A. course of Delhi was very encouraging; a second degree, Bachelor of Commerce, was added in 1970.

The Kothari Commission (1964–66) recommended that opportunities for parttime education through evening colleges and owntime education through correspondence courses be extended as widely as possible—in order to reduce the capital costs of expanding higher education. Delegates were sent to the USSR in 1967, 1968 and 1971 to study their scheme of correspondence education and to gain necessary expertise. Correspondence education was recommended as the only answer to the problem of increased demand for higher education. Prompted by the successes achieved by the Delhi and Punjab Universities, a number of other universities instituted correspondence programmes.

Current Status of Correspondence/Distance Education

At present in India, twenty-four Universities, four major Institutes and innumerable private institutions have started undergraduate, post-graduate legal and teacher training courses, with the basic aim of providing a "second chance" at a distance to those who have missed opportunities for higher education. The total enrolment in the universities during 1981–82 was 2.25 lakhs (225,000 students); Madurai-Kamaraj and Mysore Universities together accounted for 66,184 students. Madurai-Kamaraj University, in Tamil Nadu, has 35.2% of the total student population, though it only started in 1971; this university was the first to use radio to supplement lesson units. The various programmes offered lead to certificates, diplomas and bachelor's and master's degrees in virtually all the humanities and social sciences, as well as law, business, library science and other professional and vocational training areas.

The non-semester pattern, introduced at the University of Madras in 1984-85, is preferred by many students. Also, there is a need to develop certain non-traditional, job-oriented programmes, as is done in other countries, instead of just duplicating the courses of the formal system. This is especially important for female students, within a distance education climate that is still male-dominated and urban-oriented.

Universities Offering Correspondence Courses in India

- Allahabad University
- Andhra University
- Andra Pradesh Open University
- Annamalai University
- Bhopal University
- Bombay University
- Central Institute of English and Foreign Languages
- University of Calcutta
- University of Delhi
- Himachal Pradesh University
- Indira Gandhi National Open University
- University of Kerala
- University of Madras
- Madurai Kamaraj University
- Meerut University
- University of Mysore
- Osmania University
- Panjab University
- Patna University
- Punjabi University
- SNDT Women's University
- University of Rajasthan
- Regional College of Education
- NCERT, Mysore
- Udaipur University
- Sir Venkateswara University
- Utkal University
- Central Institute of Indian Languages, Mysore
- Central Hindi Directorate
- Rashtriya Sanskrit Sansthan
- Indian Institute for Workers Education
- National Institute of Educational Planning and Administration
- University of Jammu
- University of Kashmir

Innovative Programmes in Distance Education

Distance Education Through Radio—An Experiment

All India Radio (AIR) puts out a variety of programmes based on the interests and demands of the listeners, the most popular being music, which fills about 40% of total broadcast time, and news and entertainment. Popular music has a prominent function in much of our distance education by both radio and television. Radio occupies a key place among the daily mass communication media. Weather bulletins are broadcast daily for the benefit of farmers and a daily programme on agriculture is broadcast for 45 to 55 minutes from sixty-one farm and home units located in different rural stations. A syllabus-oriented programme for farmers is broadcast from thirty-one AIR stations, to impart skills and knowledge about new agricultural practices. These AIR farm schools provide stepwise guidance and instruction, backed by printed instructional and information material.

Radio Rural Forums

Based on the Canadian experience in 1956, India started rural forums on a pilot basis, near Pune, Maharashtra State, as a coordinated effort between UNESCO, the central government, All India Radio and the state government. In all, 144 radio forums were organized in colleges spread over the districts around Pune, each comprised of 12 to 20 members, mainly farmers drawn from different socio-economic groups, who worked with a convener. A special half-hour programme on the practical aspects of rural life was broadcast for the forums from the Pune Station twice a week over a period of ten weeks. Forum members assembled with the convener half an hour before each broadcast time for preliminary comments and preparation for the programme. After the programme, the forum discussed the content of the broadcast, raised questions and submitted a report to the Pune station. In this way there was continuous feedback from the forums and interaction between the broadcasters and recipients of the message.

The Radio Rural Forums proved to be an effective experiment in the utilization of radio for communicating with village people, and by 1969 the community listening forum had extended to many other areas in different states. Nevertheless, in 1969 the government of India discontinued the scheme of subsidizing community sets. With the advent of the transistor era, the number of private sets increased rapidly and the relevance of the community listening lost its official character in most states. This problem was compounded by regional variations in the distribution of the community sets; for example, Tamil Nadu and Maharashtra states alone account for nearly half the total number of community sets in the country. Nevertheless, systematic evaluation clearly indicates that radio has been an effective mode for agricultural education. Indeed, high yield varieties of seeds are now popularly known as "Radio Seeds" and fertilizer mixes as "Radio Khad."

Mother-Childcare Programme through Radio

In 1974 a National Policy for children was laid down which emphasized healthcare; a major programme, Integrated Child Development Service (ICDS) was launched to establish childcare centres— "anganwadies" and "balwadies"—for the rural population. An organized communication support system was provided through radio to inform, educate and motivate expectant and nursing mothers to make the best use of the available services under the ICDS and to adopt new practices and values to improve their own and their children's health. The planning and delivery of these communication support programmes involves representatives of the central ministries of education, social welfare, health and family welfare, rural department, the Ministry of Education and Broadcasting, the UNICEF regional office in New Delhi, and many voluntary agencies all working in cooperation with All India Radio.

Recently, radio workshops were organized, in collaboration with UNICEF, based on discussions of various dimensions of motherhood and childcare and visits to a number of "anganwadies" to study the problems in actual field situations. On the basis of these visits and discussions, twenty-six subjects were chosen for broadcast; the weekly programmes were launched in January 1984. Twelve to twenty women in each "anganwady" in the selected development blocks listen to the programmes as a group, each block being provided with a transistor set by UNICEF. The anganwady in charge is responsible for facilitating the weekly discussions on the broadcast theme and forwarding reactions to All India Radio for discussion in subsequent broadcasts. Feedback is also received through letters from listeners and through communications with staff. Subject matter specialists produce the programmes; air time is divided between specialists discussing the theme of the week, answering listener inquiries and presenting folk songs composed specifically on the themes of the broadcasts.

Although it is too soon to measure the effects of this programme on changes in attitude and behaviour, many appreciative letters have been received and there has been a substantial increase in the number of mothers utilizing the services of anganwadies.

The Use of Television in Distance Education

In 1975–76 an ambitious project, the satellite instructional television experiment (SITE), was launched to improve communications with the rural masses. The United States Satellite ATS–6 was used to beam instructional programmes on agriculture, health, hygiene, family welfare, science and education, in four Indian languages for four hours daily during one year. Morning programmes of ninety minutes were broadcast for school children, and two-and-a-half-hour programmes were broadcast in the evening for general audiences in the villages. About 2,400 villages spread over six states (Rajasthan, Mathya Pradesh, Orissa, Bihar, Andhra Pradesh and Karnathaka) were provided with community viewing facilities. SITE was a major collaboration by the central government, state government, Indian Space Research Organisation, the Department of Agriculture, Rural Development, Health and Family Welfare, and Education and Science Technology. The SITE experiment has been hailed as a quantum leap over traditional media and, as the largest and most courageous experiment in television, has made it possible for three million rural and illiterate people to watch television every day as India's first generation of mass media participants.

Evaluation of the SITE project confirmed that 1) educational programmes must have entertainment value beyond pedagogical considerations; 2) illiterate people learn effectively from TV; 3) women made significant gains in language development and primary school teacher training; 4) caste distinctions tended to blur among those viewing programmes together; and 5) the programmes effectively encouraged adoption of new agricultural, health, hygiene and family planning practices.

India also has her own satellite INSAT-IB, which has provided tremendous impetus for developing television broadcasts; the success of SITE encouraged the government to expand TV facilities. At present TV reaches nearly 70% of the population and sets have been provided to facilitate TV viewing in rural communities. Seven SITE centres have their own programmes with agriculture, health education and family welfare components. A half hour programme known as "Krishi-darshan" is broadcast from Delhi five days a week with strong emphasis on agricultural productivity, health, hygiene, family welfare, adult education and literacy. Entertainment components, including film songs, are the most popular TV offerings. "Krishi-darshan" is now a regular feature of Delhi TV, and systematic evaluation confirms the programme's importance as a source of information, education and entertainment for rural audiences.

Literacy Through Television

In 1974, a pilot project for literacy and adult education was conducted jointly by the Bombay TV Centre, the Bombay City Social Education Committee and the Institute of Communication Arts of St. Xavier's College, with thirty-eight television sets installed for community viewing in selected low-income communities where literacy centres were in operation.

In 1978 the Department of Adult and Continuing Education, University of Madras, Television Madras, the Directorate of Rural Development and the government of Tamil Nadu launched a literacy/adult education programme through television. Called "Education for Life," the programme is designed to transmit knowledge and skills and to create opportunities for self-fulfillment for those who have no formal education. The programme has three major components: a) awareness, functionality and vocational skills; b) literacy; and c) numeracy. For this project, the state government provided TV sets to 269 villages in Chingleput District for community viewing. Animators were in charge of operating community sets, which were located in central places such as schools or village council offices. Preliminary results of an evaluation study again show the effectiveness of television as a medium of communication in areas of health, nutrition, family welfare, agriculture and literacy.

A new multi-media experiment was recently developed through the Department of Adult & Continuing Education, University of Madras, in collaboration with All India Radio, Madras, and Doordarshan Kendra, Madras (Television). Its goal was to measure the impact of multi-media forum on adult learning and attitudes in selected villages of the Chingleput District in Tamil Nadu. This milestone study in distance learning in India will help in further programme development through open school and open university systems. It should be noted that in addition to radio and television, Cinema and Folk Arts are also being effectively integrated with distance education programmes. Documentary films, in particular, are intended to serve educational functions and contain strong motivational messages aimed at illiterate people and others wishing to expand their knowledge.

Conclusion

India gives high priority to education as a facilitator of the development process and, because of the massive problems of illiteracy, our country has utilized the broad capabilities of technological distance education delivery systems. Television is also used to supplement educational programmes at high schools and colleges. Evaluation of the varied means of programme delivery suggests that we now face the challenge of integrating these systems. All the communication inputs through radio, audio-visuals and interpersonal channels need to be linked to achieve effective interface and interplay of information through different sources for optimum results, through the distance education mode.

References

Agarwal, Binod C., *et al.* (1977). *Satellite Instructional Television Experiment, Social Evaluation-Impact on Adults*. Bangaore: Indian Space Research Organisation.

Bombay City Social Education Committee. *Annual Report*. 1973–78 and 1980–81.

Jayagopal, R. (1984-86). *Study of Impact of Multi-Media Forum on Adult Learning in Chingleput District Through Parliamentary Approach*. University of Madras, Department of Adult & Continuing Education, UGC Research Project.

Mani, Gomathi. (1983). "Evaluation of the P.G. Programme of the M-K University Participants." Ph.D. thesis, Madras University.

Mathur, J.C. and Paul Neurath. (1959). *An Indian Experiment in Farm Radio Forums*. Paris: UNESCO.

SNDT Women's University: Programmes for Women Through Distance Education
by
Kamalini H. Bhansali
and
Jyoti H. Trivedi

Editor's Note: Gratitude is extended to Dr. Uma S. Vandse, Director, Department of Correspondence Courses, SNDT Women's University, for her assistance in compiling the information in this article.

Background

When Dr. Dhondo Keshav Karve established his Indian Women's University in 1916, he gave it a distinct identity which set it apart from other institutions of higher learning in a country which had adopted a traditional pattern under the British rule. One of the main characteristics of this new school was the introduction of external or private studies as a complement to formal classes, enabling students to study at home and appear for the examinations conducted by the university. This was the first, modest step in the direction of distance education, a pioneering move to meet the acute needs of women of those times, making them economically and socially more independent and self-reliant in a society where a woman faced several social constraints.

The co-founders, Sir Vithaldas Thackersey and his wife Dr. Premlila Thackersey, supported the forward strategies of Dr. Karve, when they joined with him in 1920 to strengthen the University financially when it came to be known as the Shreemati Nathibai Damodar Thackersey Women's University (named for Sir Vithaldas Thackersey's mother). They firmly believed that the progress of a nation was closely related to the development of its women, and education played an important part in this achievement. During the national movement, when women of India were encouraged by Mahatma Gandhi, father of the nation, to come out of their homes to fight for the independence of the nation, they aspired to be part of the mainstream. Education was the instrument which would enable them to achieve this goal. The external or private studies system of the women's university was a boon to such women, who graduated and held key positions in educational and social welfare organizations.

With national independence, the university also achieved a statutory position; in 1951 the university was put on the statute book and came to be known as the SNDT Women's University, with headquarters in Bombay. The system of private studies continued in the liberal arts stream; at the same time the university continued expanding the various other disciplines through its formal structure.

The Open University Programme of SNDT Women's University

The sensitive and dynamic approach of the university to the needs of society led to the launching of the Open University programme in 1979 through the establishment of the Department of Open University Programme and Correspondence Courses. This was a landmark decision taken by Dr. Madhuri Shah, former Vice-Chancellor of the university and thereafter Chairperson of University

An Indian Experience

Grants Committee; the move was strongly supported and developed by Dr. Jyoti Trivedi, who succeeded Dr. Shah as Vice-Chancellor. To expand the effectiveness of the programme through a network structure, a sub-centre was established at the University's Poona Campus and another was in the offing in the State of Gujarat. The network consists of twenty-four examination centres spread over the states of Maharashtra and Gujarat. The location of examination centres near students' homes is an important benefit offered by the university, which encourages women to take advantage of this programme.

Since the inception of the Open University Programme in 1979 it has continued to grow. Registration in the first year was 784; it has risen to 4,430 in 1986-87, bringing the total number of students who have gone through this programme to nearly 22,000. The main objective of the Open University Programme was to provide a second chance to those women who had missed the opportunity to take advantage of higher education. Women who for one reason or another could not complete their formal schooling now had access to university education. The programme provided an entry to all women who were 21 years and above at the time of entry, irrespective of their formal qualifications.

In India, the formal education system follows a 10+2+3 pattern. Thus, after ten years of primary and secondary schooling, the student undergoes two years of Junior College or Higher Secondary and qualifies for entry to the three-year degree course. However, because of the cost of education, inflexible class schedules, geographical barriers and sociological factors, education in general and higher education in particular remain unrealized aspirations for large sections of the population, especially women. In addition, the formal system of higher education in India, with its 133 universities and over 5,000 colleges, has not been able to meet fully the needs of the growing student population.

The programme offers a bridge course of one year's duration, beginning in June and culminating in a university entrance test in May. Successful candidates then become eligible for more formal education, that is, degree programmes leading to Bachelor of Arts and Bachelor of Commerce either as fulltime or correspondence students. The Open University Programme in Arts offers three foundation courses for language competency, second language and general studies. The Commerce programme includes language competency, general studies and general commercial knowledge.

Correspondence Courses

The courses offered are B.A./B.Com. degree courses of three years duration; the contents and examinations are similar to fulltime courses but the approach is different. During each academic year, a minimum of 20 units of reading material along with assignments in each subject are sent to the students in correspondence courses. These are supplemented by face-to-face sessions under the contact lecture programme. The students return their assignments, which are corrected and sent back. Experienced faculty help in preparing the reading material and offering contact sessions. In order to enrich experiences, the Department of Correspondence Courses organizes workshops from time to time for course writers, script writers or teachers conducting contact sessions, on subjects such as Developing Instructional Materials, Psychology of Adult Learners, Preparation of Audio Scripts and so on.

The department has started preparing audio-cassettes to supplement the contact sessions and for students who find it difficult to attend the contact sessions. There is a proposal to set up a network of centres where audio-cassettes can be provided in rural and remote areas. In addition, library facilities at the university campuses and colleges are made available to correspondence course students for reference work.

The university has adopted four languages for instruction, and material for distance education is also provided through these: Marathi (regional language of Maharashtra State), Gujarati (regional language of Gujarat State), Hindi (national language) and English (language of communication). Among the course writers, script writers and translators, 95% are women who are engaged on contract basis for the work assigned.

The correspondence courses have proved valuable; between 1982-83 and 1986-87, an average of 6,000 students have registered each year for the three-year degree programme.

Students of the Open University

Students are usually between 25 and 40 years of age, although some are in their 50s and 60s. Although the university caters to the needs of women of varied ages and with diverse interests, students can be categorized into two main groups—about 40% are working and 60% are housewives. The working section includes mainly preschool or primary teachers, nurses, *peons,* and so on. About 20% of the women are divorced or were deserted. Sixty percent come from middle and lower socio-economic groups and 40% are from higher strata.

Women joining the open university programme are different from those taking fulltime education. For one reason or another, the former have not been able to complete their basic education. They often value education greatly, and they wish to become self-reliant. Others have a desire to help the family or want to be qualified for a job or further education. There are others who are divorced or deserted and look towards education to solve their social problems. Thus, the main motivations for entering the open university programme include: promotional, to go higher up in life or achieve promotions at work; aspirational, to achieve something for its own sake or to help train one's children; self-sufficiency, to achieve the independence to face social problems like dowry, divorce, desertion and so on; and economic, to augment family resources.

On the whole, the correspondence course students have compared well with fulltime students. This is because the motivation in adult learners is strong and they enter the learning situation voluntarily to solve their immediate problems and overcome any sense of inadequacy.

New Thrusts

There have been demands from correspondence course students for personal enrichment courses through the distance education technique. Areas of interest include Banking, Insurance, Budget Preparation, Legal Literacy, Secretarial Practice, Nutrition, Script Writing and Proof Reading, Language Competency and so on. A course titled Improve your English has been developed and will be offered shortly for language competency through correspondence lessons, audio-cassettes and a contact programme. Two other programmes are being developed, namely Family Savings Investments and Laws for Women. Over fifteen years ago, the university established its Department of Continuing and Adult Education and has offered a number of need-based courses and programmes through non-formal channels. Several of these courses will gradually be offered by the Department of Correspondence Courses, thus reaching a much wider audience. Over a decade ago, the university set up a Research Centre for Women's Studies to conduct studies on Women's issues and prepare a curriculum of women's studies. Today, the university is offering courses reflecting aspects of women in different disciplines, for example, Sociology of Women, History of Women or Psychology of Women; the first two are also offered as correspondence courses.

Conclusion

Distance education in India is offered almost solely through correspondence education, and it generally only provides higher education. Ninety-eight percent of correspondence courses are in Arts and Commerce, while vocational courses comprise only 2%. Science subjects are not offered in this mode. The emergence of Indira Gandhi National Open University is an important milestone in the field of distance education of the country; such a national, centrally governed organization is sure to offer leadership.

According to the 1981 census, literacy among women in India is 25%. Less than 3% of women take advantage of higher education. There is a great need to tackle women's education through formal as well as non-formal channels. In fact, more open university programmes are needed to provide university-level education for those women who are capable of it, regardless of their status or previous academic qualifications. Thousands of adult women would have been denied this second chance but for the innovative and bold step of the SNDT Women's University to provide programmes to the women at home in urban and rural areas.

In India, the campaign against eradication of illiteracy is marching ahead. The goal is to end illiteracy completely by the end of the century. With the spread of literacy, the percentage of women taking higher education will also increase, and consequently distance education will expand further.

Under these circumstances, the SNDT Women's University must provide more opportunities for women, expanding their horizons by designing an educational system which would be available for women throught their lives, allowing them to move freely between family responsibilities, study and work. The aim of the SNDT University is not only to achieve the highest academic progress but also to identify and develop other emerging and important social and educational needs; distance education will be one important means of achieving this goal.[1]

Note

1. Considerable research is being carried out about distance education in India, including the following unpublished papers and reports: Dr. Rajni Asher, "Evaluation Methodology in Distance Education"; Dr. A.W. Oak, "Summary of Report on the Study of Dropouts in the Open University Programme Organised by SNDT Women's University, Bombay"; Dr. Uma S. Vandse, "Distance Education and Evaluation"; and Dr. Vandse, "Hurdles in the Way of Distance Education." One published report is by Dr. Rajni Asher and Dr. A.W. Oak, *An Investigation into the Study-Habits of Adult-Learners of Open University Programme of SNDT Women's University and the Study of Impact of Guidance on their Study-Habits* (Bombay, India: SNDT Women's University, 1985). A proposed study currently under investigation is "A Study of Application of Advanced Organiser Model to the Reading Material and Contact Lectures Organised for Distant Learners."

Experience of Women Distance Learners in India
by
Gomathi Mani

Editor's Note: Dr. Gomathi Mani made the following observations about women distance learners as part of face-to-face interviews about distance education conducted during her research at the University of Madras.

Research showed that distance education students are better motivated than their counterparts in traditional systems. Most students continue their studies to improve their career opportunities, to qualify for promotions in their present occupations, to increase their social status, or to spend their leisure time usefully. Many students, especially those away from their studies for some time, feel the need for understanding, sympathy and encouragement; some need guidance and counselling, either by the faculty or by trained counsellors, to enable them to gain more self-confidence. An overwhelming majority of women students are either teachers or low-paid employees, and many of them have to shoulder heavy family responsibilities in addition to their work and studies. They receive limited financial assistance during their studies and few concessions for their expenses. When interviewed, women distance learners commented on the need for the following changes in the nature of distance education.

Women asked for increased flexibility in the choice and time of contact seminars. Pregnant women or mothers with young infants should be able to defer their seminar work until they are physically able to travel to the course. Some women preferred the contact seminar to last one week at the end of each semester; others wanted two-week sessions only once during a course; and a minority preferred not to have any seminars at all.

Women felt that their participation in contact seminars was limited or hindered by the difficulty they had obtaining leave from work or finding adequate care for their children while they were away from home. Students living near the seminar location found the long days awkward, because they would often not leave the class until the evening, when it was unsafe on the streets, or they would have to attend in the morning, after completing their domestic chores.

Most of the distance learners felt that they could not afford the costs of boarding, lodging and transportation needed to travel to contact seminars. They were also concerned about safety in lodges and hotels. Students requested accommodation in university residences and transportation concession fares on trains or buses to save money.

Most female students expressed their dissatisfaction with the classrooms used for required contact seminars. They complained of inadequate accommodation and overcrowded classrooms, the lack of proper ventilation and lighting, unsafe drinking water and unhygienic lavatory conditions.

Many women felt the need for local study centres, with lesson units, radios, audio-cassettes, TV and videotapes, a proper library and a teacher or reference assistant all available for students to use during their free time. Mobile library units and lending library services were also valuable ideas. Students also asked that library facilities in major centres be extended and improved to enable students to work more extensively at the undergraduate and postgraduate level.

Women asked that radio and TV programmes supplement and support distance education programmes; they indicated a preference for interesting programmes such as plays, dramas and discussions, rather than simply readings of lessons. The students also asked that programmes be offered at times more convenient for working women and women with daily family responsibilities: early evenings were considered better than late at night, and holidays were also preferred.

The Indian Experience

Women felt that distance learners should receive financial assistance to enable them to continue their studies; national loan scholarships should be extended to distance students, and tuition fee concessions could be offered in deserving cases. Students also asked that lesson units be sent as one group at the beginning of the course or well in advance of the contact seminar. Many students indicated that they did not receive some materials before their examinations.

Women requested that sample answers be provided for questions if the student's work is not adequate, so that she can see the accepted norm and adjust her work accordingly. Students asked for the opportunity to provide extensive feedback on courses and wanted programmes reevaluated and changed whenever necessary.

While many advances continue in the development of distance education in India, systems need to be improved so that Indian women can benefit from education systems and succeed in this otherwise male-dominated society.

Chapter 12

BY PRINT AND POST: VOCATIONAL TRAINING FOR ISOLATED WOMEN

by

Paulene Heiler and Wendy Richards

Paulene Heiler, B.A., Dip. Ed., M. Ed., has a number of years' experience as a high school teacher and research assistant in educational research at the University of Sydney, particularly in areas of distance education and education for women and girls. Currently she is responsible for promoting women's access to vocational training in TAFE through distance education modes. Born in the country, she has continuing interest in education issues concerning rural women. She is currently the Women's Access Coordinator of the External Studies College, New South Wales (Australia), Department of Technical and Further Education (TAFE).

Wendy Richards, B.A. (Hons.), has a background in educational research and evaluation and university tutoring in feminist and social theory and social science methodology. She has completed two years towards her doctoral thesis on women on the land in Australia since the 1930s and is currently evaluating a TAFE women's access programme. Like Paulene, Wendy was born in the country, and she maintains strong links with rural people and issues. She is currently a Research Officer with the Women's Coordination Unit of TAFE.

Introduction

Australian technical and vocational education has recently seen the implementation of an external course for isolated and rural mature women to draw them into the building and construction field. The course, Introduction to Technical Occupations (*Distance INTO*—Building and Construction), was developed by the New South Wales state Department of Technical and Further Education (TAFE). The guiding principle behind this unique Australian course has been that the course design, development and implementation should be determined by the characteristics and needs of the target group: mature rural women.

The pilot phase of the course was introduced in three regional centres in New South Wales in March 1986; eight months later, in November-December, a formative evaluation was undertaken with students and staff at those centres. Drawing upon some preliminary findings from the evaluation, this paper reviews some of the original decisions made during the course design and production and examines the extent to which the outcomes of these decisions have met the needs of the target group.

Background

From a growing recognition of the many disadvantages experienced by women in public and private life, the New South Wales state government and its departments have initiated a variety of programmes and policies designed to improve women's social and economic positions. The Department of TAFE's *INTO* course represents a response within the technical and vocational education field to women's need for greater access to training in occupations which have been traditionally closed to them. The *INTO* course, developed by TAFE's Women's Co-ordination Unit, recognizes that women who wish to train and work in a non-traditional area often require specially developed bridging courses to help them gain entry into their chosen field.

The *INTO* course model was designed to provide industry-specific applications of the course in fields such as building and construction, rural studies, electronics engineering, and business studies. It was initially developed within a metropolitan context as a face-to-face course, offered at large metropolitan colleges over 18 weeks for 24 hours per week.

A number of barriers confront rural women in gaining access to vocational training and employment in Australia; some of these they share with their urban counterparts, while others are largely the products of the environment in which they live. The most obvious of these is the barrier of physical distance—from employment opportunities, from properly equipped colleges and qualified teachers, and, most importantly, from other women with similar aspirations, in similar situations. To provide non-metropolitan women with access to non-traditional training and employment opportunities, a different *INTO* course structure was required, one which could overcome the particular barriers facing rural Australian women. The *Distance INTO*—Building and Construction course was developed by TAFE for this purpose.

The Significance of Distance

In part because of the arid and inhospitable nature of much of its interior, Australia is one of the most highly urbanized countries in the world, and its relatively small rural population is scattered over vast distances. According to the 1981 census, only a quarter of the New South Wales female population lives outside the densely populated coastal stretch of the neighbouring Sydney, Newcastle and Wollongong metropolitan areas. While some of these women live and work on farms, the majority of them live in a few large regional centres and many small country towns and villages spread over seven thousand square kilometres within the state. Local conditions such as bad roads, inadequate public transport, and the generally higher costs of fuel in country areas restrict their mobility and access to the limited health, welfare and educational services available to them. Thus, for rural Australian women, distance and isolation usually go hand in hand, greatly affecting their chances to gain education, training and employment.

Rural Women in the Labour Market

Australia has one of the most sex-segregated labour markets in the Organization for Economic Co-operation and Development (OECD) group of nations, and Australian country women, no less than urban women, are concentrated in a narrow range of typically "female" occupations. Just over half of Australia's female workers are in three occupations—clerical, service (where the majority are cooks, waitresses and cleaners), and professional/technical (principally teachers and nurses). The result of this ghettoization of women workers has been consistently lower status, lower pay and lack of career options within most of these occupations, many of which are also now under threat from technological innovations and the reduction of fulltime jobs to parttime and casual hours of work. During the last decade, the movement of labour-intensive industries to cheaper overseas labour markets has drastically reduced work opportunities in heavily female industries such as textiles and footwear.

For women living in rural areas, the overcrowding of the female workforce into a narrow range of occupations is worsened by the highly centralized nature of Australian commerce and manufacturing. Regional centres and country towns usually support considerably fewer industries and enterprises than metropolitan areas. Thus the opportunities for rural women's employment are not only narrow in terms of occupational areas; they are also limited in terms of numbers. Federal government employment agency figures show that unemployment is high amongst country women and girls, even though, as is often the case with women's employment statistics, these rates do not take into account the hidden unemployment of women who do not register as unemployed, who cannot work because of lack of childcare, or who are underemployed in parttime or insecure jobs.

Rural Women in Education

The economic vulnerability of rural women is also evident in their low levels of education and training. In the 1981 national census, 73% of country women reported having no accepted qualifications for jobs. The distribution of credentials of those who had gained training and qualifications after leaving school reflects the sex-segregation of the labour market: 55% held qualifications in education or medicine and health (that is, teaching and nursing), and 28% held qualifications in business and related studies (usually typing, stenography and business procedures). Conversely, the rate of movement of rural women into male-dominated fields of employment has been minimal. In 1981, 60% of country men with employment credentials were qualified to work in the three related fields of engineering and technology, architecture and building, and manufacturing and construction. Only 3% of country women were qualified to work in these fields.

Rural Women in TAFE

The Department of Technical and Further Education is the major provider of technical and trade training in New South Wales. However, while TAFE colleges across the state offer a wide range of trade and technical training options, most country women enrol in courses which provide training in secretarial and clerical occupations. Moreover, more rural than urban women enrol in these courses, even though three-quarters of all secretarial positions are found in the metropolitan areas of the state. Apart from training in hairdressing, almost no country women are enrolled in the wide range of TAFE trade certificate courses offered by country colleges which service local industry training requirements. It would seem that local employers are still reluctant to apprentice women in male-dominated trades, as the few available apprenticeships in country areas continue to be taken by young men.

While access to trade training is made difficult for rural women by the limited availability of local apprenticeships and the sex-segregation of the labour market, access to technical certificate courses is difficult for country people generally. Few country colleges offer certificate courses which provide an opportunity to train for middle-level technician positions. To overcome these gaps in course provision in country areas, certificate-level courses are offered via distance education modes through TAFE's External Studies College. However, just as there are few women enrolled in these courses when offered face-to-face, there are also few women enrolled when they are offered externally. On average, female external enrolments in these courses are less than 5% of the total enrolment.

The *Distance INTO*—Building and Construction Course

The guiding principle during the developmental stages of the *Distance INTO*—Building and Construction course was that the course design should be determined by the characteristics and needs of the group for whom the course was intended. These factors included:

- their high rate of unemployment;
- their overrepresentation in a limited and insecure range of occupations;
- their difficulties in gaining daily access to face-to-face vocational training;
- their lack of practical experience and language basic to an understanding of many mathematics- and science-based skills and concepts.

However, while feminist researchers over recent years have built up a complex and detailed picture of women's education and employment generally, little is known about the specific issues of adult women (and particularly isolated adult women) learning in a non-traditional field. Therefore *Distance INTO* course designers based decisions about content and delivery questions on assumptions, as well as known facts, about the characteristics and needs of the target group. For example, important decisions were based on assumptions that rural women studying in a technical and male-dominated field:

- may lack support from family, friends and community and may experience the essential loneliness of external study more severely than if they were studying in a field more socially acceptable and culturally familiar to them;
- had made a focused and informed vocational choice (unlike women re-entering education and employment in an undirected way) and, despite potential lack of support, would be confident in this choice and aware of its implications;
- would have well-developed communication and inquiry skills;
- would be highly motivated and anxious to move on to further training and/or employment.

This combination of facts and assumptions about certain characteristics and needs of rural women shaped many of the features of the *Distance INTO*—Building and Construction course. The most important of these was based on the belief that a bridging course offered through distance modes for rural women would provide a solid foundation for later technical training and should improve their employment options.

It was also argued that such a bridging course should efficiently and effectively improve women's access to study and employment in predicted labour market growth areas. The Australian Bureau of Statistics has produced data which indicate that in New South Wales there has recently been growth in the building and construction industry. Work in this industry is likely to be located within reasonable distance of most members of the target group. The industry also encompasses a wide and varied range of occupations, many of which rural women have already expressed an interest in pursuing, such as town and environmental planning, health inspection, building restoration, farm and domestic construction, construction management, and furniture design and manufacture. Information from regional government employment agencies also suggests there is work available in their local areas for experienced technicians in this group of occupations. For these reasons, the building and construction industry was chosen as the focus for the first *Distance INTO* course.

Course Objectives, Content and Delivery

The objectives of the *Distance INTO*—Building and Construction course are:

- to develop skills, technical knowledge, understanding and confidence associated with training and employment in the building and construction industry;
- to provide assessment, guidance and counselling to assist entry into occupations in the building industry which offer the opportunity for future employment, advancement, security and personal satisfaction;
- to enable students to gain self-confidence, awareness and motivation in relation to study, training and work;
- to provide access to the practical skills and theoretical knowledge associated with the building and construction industry through a range of learning modes.

In the process of establishing these objectives, course developers referred to the significant features of rural women's education and employment opportunities and acknowledged the obstacle of physical distance. However, the course objectives also acknowledged the problem of psychological distance and emphasized the provision of appropriately designed content, as well as personal support and counselling.

Decisions about course content relied as much on the notion of psychological distance as on the facts of physical distance and geographical location. Because these women would be approaching a non-traditional and, therefore, unfamiliar area of study and possible employment, the subject matter they were studying would probably be culturally and therefore psychologically distant from their previous work and learning experiences. In support of this assumption, statistics show that few mature age women in Australia will have had any training at school in carpentry or technical drawing, and few will have experienced a school curriculum designed to help them become confident and familiar with the language, concepts and skills integral to a maths- and science-based education and training (ACITCA, 1980). This lack of a theoretical background is reinforced by an almost complete absence of hands-on experience. The occupational streaming of women into clerical and service work areas would suggest that few women receive any consistent training and expertise in the practical skills associated with male-dominated occupations such as those found in the building and construction industry. This second dimension of distance therefore suggested the need for a course content which would provide students with basic mathematical and science skills, concepts and vocabulary necessary to enable them to complete all course components satisfactorily. It also suggested the need for a curriculum comprising a broad mix of subjects which would provide an overview of the range of theoretical and practical knowledge and skills used in the building and construction industry, as well as information about the full range of further training and employment options within the industry.

To provide this theoretical and practical overview, the *Distance INTO*—Building and Construction course is made up of thirteen components:

>Construction Theory
>Building Materials
>Elementary Quantity Estimation
>Introduction to Architectural Drafting
>Introduction to Surveying
>Controlling Authorities
>Introduction to Small Business Management
>   in the Building Industry
>Technical Communications
>Career Opportunities
>Mathematics
>Science
>Introduction to Basic Hand Skills
>Site Visits

The course is considered equivalent to the 432 hours of instruction given to face-to-face students, with additional hours available in the distance course for face-to-face practical instruction in handskills training and visits to building sites.

The psychological distance of the subject matter from the women's everyday lives required an appropriate style of presentation as well as suitable course content. Therefore, the course material was written from a "women-friendly" approach which assumed no prior knowldge of the subject matter, used non-sexist, non-jargonistic, non-patronizing and accessible language and format, and wherever possible incorporated examples related to women's daily lives.

Therefore, course developers were required not only to consider the unfamiliarity of the target group with the subject matter but also to acknowledge and utilize women's considerable experience and skills in other areas. For example, it was assumed that the women would be likely to have strong communication, inquiry and organizational skills and that their interest and involvement in the course would be maximized if they were encouraged to develop these skills through research and writing assignments. *Distance INTO* students were also assumed to be highly motivated, well-organized, keen to re-enter employment, and therefore likely to complete both the correspondence work and the face-to-face subjects within one year. Therefore, the course was developed within the same time schedule of 432 hours (18 weeks by 24 hours per week) as instruction given to face-to-face students.

The target group is physically distant from college centres; the difficulties of travelling long distances on a daily basis and the time constraints of women's domestic responsibilities clearly indicated the need for a course delivered externally. While it was possible to teach most of the knowledge and skills externally through print materials, some practical skills obviously needed to be demonstrated to the students, and experienced by them, in face-to-face classes. It was therefore decided that two subjects, Introduction to Basic Handskills and Site Visits, would be taught by fulltime TAFE teachers in properly equipped local college workshops. To ensure sufficient numbers to run regular face-to-face classes at a college, students within two to three hours travelling distance of that college were encouraged to enrol in groups, and the face-to-face component of the course was made compulsory.

One of the course objectives is to provide guidance and counselling that will help women enter a male-dominated industry. The Career Opportunities subject was therefore timetabled for the end of the course, to provide necessary information and assistance just prior to the students' next step into further training or employment. It was assumed that because *Distance INTO* students had made a considered decision to enter a male-dominated industry, the personal alienation of studying non-traditional subject matter would be minimal for them; therefore formally structured and continuing support during the course would not be necessary. However, since correspondence study of itself is a lonely undertaking, and possibly more so for women studying in a culturally alien field, provision was made for regular, informal personal support and reassurance during the course. Thus, while the face-to-face classes were designed for the primary purpose of skills training, a second function of this component would be to provide students with the opportunity to gain informal support and solidarity from regular contact with each other.

The *Distance INTO* Evaluation

The pilot phase of the course (1986-87) is being delivered to three groups of rural women (approximately ten in each group) who enrolled in the course in March 1986 through the TAFE External Studies College in Sydney. The students are receiving print material from and are returning assignments to the Sydney college, and they are attending practical skills classes on a one-day-per-fortnight basis at a local TAFE college. Teachers of these classes are fulltime TAFE teachers in the School of Building. By December 1986 the students had completed their scheduled practical classes but, contrary to expectations, had completed only one-third of their written assignments.

A formative evaluation of the course was conducted at the three colleges in November-December 1986. Extensive interviews were held with the students and with the local course teachers to assess their satisfaction to date with the course materials and delivery system. A preliminary examination of some of their views of the course are used in this paper to test the assumptions about the characteristics and learning needs of these women, assumptions which formed the basis of the course design.

Evaluation Findings

The evaluation findings show that the combination of delivery mechanisms (correspondence mode, compulsory face-to-face component, group enrolment) does overcome the lack of access to education which is a consequence of physical isolation, and it does provide opportunities for practical skills training. The students have reported that without the course materials delivered to them in this fashion, they would have been unable to gain any worthwhile knowledge and experience in this field. As well as skills training, the compulsory face-to-face component of the course has provided, as intended, an opportunity for informal group support amongst the students. Those interviewed felt that the chance to meet and talk as a group has become an important aspect of their fortnightly face-to-face classes, and that many of them are forming supportive bonds with each other as a result of their unique common experience. The students have also reported satisfaction with the subject mix. The presentation, level of difficulty, sequencing and approach of the materials have provided easy and effective access to the content of each subject.

However, while the combination delivery has fulfilled its purpose, and the students report no difficulties with the presentation of the course material, two patterns have developed that are a consequence of problems they are meeting in the course. The students are:
- taking a lot longer than they or the course developers anticipated to complete each unit of correspondence lesson material;
- bringing both educational and personal needs (that is, for assistance with technical questions, and for support with their experiences as women entering a non-traditional field) to the face-to-face handskills and site visits classes.

The fact that they are taking longer than expected to complete assignments has been of growing concern to both the women and the course developers. The original assumption that they would be highly motivated and anxious to complete the course in minimum time has been supported by the statements of the women themselves. Their slow movement through the course is therefore probably not related to lack of motivation but to the fact that they are women studying subject matter which is culturally and psychologically alien to them and to the fact that they are studying most of the course at a distance, through print and post.

Discussions during the evaluation suggest that their slowness in absorbing the course material, and in utilizing it in assignments, stem from difficulties with visualizing new and culturally unfamiliar concepts and practices. This lack of familiarity also inhibits development of the facility to "see" these concepts at work in the real world. These difficulties are compounded by the need to understand and use strange terminology and by their lack of experience with assignments and written work in technical subjects.

The expectation that the target group would have strong communication and inquiry skills contributed to unrealistic demands on the students and slowed the pace of their movement through the course material: assignments often demanded not only a great deal of research but also well-developed written communication skills. The assumption that women are likely to have such skills ignored the fact that communication is a complex written and oral, verbal and non-verbal exercise. Thus, a person with strong verbal communication skills will not necessarily also have strong written communication skills, and distance education relies heavily on written communication. One or two of the most articulate women interviewed during the evaluation are also among the slowest to return written work. It could even be hypothesized that women interested in non-traditional and often manual skills-oriented occupations such as building could also be less interested and skilled in work based on written communication. One conclusion that can be drawn is that it is not useful for the purposes of external course design to suppose that women's socially developed communication skills include ability and confidence with writing.

The problems associated with psychological distance from the subject matter, and the complexity and length of assignments, are exacerbated by the nature of external study itself. Even with the use of two-way telecommunications systems for delivery of lesson materials, distance education cannot allow instant identification of and solution to problems, which is possible in face-to-face classes. Distance educators can only monitor students' progress and welfare through the written word; therefore they cannot provide the immediate personal guidance and reassurance that can be part of the student-teacher relationship. Neither are there opportunities for the informal teaching and learning exchanges that go on amongst students in face-to-face classes, which can increase the rate of comprehension and absorption of information.

While these problems have slowed down the pace of the women's progress through the course, they have certainly not resulted in the submission of below-standard work. Just as course designers have been demanding of students, so have the students been demanding of themselves. They have produced assignments which External Studies College markers consider not just good but often excellent and certainly beyond expectations. The assumption that *Distance INTO* students would be extremely interested in the course material and highly motivated to complete it successfully has proven to be correct. However, in producing work of such overall high quality, their motivation and interest may also be linked with lack of experience in assignments associated with technical subjects and the limitations of receiving training at a distance. Lack of daily contact with each other leaves them with no way to judge the standard of their work against that of others.

Not only educational needs are served by the classes. During the evaluation they spoke of a great need to spend time with each other, discussing their individual yet common experiences as women entering a non-traditional field. However, there is little time during the face-to-face classes to explore these issues fully, which has proved to be a frustrating inhibition to the development of informal group support and solidarity. Although it was correctly assumed that women studying in a non-traditional area would need the support of other women studying similar material, the extent of this need was underestimated. The strategy of local group enrolment was originally developed to provide each of the students with an accessible support network, as well as to form the basis for hand-skills classes. However, a related assumption about the characteristics of the target group has proved incorrect. It was assumed that *INTO* students generally, having chosen a non-traditional area of study, would not need formal class discussion time in which to explore the issues surrounding this choice. Therefore, although the *Distance INTO* students were required to form local groups for practical classes, which would also facilitate group support, it was felt that no formal face-to-face discussion time would be needed.

The decision not to provide time, space and guidance during face-to-face classes for discussions of this nature has particularly serious implications for rural women studying in a non-traditional field, in comparison with their urban sisters. Metropolitan women have greater access to informal support networks, both inside and outside college, and are part of a much greater number of women studying and working in non-traditional areas. For rural *INTO* groups, physical isolation prevents any meaningful contact with each other outside the once-per-fortnight face-to-face classes during the course. Like metropolitan women, they need to deal with the issues of women in non-traditional work through discussion and communication with other women, but they have far fewer means of meeting those needs. For nearly all rural women, the realities of physical isolation limit face-to-face contact to no more than one day per week, and often one day per fortnight.

Conclusions

This preliminary analysis has shown that the combination delivery methods of correspondence mode, group enrolment and a compulsory face-to-face skills training component do overcome access difficulties for isolated women and provide practical instruction, experience, and opportunities for informal group support. However, the students are spending more study time per unit than expected, demanding technical feedback on correspondence material from the local handskills teachers, and expressing the need for formal discussion time during face-to-face hours to consider their experiences as women entering a non-traditional field. Thus, although the course objectives, design and delivery do provide rural women with an introduction to the building and construction industry, they have not been able to satisfy all aspects of the educational needs of the target group and have placed unexpected burdens on the students.

An obvious solution would be to provide more face-to-face time within the course, for assistance with technical questions related to the correspondence units and for discussion, guidance and support regarding the issues of women and non-traditional work and training. However, this simple solution is not possible in the lives of isolated women who cannot attend such classes more than one day per week. Therefore, a combination of strategies needs to be considered, with the aims of minimizing time taken to complete the correspondence units, using more efficiently the limited time for face-to-face contact, and improving the amount and quality of support and guidance available to students.

Strategies to reduce the time spent on correspondence work include:

- reviewing the structure of course content with a view to optionalizing some subjects;
- making assignments shorter and simpler and providing more guidance regarding their requirements;
- establishing more effective communication channels between markers and students for feedback on progress; and
- providing more visual material to help students "see" building and construction theory at work.

Reorganizing face-to-face time for greater use would involve:

- linking correspondence units with face-to-face classes and providing adequate time during the classes for tutorials on unit content; and
- establishing the role of tutor by briefing local TAFE building and construction teachers to provide technical feedback in tutorial time.

Improving the degree and nature of personal support and guidance to students suggests:

- setting aside regular face-to-face time for discussion;
- involving local female TAFE teachers, especially those experienced in adult women's education, in these discussions (and, if possible, bringing in women already involved in the industry);
- timetabling the Career Opportunities subject at the beginning of the course rather than at the end; and
- providing staff development for local tutors, handskills teachers and external studies markers on the issues surrounding women's education and employment in non-traditional fields.

The *Distance INTO*—Building and Construction course for rural and isolated women represents a pioneering move in distance education and women's vocational education in Australia. The design and implementation of *Distance INTO* presented course developers with a complex mix of issues related to distance education provision, adult women's learning, and the movement of women into non-traditional fields. The processes of course development also highlighted the difficulties course developers face when making decisions about the educational needs of a particular group, in the absence of any comprehensive knowledge about those needs.

The students' positive response to the course delivery and content verifies that it is possible to provide technical training to isolated women through distance education. The challenge to course developers and providers concerned with isolated women's vocational training, in Australia and elsewhere, is to tailor both course delivery and content as closely as possible to the characteristics and needs of the students, so that real improvements in women's education and employment can eventually be made.

Reference

Australia Committee of Inquiry into Technological Change in Australia (ACITCA). (1980). *Technological Change in Australia Report*. 4 vols. Canberra: AGPS.

─────── Chapter 13 ───────

WOMEN IN TURKEY AND THE POTENTIAL FOR OPEN LEARNING

by

Ülkü S. Köymen

> **Ülkü S. Köymen** works as an assistant professor at Çukurova University, Faculty of Education, Adana/Turkey. She received her B.A. from Ankara University, majoring in Sociology, Psychology and Education; her M.A. from Hacettepe University, majoring in Curriculum Development; and her Ph.D. from Syracuse University, majoring in Instructional Design, Development and Evaluation. Her published articles include: "Scientific Basis for the Written Instructional Materials Prepared for Open University in Turkey," "The Role and Function of Instructional Technology for Effective Teaching" and "Student and Faculty Perceptions of Turkish Open Learning System."

Introduction

There is a straighter and more secure path for us to follow. This is to have Turkish women as partners in everything: to share our lives with them and to value them as friends, helpers, and colleagues in our scientific, spiritual, social and economic life.   — Atatürk

This paper will focus on the problems of women's education in Turkey in the context of other social events and will examine the potential of the "open learning" system for solving these problems.

Background

Serious women's liberation began after Kemal Atatürk founded the Republic of Turkey in 1923. Atatürk, president of the Republic from 1923 until his death in 1938, was considered the "father of modern Turkey." He introduced several reforms concerning religion, society, education and the law, reforms which transformed the entire nation into a new and modern society. These reforms began with secularization, which led to a transformation of Islamic heritage. Islam had always been more than just a religion to its believers; it had encompassed all aspects of human thought and behaviour. Atatürk saw secularization not as the elimination of religious institutions and beliefs but rather as a means to a more scientific or rational approach to life (Köymen, 1984). Atatürk also abolished *medreses,* or religious schools, which had been powerful religious institutions, in his effort to change the concept of authority in society and encourage individuals to develop independently.

Another important reform Atatürk introduced was the adoption of the Latin alphabet, which resulted in a more favourable attitude toward learning to read and write. For Atatürk, education was a way to end illiteracy and achieve success in everyday life. He constantly emphasized the value of education for national development, and he always stressed the importance of providing equal educational opportunities for both men and women and for every social class. As he said in his historic speech, given in Kastamonu in 1925:

> Is it possible that one half of the nation can be developed and the other half neglected, if we are to have a truly developed country? Is it possible that one half of the nation can be uplifted while the other half remains rooted to the ground?

Another significant reform was the abolition in 1925 of the *fez,* or skull-cap, the traditional symbol of male dignity during the pre-Republic period (Kazamias, 1966). Later, abolition of the veil and the introduction of civil law (1934) changed the legal status of women in the family and in marriage, granting them greatly amplified rights. In 1934, family-name reform was also accepted, and women could use both their maiden name and their husband's name, as in Western countries.

As a result of Atatürk's reforms, Turkey became the first Muslim country which encouraged and supported women's rights. Atatürk's ideas were considered as a model for modernization, and Turkey's reforms were adopted by several Muslim nations (Caporal, 1982).

Despite all these important reforms, however, the position of women in Turkish society is still low, especially in the countryside, where the impact of reforms is felt less than in urban areas. While more opportunities are available for the men and boys, and they are generally encouraged and supported by families and society, women and girls are still greatly neglected. Throughout the period of the Ottoman Empire, from the 1300s to 1923, only girls from the urban upper classes received any education, and even at this level, the number of educated women was quite limited (Caporal, 1982). While there has been a certain increase in the number of educated women since the establishment of the Republic, the imbalance between female and male education does still exist. Thus, Atatürk's reforms have not fully succeeded, perhaps because of the vigour with which Turkey still retains its Islamic heritage.

Women in Muslim Society

Islamic religion has always had a negative influence on women, even though it is considered a reform of pre-Islamic practices. (For example, female babies are saved from being buried alive by an Islamic principle contrary to a common practice among Arabs [Coulson and Hinchcliffe, 1978].) The Koran itself gives high respect to women, particularly to mothers, and it accepts women and men as equal. However, authority in the family was always given to men because of women's "weak" nature. Men had been allowed up to four wives in Islam, as long as they could treat them all equally. But since fairness was considered almost impossible in practice, reformers thought it would be better to allow only one spouse. Leaders of this approach also believed in the necessity of education for both men and women and the veil and covering for women were deemed unnecessary. As the Koran was reinterpreted and misinterpreted, women's status changed; they started losing legal rights, suffered from lack of education, and became second-class human beings. Kasim Amin explains this situation, saying that "if women do not know their rights, this is the result of misusing and misinterpretation of Islamic principles by men" (Caporal, 1982:33). Even in modern Turkey we can easily see the traces of old (and strong) Arab and Muslim characteristics, which are even more noticeable in rural areas.

Women in Education

There is no obvious discrimination against women in education in Turkey. By law, primary education is compulsory for all; however, in practice this policy is not enforced with equal vigour for both girls and boys. In 1985, for example, girls made up 40% of the national enrolment, and according to UNESCO figures the differential of 35% illiteracy between men and women in Turkey is the highest in the world (1980). This is mainly because most of the secondary and high schools are located in urban areas and can absorb only a limited number of students. Many rural girls, especially in small towns and villages, are automatically excluded from education. This is also true for higher education. In general, rural-urban residence and socio-economic status have had a greater impact on women's educational opportunities than on men's, and usually only talented women from the privileged socio-economic class can manage to attain higher education.

Erkut (1982:121) summarizes her observations on the educational status of Turkish women in three points:

1. Relative to men, women display substantially lower levels of educational attainment.

2. Again relative to men, women who go on in school beyond primary levels show more persistence and achieve greater success.

3. Despite the low level of educational attainment for women in general, substantial numbers of Turkish women obtain professional degrees and practice in what are considered to be male-dominated occupations.

Educational Reforms

The year 1960 was a turning point in Turkey's educational development: by adopting the Constitution of 1961, Turkey established itself as one of the few countries seriously attempting to create a planned democratic society. The new Republic faced three fundamental problems:

1. How to provide equal educational opportunities for everyone.

2. How to enlarge these opportunities.

3. How to foster an enlightened and creative citizenship.

In order to solve these issues, a planning board was established, and as a result of their successive five-year plans begun in 1963, many educational problems were resolved. The literacy rate increased, as did the number of primary, secondary and high schools, and universities. However, these improvements were not enough. By the end of the 1970s, universities were able to absorb only a fraction of the number of students who demanded higher education. Students from rural areas, often taught by under-qualified teachers, were unable to pass necessary university entrance examinations.

The expansion of primary and secondary school systems has resulted in a large number of students planning to enrol in the universities. Unfortunately, the capacities of the universities have not developed in proportion to this increase. Even today, more than half of the high-school graduates in Turkey are left out of the higher education system every year (Köymen, 1984). And although the quality of education varies in different levels and branches in the universities, higher education in Turkey cannot be considered satisfactory. The poor quality of education in most universities can be attributed to many factors, including the insufficient number and quality of the teaching staff, poor curriculum and inadequate instructional methods.

As a result, both the youth who are unable to enrol in the universities and students dissatisfied with the quality of university education became frustrated. They became politically active and stimulated by the low credibility of the government, and they participated in strikes, boycotts, demonstrations and violence. During this period, universities were often closed down, and educators and legislators were forced to look for immediate solutions (Köymen, 1984).

Another attempt was made to reorganize the Turkish Higher Educational system in 1981, by Law 2547. A Higher Education Council was established; its goal was to increase educational availability and equalize educational opportunities across social classes through formal and non-formal education. As a result of this reform, the number of universities increased from nineteen in 1980 to twenty-seven in 1982, and the Turkish Open University (Açık Öğretim) was established in 1982 in the city of Eskişehir (Karagözoğlu, 1986).

Open Education in Turkey

Traditional educational systems do not meet the needs of developing countries. Like other developing countries, Turkey cannot afford to open as many higher institutions as needed. Therefore open learning has been accepted as an economical alternative.

The Turkish Open Education Faculty, established in Anadolu University, aims to provide access to higher education for a wider section of high school graduates who have not been absorbed by the existing traditional systems. As a very young faculty, it offers only two degree programmes: Business Administration and Economics. It functions on a multi-media basis but the primary medium of instruction is printed material. There are twenty study centres located in eighteen cities throughout Turkey which provide tutorial assistance as well as supplementary lectures and materials.

Despite its short history, open education in Turkey has grown rapidly. Following are the student enrolment figures:

Table 1: Students Enrolled

Year	New Registration Total	Female	Male	Total	Total Female	Male
1982-83	25,000	—	—			
1983-84	19,009	4,660	14,349	40,874	10,447	30,427
1984-85	31,084	7,693	23,391	65,774	16,529	49,245
1985-86	40,590	11,126	29,464	104,063	26,515	77,548

Although girls made up only one-third of the entire enrolment, the increase in female participation is meaningful for such a short period.

Additional Open Learning Programmes

There are two additional projects carried out through the Open Education Faculty. The first is "The Primary School Teacher Training Project," which started in 1986 with 46,000 students and strives for a total of 130,000 in 1987. It is a two-year certificate programme carried out with the cooperation of the Ministry of Education and Anadolu University. The second project of the Open Learning Faculty is "Training Turks in Germany." This project is designed to educate two million Turkish families who are working in Germany.

The Potential of the Open Learning System for Meeting the Needs of Women in Turkey

Learning itself involves not just conventional education, including an academic and scientific body of knowledge and/or some subjects taught in schools, but also the development of human resources. And today, new and changing forms of both media and technology increase the potential of education since they help the instructional system reach almost everywhere, changing attitudes and values across the whole nation, which is what is needed in Turkey at present.

Despite all the reforms and efforts that have been made regarding women in society, however, male/female equity has not been achieved. Recent research carried out in Adana, in the southern part of Turkey, confirmed the low social status of the younger generation. According to this study, there is a significant difference between the self-image of females and males from 16 to 19 years old, with girls having a less positive self-image than do boys. In particular, girls' social self-image (social relationship, moral, and vocational and educational goals) is substantially lower. This is also true for their sexual self-image (Inanç, 1987). We should not forget that, in Turkey, women's rights have essentially been given to them by Atatürk; Turkish women did not have to fight for themselves. Today, women need to fight for changes, participating actively of their own free will and combating the nation's strong resistance toward change and improvement.

Conclusion

The Turkish Open Learning Faculty is a very young establishment. Despite its short experience, however, it has already attempted to solve some of the important educational problems in Turkey. The potential of the Turkish Open Learning Faculty for solving these problems could be summarized as follows:

- It has the potential of providing educational opportunities to women who are disadvantaged by religious, socio-economic and geographical conditions.

- It has already attempted to give higher education opportunities to elementary school teachers, the majority of whom are women, who will be able to get a higher education diploma, raise their retirement benefits and develop themselves as they educate the future women of Turkey.

- It has the potential to provide educational opportunities to Turkish women in Germany, who are squeezed between two cultures and have lost their own identity.

Although the Turkish Open Learning Faculty has only two degree programmes at present, they could be extended to include the following courses for rural women:

- literacy education
- maternal and child healthcare
- nutrition
- sanitation
- family planning
- housing improvement
- small-farm management
- cultivation of vegetables and fruits on family land or garden
- basic consumer economics

Open learning in Turkey has the potential to support and facilitate the realization of Atatürk's principles by providing education to Turkish women through its own special structures.

References

Ahmed, L. (1982). "Feminism and Feminist Movements in the Middle East, a Preliminary Exploration: Turkey, Egypt, Algeria, People's Democratic Republic of Yemen." *Women's Studies International Forum*, 5(2), 153–68.

Atatürk, K. (August 30, 1925). "Second Speech to the Women of Kastamonu."

Caporal, B. (1982). *Turkish Women in Kemalism and Post-Kemalism Period.* Ankara: Tisa Matbassi.

Coşar, F.M. (1978). "Women in Turkish Society." In L. Beck and N. Keddie. (Eds.). *Women in the Muslim World.* (pp. 124–40). Cambridge, Mass.: Harvard University Press.

Coulson, N. and D. Hinchcliffe. (1978). "Women and Law Reform in Contemporary Islam." In L. Beck and N. Keddie. (Eds.). *Women in the Muslim World.* (pp. 37–51). Cambridge, Mass.: Harvard University Press.

Erkut, S. (1982). "Dualism in Values Toward Education of Turkish Women." In. Ç. Kağitçibaşi. (Ed.). *Sex Roles, Family and Community in Turkey.* (pp. 121–32). Bloomington, Ind.: Indiana University Turkish Studies.

Inanç, B. (1987). "Turkish Adolescents Self-Image." In D. Offer, E. Ostrov, K.I. Howard & R. Atkinson. (Eds.). *The Teenage World: Adolescents' Self-Image in Ten Countries.* New York: Plenum (in press).

Karagözoğlu, G. (1986). "1981 Higher Education Reform of Turkey after Five Years of Practice." Unpublished paper, Ankara, Turkey, November 1986.

Kazamias, A.M. (1966). *Education and the Quest for Modernity in Turkey.* Chicago: University of Chicago Press.

Köymen, U.S. (1984). "A Model for Organizing Written Instructional Materials in the Context of a Proposed Model for an Open University in Turkey." Ph.D. Diss., Syracuse University, New York.

Murphy, K. and M. McIsaac. (1987). "Turkey: Turkish Open Education Faculty." Paper presented at the Association for Educational Communication and Technology, Atlanta, February 1987.

Turkey. (1985). Education and Youth and Sports Statistics. Ankara.

Turkey. (1986). 1983-1984 Academic Year Higher Education Statistics. Ankara.

Turkey. (1986). 1984-1985 Academic Year Higher Education Statistics. Ankara.

Turkey. (1986). 1985-1986 Academic Year Higher Education Statistics. Ankara.

―――――――――――― Chapter 14 ――――――――――――

PROBLEMS AND POSSIBILITIES: CANADIAN NATIVE WOMEN IN DISTANCE EDUCATION

by

Barbara Spronk and Donna Radtke

> **Barbara Spronk** has worked at Athabasca University since 1975 in a variety of positions, including Director of Regional and Tutorial Services. At present she is teaching anthropology and working as a member of the task force that is putting together a programme geared to the needs of Native peoples in northern Alberta.

> **Donna Radtke** worked at Athabasca University from 1980 to 1986 in several positions, including Head of Student Services. While with the university she was a member of the task force that put together proposals for a programme geared to the needs of Native peoples in northern Alberta. She is presently employed in Kingston, Ontario.

Introduction[1]

The objective of this paper is to describe education at a distance for Native women, as it is organized at Athabasca University. This description has three components:

1. a description of the special mode of delivery that characterizes programming for Native people at Athabasca University[2];

2. a discussion of the obstacles to learning in this mode which Native students encounter, in particular problems with learning and study skills; and

3. a discussion of those obstacles which arise from students' lives beyond the classroom, with special attention to the problems of female Native students.

First, a note about the title of this paper. The title reflects the fact that, at Athabasca University (AU), distance education for Native people, although not specifically directed at women, is largely taken up by Native women, who comprise more than four-fifths of the Native students who enrol in the programmes the university offers at Native Education Centres throughout the province.

One possible explanation is that Athabasca's courses attract more Native women than men for the same reasons that AU's programmes, whether home study, teleconferenced, or classroom-based, generally attract more women than men. Over the past decade, the proportion of Athabasca's female students has remained more or less steady at two-thirds. Several features of Athabasca's model make it particularly attractive to women. First, the possibility of home study and self-pacing makes AU's courses accessible to women at home with small children or women who work outside the home as well as at domestic tasks. Second, AU's policies of open admissions and coordination of credits earned at other institutions enable the woman whose educational career has been interrupted by marriage, childbearing or a partner's job-related transfers to pick up her education where she left off. And third, AU's free and freely available student services provide advice and counselling on career change, programme choice and financial aid, which have particular relevance to women (see Coulter *et al.*, 1983).

Native women living in rural areas tend to be even less mobile than their non-Native counterparts, because of relatively early marriages, large families and close ties to and dependence on a close-knit network of kin and affines. Employment opportunities in rural areas are limited, and educational opportunities almost nil. Going to school may be the only immediate opportunity for Native women to earn money on the reserve, since the federal Department of Indian Affairs pays not only tuition fees but also a subsistence allowance to status Indians who are enrolled as full-time students in an educational programme. Even more important than the income for many Native women is the opportunity for more education that is provided by the programmes organized by Native Education Centres such as those with which AU cooperates. As the growing literature on Native American and Canadian women documents (e.g., Cruikshank, 1971; Green 1980, 1983a, 1983b), Indian and Métis women take an active and often leading role in their communities in accepting and engineering change. Education can help them increase their participation in directing such change.

Athabasca University's Native Programmes

Given the aspirations of Native peoples to self-government, the demand for trained and professional Native personnel to staff administrative, educational, social services and health care positions on reserves has become urgent. Athabasca University, like many other post-secondary institutions throughout Canada, has responded to the challenge. In 1976, AU was asked by a Native Education Centre in northeastern Alberta to provide a range of courses that would lead to a university degree. AU said "Yes" to this invitation, as well as to similar requests from five other centres in the decade that followed. Of the resulting programmes, three are currently active.

AU's mainstream programming is aimed at the adult parttime student, working in her home at her own pace, with a package of instructional materials and the assistance of a tutor who can be reached by telephone. It quickly became apparent that this mode would not work well for Native students, at least for those new to university-level course work. English (the language of instruction) is usually neither their first language nor the language they usually speak at home; this combined with the typically low quality of their grade-school education results in extreme difficulties in coping with the amount and level of reading and writing required by AU's packaged courses. Therefore, these students need more intensive support. In addition, many students' homes lack a telephone, which makes tutoring by some other means imperative.

As a solution, the first strategy was to group students in a classroom at the centre, where they were expected to come each weekday for prescribed hours to work individually on their packaged courses. In addition to the telephone tutor, whom they could call (but seldom did) and who graded their assignments, these students were provided with a classroom tutor, not necessarily an expert in any of the subject areas, to assist students with generic reading, writing and study skills.

This mode proved frustrating for all concerned: students were still finding the materials too difficult; the classroom tutor was finding it impossible to give each student the intensive help she needed; and telephone tutors were unable to make any meaningful or continuing contact with students or provide them with adequate feedback on their progress.

The next solution was to provide for each course a classroom tutor in place of a telephone tutor. This mode, with several transformations, has prevailed. Originally these classroom tutors (at that time called "instructors") were hired from all over Canada and brought to the centre to teach a course or courses, living there for a three-week period, teaching their course all day five days a week. They often had considerable latitude in what they taught and in many cases even designed their own courses, since the university had few packaged courses at that time. This mode, although a considerable improvement over both home study and the study skills assistant models, presented several difficulties. Qualified tutors were difficult and expensive to recruit; the in-house academic coordinator, who was responsible for the subject area, had little control over what was being taught, who was teaching it, and overall curriculum design and development. Both the university and the students were concerned that because centre students were receiving different materials from those provided to home study students, and were compressing so much material into three weeks, they risked receiving substandard or fewer materials and hence an inferior education.

The now standard classroom mode of delivery has the following general features (with local adaptations and changes):

1. Classroom tutors (now called "seminar tutors") are hired for six months. For thirteen weeks of those six months they spend one day a week with their class. For three hours of that day they meet with the class as a whole, and for an additional three hours they meet individually with students to help them with specific problems. For the remaining months, they remain available for grading any assignments or exams written after the end of scheduled classroom sessions, by students who elect to revert to home study from the seminar-support mode. Seminar tutors are expected to "support" rather than teach the course materials, on the assumption that the materials are designed to teach themselves. For example, seminar tutors may lead discussions on points raised by the course materials, show films, bring in guest speakers, or even give mini-lectures on difficult aspects of the course. However, they are discouraged from lecturing. They may make some modifications to the course, with the approval of the course coordinator, to accommodate the compressed time period or the students' particular interests and needs, but such changes tend to be minor.

2. The Native student is paid, by Indian Affairs via the centre administration, for coming to class. Generally, if she does not come, she is not paid. Typically she takes three classroom courses at a time. On the days she is not attending classes, she is expected to come to the centre to work under the supervision of the fulltime tutor on staff, either on her current classroom courses or on assignments in her home study courses. As a result of the mix of classroom and home study, she may in fact be enrolled in as many as six courses at one time.

This mode, although more effective than the ones that preceded it, still presents a number of problems. The packaged course offers great flexibility in mode and pace of delivery, but it imposes considerable constraints both on the tutor hired to support it and on the learner whose needs it may not meet. For example, it is difficult to adapt a packaged course to suit the life situation and special interests of a Native population short of extensive rewriting, for which there is little time and no resources. Some problems arise from the classroom situation itself. Students in a classroom setting expect to be taught, not merely "supported," and tutors, accustomed to "teaching" rather than to "facilitating learning," feel torn and frustrated. In addition, although completion rates in seminar-supported courses tend to be no lower and often somewhat higher than the average for the home-study mode, the face-to-face contact on a continuing basis with students who later "fail," or simply disappear, makes each failure more painful.

Finally, as one would expect given their historical and social situation, Native students labour under even greater burdens than do the average adults returning to formal schooling. Some of these, in particular learning and study skills problems and problems arising from students' lives outside the classroom, are described in more detail below.

Learning and Study Skills

Almost since the beginning of AU's relationship with Native Education Centres, staff and students at the centres have requested workshops on study skills, as Native students tend to have especially great needs in this area and are often uncomfortable and unwilling to obtain help by telephone. Their cultural values place great importance on the quality of one-to-one personal interaction and are equally strong for men and women. The university's initial response was to provide the "standard" study skills workshop to students at these centres. This standard workshop is typically offered either on a weekend (a seven-to-eight-hour day) or on two consecutive evenings. Students are usually asked to pay a small fee and to register in advance. The workshop tends to be very fast-paced, covering time management, reading and study skills, essay writing techniques, and preparation for and writing of exams. The emphasis is on "how to's," with some theory provided but also some practice. Presentation formats include lecturettes, small group discussions and exercises, individual exercises, and question and answer sessions. This standard workshop, which seems to work well with AU's "mainstream" students, has not been a success with Native students. These students do not seem interested; they rarely speak or participate and tend to drop out before the end.

In an attempt to increase the effectiveness of these workshops and to tailor them to the needs of AU's Native students, one of the authors (as Head of Student Services at AU) offered to do a series of free workshops (three sessions of 2 1/2 hours each) at one of the Native education centres with which AU cooperates, in exchange for the opportunity to do some related pre-testing of the students who signed up for the series.

Sixteen students attended the first session, nine of them Native (mostly women) and seven non-Native. At this session, the presenter explained that her interest in doing this series of workshops as a research project was both to be of immediate assistance to them and to learn how the workshops could be improved to meet their needs more effectively. She then asked them to fill out: 1) an informal needs assessment (Lampikoski and Mantere, 1978); and 2) a standardized psychological measure *Survey of Study Habits and Attitudes* (SSHA) (Brown and Holtzman, 1965). At the close of each session students were also asked to fill out an evaluation form. The results of these pre-tests were then used in the second and third sessions to direct presentations, materials and discussions towards the needs and interests they revealed.

The results of the needs assessment showed almost equal degrees of concern on the part of students regarding motivation, their ability to assimilate and remember material, doing homework assignments, and organizing their studies, with no strong differences emerging between Natives and non-Natives. This was not the case, however, for the SSHA. The SSHA questionnaire consisted of one hundred statements about the respondent's attitudes and approaches to study, indicating if the statement applied rarely, sometimes, frequently, generally or almost always. The statements and responses were grouped under two general headings:

1. *study habits,* a combination of delay avoidance (promptness on assignments, lack of procrastination and freedom from wasteful delay and distraction) and work methods (use of effective study procedures and efficiency in doing assignments); and,

2. *study attitudes,* referring to teacher approval (students' opinions of teachers' behaviour and methods) and educational acceptance (students' approval of the educational objectives, practices and requirements to which they are subject).

Under the category *study habits,* Natives and non-Natives scored about equally but well below the North American norm.[3] Under the category *study attitudes,* Natives' and non-Natives' scores indicated quite different feelings, non-Natives scoring considerably above the North American norm (at about the 60th percentile), and Natives scoring well below the North American norm (at about the 25th percentile).

As a consequence of the results of the needs assessments, SSHA, and the session evaluations, as well as discussions with students and experiences in previous workshops, a number of changes were made to the standard workshop format and content:

1. *Smaller group.* The group taking the workshop series was intentionally kept small, given both the Native students' preference for learning in a group rather than individually and the presenter's experience that Native students even more than non-Natives seem more open to discussing problems in a small group.

2. *Slower pace.* Although the presenter's experience has been that most students would prefer more time to cover and practice the concepts taught in the workshop, most AU students will accept a fast pace on the understanding that it is necessary to cover the territory. However, workshops given to a largely Native group work only if the pace is slowed, with frequent breaks. Even at half speed, Native students state that they would like more time for discussion. This is by no means an indication of

any mental "slowness" on the part of Native students but is rather a function of some problems with English, unfamiliarity with the concepts being discussed, and the need for interpretation of these concepts by the instructor and students in the context of Native culture.

3. *Time management.* For AU students of Northern European ancestry, the pace of life and setting of priorities tend to be hectic, geared as they are to the exigencies of factory production. Life for Native women can be just as hectic. (See the closing section of this paper.) However, Native people have a different approach to time from people of Northern European ancestry, who tend to approach time in linear fashion, tackling activities systematically, one at a time. Standard workshops on time management and study skills tend to be based on this assumption, that it is most efficient to tackle tasks one at a time, completing or dealing with the first in some way before moving on to the second, and so on. Within the Native context, however, people are adept at engaging in a number of activities simultaneously, with more concern for the quality of their work and of their interactions with other people than for efficiency or the quantity of tasks accomplished (see Hall, 1984). To acknowledge this difference in approaches to time, that portion of the standard workshop dealing with prioritizing "to do" lists and making schedules was omitted or downplayed in the revised workshop series. In addition, commitments to family and community assume an even higher importance for Native students than for non-Natives, and many students experience conflict between long- and short-range commitments, such as studying to be a teacher in the future versus being a mother now. As a result, the revised workshop focused on making the best use of one's time and trading ideas such as pooling childcare to allow more free study time.

4. *Time required for studies.* Native students appear to lack knowledge about the time required for studies, probably because of a lack of familiarity with people who are studying fulltime. As a consequence, the revised workshop provided more information than usual about the hours of work per week required for fulltime studies and, for example, the number of pages it is possible to read in an hour.

5. *Anxiety.* Although most adults returning to school are anxious about their ability to do the work, Native students appear to be

more so. Therefore the revised workshop devoted more time to dealing with "internal distractions," such as anxiety, and "cures" for procrastination.

6. *Teachers' expectations.* The attitudes evident from Native students' responses toward teachers and education as indicated on the SSHA seem to indicate some lack of understanding of what teachers in particular and the university in general are looking for. Therefore, in the revised workshop more time was spent on explanations of "the inside story"—how papers are marked, what to expect on exams, and so on.

This is by no means the final chapter in developing learning and study skills workshops for students at Native education centres. Despite the revisions, attendance over the series of workshops described above still dropped, although only to half the original number of participants and not to zero. And, by the end of the workshops, the level of discussion was excellent, students stayed through the entire session, and the evaluations were very positive. Work will continue on improving the workshops, and changes will include experimenting with the inclusion of discussions with successful Native students of the attitudinal differences pointed out by the SSHA results.

As a postscript to this discussion of the delivery model and learning and study skills needs, it is gratifying to note that AU is putting to work what it and its sister institutions have learned over the past decade, about how and how not to design and deliver distance education for a rural Native population, by developing a number of Native-oriented degree programmes. A joint committee of university and Native leaders is now seeking funding for the project, which proposes to deliver these programmes via a number of modes to remote communities in northern Alberta. Incorporated into the programmes will be an intensive counselling and tutoring component on-site in each community, and we will work closely with community members to ensure that both the content and implementation of the programmes meet community needs.

Beyond the Classroom

Over and above learning and study skills difficulties, Native women experience all the problems that affect any woman returning to school, and more. This was apparent from interviews with several Native women students over a period of two months. The experiences of four of these women are summarized below. The women are Rose, a middle-aged woman with a large family and a spouse; Theresa, separated and mother of three; Jeannette, mother of three and in reality if not legally a single parent; and Mary, a young woman as yet unmarried.[4]

First, family obligations. As mentioned above, Native students devote a great deal of time and energy to support for the family. "Family" for Native students tends to mean the extended family, often resident in the same household. Mutual help is expected, especially of women. Rose's situation is not uncommon. In addition to the four children still at home, Rose is mother to the three children of a daughter who died in an alcohol-related accident. Rose describes the resulting demands on her time this way:

> You have to work twice as hard with an extended family like that, with your own daughters and their families. It makes twice as much [work]. Like today: besides going to Indian Affairs [on behalf of one of her married daughters], one of my other daughters wants us to run her into town to do a little bit of business. We do that kind of [thing] for our children.

Rose, like all the women we interviewed who are also mothers, devotes a great deal of energy to her children, and not just in the home, but in the school, and in supporting her children's involvement in numerous sports.

Community obligations are also time-consuming. Events such as marriages and funerals usually involve the whole community. Family connections extend not only to most members of their own reserve but also often to members of neighbouring reserves. Death on the reserve is followed by night- and day-long wakes. Often deaths are associated with crises in the community such as suicide, which is especially high among adolescents and young adults, or violence caused by alcohol and drug abuse. At such times people gather and try to help each other. In the month in which I spoke with Rose, she had attended several funerals, of people who were "not directly [related] but close enough so that I had to go, like my mother's relatives, and Paul's relatives [Paul is her husband]. That's one of the unexpected things [that interfere with studies]."

Family and community obligations could be called "positive" problems, since they bring their own rewards. The "double burden" of domestic and salaried or wage labour that is central to feminist analyses of women and work does not figure as prominently in Native women's political agendas. As Sioux scholar and activist Rayna Green puts it,

> Overcoming the barriers their status as Indian and female places on them in this world is a theme that runs throughout their words, but an equally strong theme is the advantage of that status. Such words will surprise some who believe that Indian, reservation and female life is burdensome. For example, Canadian Native women [are fighting to] try to retain that status when, simply by marrying a non-Indian they can lose it (Green, 1983b:12).

The aspirations of the women we interviewed are to combine the best of two worlds, to use what they learn from their books and tutors to improve life for their people, in the context of their struggles for self-determination and tribal sovereignty over land. Theresa, for example, has worked as a teacher's aide and wants eventually to be a teacher in a band-controlled school. Rose hopes to become an addictions counsellor, to help prevent the kind of accident that took her daughter's life. Jeannette, even though she has moved away from the reserve and has no plan to return, also plans to become a counsellor working with Native people and is intent on helping her children learn and practice the ways of their people, especially the language, which she speaks with them at home.

Thus, however much family and community obligations may interfere with their studies, the women interviewed expressed no wish to escape from them. On the contrary, they looked to these family and community ties for support in dealing with the considerably more negative problems they confront. Some problems, such as lack of transportation, may seem relatively minor, but they can have a devastating effect on students' course work. Students usually live some distance from the Education Centre, and many of them, especially the women, do not own their own vehicle; nor does public transportation reach the centre. For example, Mary expressed the fear that she would not be able to finish her courses this year, because she would no longer be able to get a ride to school: "I can't get into town [any] more. The girl I was catching a ride with, she's not going [any] more. She's taking the home study a lot now....I don't have any other way of getting in."

Even more serious in its effects on study, however, is what could generally be labelled the "atmosphere" on the reserve, which is anything but conducive to study. Mary describes it this way:

> Out here, where I'm living [on a reserve], hardly anyone's going to school, so it's a lot harder for me, because all my friends [on the reserve] have nothing to do with school. It's really hurt my marks....I get a lot of work done at school. Here everybody's working and doing the same thing you are so it's a lot easier....When I was here [in town] for that week all I did was work, I had no distractions, no one asking me, "Oh, why don't you put those books away and come out and play" sort of thing....I worked my ass off, and it felt good!

Mary's boyfriend, on whose home reserve they live, appears to have been more vulnerable to this peer pressure. He initially enrolled in the same programme as Mary, but gave it up after the first semester in favour of a short-term job which, despite its temporary nature, gave him more prestige with his age-mates than did going to school. Indeed, Native females tend to persevere in the programme to a much greater extent than do the relatively fewer males who enrol.

Part of the "atmosphere" of the reserve is violence, much of it alcohol-related. Theresa, when asked what problems she faced as a student, found this one difficult to put into words:

> How should I put this....Most of the time my sister [who is a band chief] comes over and stays with us. We are bothered by people sometimes late at night. It's pretty dangerous to be alone at night-time. Sometimes we go out and stay at motels. Right now that's what we're doing. I'm hoping to get a place in town, where I can stay and settle down and be able to think.... I lived in the city for a long time. It's different, there you feel safe. On the reserve we're separated, so far apart. When I'm on my own, I get scared, I don't feel safe.

Theresa's fears are understandable. In 1982, in her reserve with a population of 2,264, there were 27 deaths. A third of these were a result of accidents, poisonings and violence, a proportion similar to that for all registered Indians in the Alberta region: out of a total population of 39,449 in 1982, there were 287 deaths, of which 108 were a result of accidents, poisoning or violence. Health and Welfare statisticians (1984:7) suspect that "the majority of these [108 deaths] were also alcohol-related, even though in 78 of them no mention of alcohol was made on the death certificate."[5] Deaths on this scale are only the surface indication of violence on a much greater scale, much of it at the domestic level. Marital violence is an overwhelming problem for several of the Native women we talked with, including Rose. However, as emotional restraint and the quiet acceptance of pain and hardship are highly valued among Native women, they do not often discuss marital violence.

Money is a final and overarching problem for these women, as it is for the majority of adults who have returned or are contemplating a return to school (CCLOW, 1984). However, for women, particularly Native women, this problem is especially serious. Government allowances for tuition and subsistence are based on individual need but appear not to take into account the actual cost of living in rural Alberta. As Theresa phrased it,

> I think that's what really discouraged me, I was always lacking money... Financially I'm getting less than what I was making [when she worked as a teacher's aide]. Kids eat a lot. Sometimes I run out [of] groceries. This $520 [a month] from Indian Affairs... sometimes my credit at the store gets up to $300. I wish my kids' father could help them, support them. They [Social Services] have been taking him to court to get some assistance from him, but I haven't heard anything from them.

Jeannette gets by on funding from her band, with supplements from student loans (a government programme for Natives and non-Natives alike), in order to "buy my kids the things they need." Funding is also unpredictable. For instance, now that she has moved to the reserve to be with her boyfriend, Mary explains that "My band has cut my funding in half now. I think it's because [on the reserve] you're not paying rent. I used to get $560, $60 [of it] for travelling back and forth [to school]. And now I only get $280 a month."

These problems are serious and abiding, and beyond our control as educators. We can do little toward solving these problems, but we can admire the strength of our students in what often seem to us to be overwhelming difficulties. We can support them in their struggles, and we can build enough flexibility into our programmes so that they become aids rather than further obstacles to our students' eventual success.

Notes

1. Another version of this paper appears in the forthcoming collection, Kathleen Storrie, (Ed.), *Women, Isolation and Bonding: Readings in the Ecology of Gender*, (Toronto: Methuen/Garamond). The research on which this paper is based was made possible by a grant from the Academic Research Fund of Athabasca University. That support is gratefully acknowledged.

2. Following Asch (1984), *Native* covers all persons who can trace their biological ancestry through at least one line to individuals belonging to societies that existed in Canada prior to European contact and settlement. The term encompasses four distinct categories: Inuit (or Eskimo); status Indians, who are registered as such under the Indian Act and entitled to certain rights under the act; non-status Indians, who have lost their rights as status Indians; and Métis, people of mixed ancestry who have developed out of cultural elements drawn from both Indian national entities and French or English settlers. The Native groups represented by students at Athabasca University are primarily Cree and Stoney, with some Métis.

3. Note that these norms were established on the basis of the responses of a population of largely white, pre-adult college students in the U.S.A.

4. In order to provide these women with some anonymity and to honour the confidence in which they told us of their experiences, they have been given fictitious names. However, their words and the experiences they describe are real.

5. For purposes of comparison, of 12,968 deaths in Alberta in 1982, only 11.31% (1,467) were the result of accidents, poisoning or violence (Statistics Canada, 1983).

References

Asch, Michael. (1984). *Home and Native Land.* Toronto: Methuen.

Barman, Jean, Yvonne Hébert, and Don McCaskill. (Eds.). (1986). *Indian Education in Canada.* Volume 1: *The Legacy.* Vancouver: University of British Columbia Press.

Brown, William and Wayne Holtzman. (1965). *Survey of Study Habits and Attitudes.* New York: Psychological Corporation.

CCLOW. (November 1984). *In Search of Opportunity.* A Report by the Women's Education Research Project to the Canadian Congress for Learning Opportunities for Women (Edmonton Chapter).

Coulter, Rebecca, Roz Delehanty, and Barbara Spronk. (November 1983). "Women and Distance Education." Unpublished paper, presented to the Canadian Research Institute for the Advancement of Women, Vancouver.

Cruikshank, Julie. (1971). "Native Women in the North." *North/Nord, 18* (6).

Frideres, James S. (1983). *Native People in Canada: Contemporary Conflicts.* Scarborough, Ontario: Prentice-Hall.

Ghitter, Ron. (1984). *Report of the Committee on Tolerance and Understanding.* Government of the Province of Alberta.

Green, Rayna. (Winter 1980). "Native American Women: A Review Essay." *Signs,* 6(2), 248–67.

Green, Rayna. (1983a). "Honoring the Vision of Changing Woman: A Decade of American Feminism." In Robin Morgan. (Ed.). *Sisterhood is Global.* New York: Doubleday and Company.

Green, Rayna. (1983b). *Native American Women: A Contextual Bibliography.* Bloomington: Indiana University Press.

Hall, Edward T. (1984). *The Dance of Life.* New York: Anchor Press/ Doubleday.

Health and Welfare Canada. (1984). *Annual Review and Vital Statistics, Alberta Region, 1982.* Ottawa: Health and Welfare.

Lampikoski, Kari and Pertti Mantere. (1978). *Final Report of the Distance Education on Development Project, Report 3.* Finland: The Institute of Marketing.

Statistics Canada Vital Statistics, Health Division. (1983). *Causes of Death, 1982.* Ottawa: Supply and Services.

Tobias, John. (1976). "Protection, Civilization, Assimilation: An Outline History of Canada's Indian Policy." *Western Canadian Journal of Anthropology,* 7(2), 13–20.

NEGOTIATING A NEW MODEL FOR ABORIGINAL TEACHER EDUCATION: ANTEP — A CASE STUDY

by

Loene Furler and Carol Scott

Loene Furler is the Course Coordinator for Art and the Lecturer-in-Charge of "New Opportunities for Women" programmes at the Adelaide College of TAFE in South Australia. In response to community requests, she has facilitated art workshops in several Aboriginal communities in the Homelands of South Australia. She is the Lecturer-in-Charge of Non-Anangu Art with the ANTEP programme.

Carol Scott is the Course Coordinator for the ANTEP programme at the South Australian College of Advanced Education. She has been involved in the field of Aboriginal Education for ten years, working in the Kimberleys of Western Australia, in the Northern Territory as the Curriculum Coordinator for an independent Aboriginal community school (Yipirinya), and in the field of Aboriginal Teacher Education. She is originally from Canada.

Introduction

This paper focuses on the Anangu* Teacher Education Program, which was designed for Aboriginal men and women from a traditionally oriented background who wish to undertake greater professional responsibilities in teaching in their own communities. Most of the enrolments in the programme since its inception have been Aboriginal females. We have examined the contemporary circumstances of these learners and have considered those factors which relate to the predominance of female enrolments. The development of the programme is described against the back-

---

* The word ANANGU refers to traditionally oriented Aboriginal persons residing in, or having occasion to reside in, a South Australian community.

ground of Aboriginal history since contact with Europeans, with particular reference to the role of education in colonizing the Aboriginal people of Australia. Finally, the programme's mechanisms for responding to clients' needs within the current climate of social, cultural and political change are examined in detail.

Profile of the Learners

The Anangu Teacher Education Programme (ANTEP) has been specifically designed for Aboriginal adults who are living a traditional lifestyle in Central Australia and who wish to undertake professional responsibilities in schools in their communities. The learners are predominantly full-blood Aboriginal adults between the ages of 18 and 40. Many of these learners have had extensive experience working in state Department of Education schools in South Australia and the Northern Territory as Aboriginal Education Workers and Teacher Aides. Among the learners at a recently established second location of the programme are several people who were integral in establishing their own independent community school in the face of strong opposition from state education authorities in the late 1970s and early 1980s. They usually speak an Aboriginal language as their first language, although all of them have been "schooled" in the Western education system and, therefore, have attained varying degrees of literacy and oral facility in English.

Significantly, 80% of the learners are women, for the programme is designed to prepare teachers for primary schools and, in spite of attempts within the last two decades to attract men to primary school teaching, the perception persists that the care of young children is "women's work." Among traditionally oriented and geographically isolated Aborigines, whose contact with Western formal education has often been through mission schools, this perception of the female role in the primary classroom is widely upheld.

The majority enrolment of women is also related to the fact that Aboriginal women generally attain higher levels of literacy and oral skills in English than their male counterparts and therefore have greater access to tertiary study. The reasons for the male/female disparity in academic skills have been insufficiently researched and documented. However, the relative continuity of Aboriginal women's role in the face of cultural change, and the tradition of sexual equality in Aboriginal culture, are probably significant factors.

> In the early culture contact period of the 19th century, women shared with their menfolk a common experience of shock and disruption caused by the sudden overpowering of their traditional lifestyle by European settlers bent on taking the land and turning it to economic purposes. This often involved European cruelty, ignorance and disease. For women, especially in isolated rural areas where there were few white women, this rape of the land was combined with degrading sexual exploitation of their own persons.... The women who survived faced the task of picking themselves up, meeting their changed life situation and grafting their former roles on to the new cultural circumstances in which they found themselves.... The women's roles in the family did at least continue, even if carried out under drastically changed circumstances, which gave their lives continuity (Grimshaw, 1981:96).

This perception that Aboriginal women experienced marginally less traumatization than Aboriginal men, as a result of the thread of continuity which childbearing and nurturing afforded them, suggests that women were in a better position to adapt to a changed situation, to learn new skills and to take advantage of the offerings of the Western education system. Moreover, the largest dropout rate among Aboriginal boys from formal Western schools occurs in the years leading up to puberty, when Aboriginal identity and manhood is formalized through initiation ceremonies. Having been "made a man," many initiated young Aboriginal men cannot accept the infantilization of students in the Western classroom. Initiation confirms young men in their Aboriginal identity and perhaps develops awareness of the colonizing aspects of Western institutions which are imposed on local Aboriginal communities, including schools.

Although the reasons are still being debated, a 1986 report on post-primary education for Anangu children, which included surveys relating to the participation and achievement of Aboriginal boys and girls in secondary schools, confirms that more Aboriginal girls than boys are rated as high achievers. High achievers were characterized "by an enthusiasm for school work, comparatively regular attendance, and strong support from their families" (Groome, 1986:13). The following tables from this report show enrolment and achievement breakdown by sex and age.

Table 1: Age Distribution of Secondary Students

Age	Male	Female
17	3	2
16	7	16
15	14	13
14	21	22
13	21	24
12	15	15
11	2	0
Totals	83	92

Source: Groome, 1986:12.

Table 2: High Achievers by Age and Sex

Age	Male	Female
17	1	0
16	1	6
15	2	3
14	2	9
13	5	9
12	2	2
Totals	13	29

Source: Groome, 1986:13.

Table 3 indicates the number of Aboriginal learners enrolled in tertiary courses who were receiving Aboriginal Study Grants assistance from 1976 to 1982. The table further identifies the number of male and female learners.

The reasons for the predominance of Aboriginal women in tertiary education courses are varied and complex. The evidence would suggest, however, that "enthusiasm" for school work, which Groome cites as one of the characteristics of high achievers, and which is identified more among female secondary students, reflects an active interest in developing the academic skills required for access to tertiary education.

Aboriginal women's interest in further education may also be affected by their contemporary political activism, which is supported by the inheritance of a tradition of sexual equality within Aboriginal society. This is related to their traditional role as economic providers and their separate ceremonial life. The contemporary activism of many white Australian women arises within the context of a marxist-feminist analysis of male-dominated capitalist society and the imposed limitations on women's

Table 3: Number of Grants Awarded, 1976-82:
Fulltime and Parttime, by Sex and Field of Study (Tertiary, Technical Colleges and Schools, and Other)

	1976 M	1976 F	1977 M	1977 F	1978 M	1978 F	1979 M	1979 F	1980 M	1980 F	1981 M	1981 F	1982 M	1982 F
Tertiary:														
Fulltime	81	95	113	129	142	193	174	245	249	449	286	467	854	
Parttime	11	12	14	13	42	70	51	114	85	220	52	95		
Technical colleges and schools:														
Fulltime	206	285	184	235	322	456	549	649	491	1225	600	1480	1505	
Parttime	96	151	67	172	94	190	236	571	244	607	394	851		
Other:														
Fulltime	164	422	303	536	442	836	840	1315	1815	1961	1388	1313	7502	
Parttime	202	528	199	486	338	1216	703	1755	1040	2471	1224	3280		
	760	1493	880	1571	1380	2961	2553	4649	3924	6933	3944	7486	3507	6354
TOTAL	2253		2451		4341		7202		10857		11430		9861	

Note: The statistics for 1982 do not enable identification of fulltime and parttime students by sex, according to these categories, following the introduction of new statistical collection procedures. Figures given are based on the level of study being undertaken by grantholders, such as Bachelor's Degree, or Trade Certificate.

Source: House of Representatives Standing Committee on Aboriginal Affairs, 1984, attachment K.

roles and power within that context. White women often perceive education as a means to acquire the "cultural capital" to achieve social, political and economic equality. Aboriginal women, on the other hand, do not appear to have the same tradition of political and economic inequality and social inferiority as white women. Some recent research suggests that Aboriginal women were accorded the status of "junior partners" to their men. However, female anthropologists Philis Kaberry, Jane Goodale and Diane Bell, relying on women as informants, discovered that Aboriginal women "considered themselves in no way socially inferior, viewing their roles as separate and complementary, but in no way subordinate" (Grimshaw, 1981:89). What is certain is that, within Aboriginal society, women have always maintained their own tradition of ceremonial life, and this has contributed to the development of a strong, separate "women's sphere" and an accompanying feminine consciousness. In addition, because Aboriginal women have always been crucial to the economic life of the society through their physical work as gatherers, Aboriginal femininity has never been equated with passivity.

Many Aboriginal women perceive the struggle for sexual equality as a white women's struggle and European feminism as irrelevant to their situation. Their focus, rather, is directed towards the liberation of their culture as a whole, and it is from this perspective that they seek higher education.

> I can't get interested in women's liberation. To me, as an Aboriginal, it's not relevant, for the simple reason that our whole people have to be liberated. I don't consider that we split forces here, between women and men. I can only identify with the idea of "lib" [sic] for the whole people (Grimshaw, 1981:87).

For Aboriginal women, then, education is a vehicle for raising the life chances of the whole group and realizing the aims of cultural self-determination and self-management. It is insufficient just to "get an education"; there is a growing interest among Aborigines in controlling the processes of education, to ensure that Aboriginal values and identity will be maintained and the colonizing effects of Western schooling will be ameliorated. During an interview in the ANTEP programme, one of the authors of this paper asked a female student why she wanted to become a teacher. Her answer was "so we can be bosses and look after our schools."[1]

In sum, the historical development of Aboriginal education in Australia must be examined within the context of colonization, viewing the institution of Western schooling as a major colonizing tool. The development of the ANTEP programme is a response to the expressed concerns of Aboriginal people who are attempting to regain control over the education of their children and searching for models aligned with broader developments in contemporary Aboriginal culture.

The Development of Aboriginal Education

Contact between Aborigines and Europeans in Central Australia is a relatively recent phenomenon, occurring in the late nineteenth century when initial exploration was followed by rapid white settlement. The immediate impact of the arrival of Western society was felt in the changed relationships which Aboriginal people had with the land. The introduction of cattle-fouled waterholes and disturbed hunting patterns, and this alteration in the economic base of the society, forced many Aboriginal families to seek work on stations in exchange for rations. The establishment of missions provided a haven for other Aboriginal groups. In both cases, patterns of settlement were beginning to emerge which could facilitate centralized control of the Aboriginal population. This centralized management gained momentum in the 1950s and 1960s under the Native Welfare Act and was given added impetus during the rocket testing at Woomera and the nuclear bomb tests at Emu Junction and Maralinga. A full-scale programme of relocation to government settlements was undertaken which forcibly removed Aboriginal people from their tribal lands.

Resettlement and centralized management policies have seriously affected Aboriginal culture. Frequently, disparate tribes and language groups were herded together in crowded living conditions, giving rise to severe social conflict. Health deteriorated as the result of the increased spread of hitherto unknown infectious and contagious diseases for which the population had no natural immunity. A breakdown of religious observance and ceremonies occurred as a result of the separation by distance from the totemic sites where rituals were held. Specifically related to the topic of this paper, centralization enabled the establishment of Western models of education which effectively modified many of the traditional socialization patterns of Aboriginal children and imposed a monocultural world view at variance with Aboriginal beliefs.

Five distinct periods in the history of Aboriginal education can be identified, all reflecting central government policies towards Aborigines at that time (Welch, 1985:11):

1. the exclusion of Aboriginal students from mainstream schools on the basis of their inferiority, a period distinguished by the establishment of mission schools which were designed to accommodate Aboriginal students but which offered a limited curriculum;
2. the forcible removal of Aboriginal children from their parents for schooling to alleviate "the harmful effects of Aboriginal adults on the educated children" (Milnes, quoted in Welch, 1985:13);
3. the attempted assimilation of Aborigines into Western culture as the result of exposure to Western education;
4. the token acknowledgement of Aboriginal culture in policies of "integration"; and
5. the development of emerging policies of Aboriginal self-management and self-determination in education.

As was reported in 1983, the gap between the educational and cultural expectations of Western schooling and the achievements of Aboriginal children was commonly interpreted as individual failure on the part of the Aboriginal children and has been attributed at various times to: the inevitable effect of belonging to an inferior species; the pernicious influences of Aboriginal parents; genetically determined low I.Q.; and the inadequacies of the home environment of Aboriginal children. Rarely was the failure attributed to white society, or to the active resistance of some Aboriginal communities to the destructive elements implicit in many of the educational programmes (SACAE, 1983:11).

Within a climate of Social Darwinism, an underlying assumption throughout the history of Aboriginal education has been that the imposition of a monocultural curriculum of Western values on Aboriginal learners would ultimately exert a "civilizing" effect. The result has been cognitive dissonance, confusion and conflict as Western models of explanation and knowledge, diametrically opposed to Aboriginal views of the world, have been introduced. In addition, an elaborate "hidden curriculum" of Western socio-cultural patterns has been transmitted which negates the essential features of Aboriginal social organization:

> By establishing schools and classrooms organized along Western structures, with children being grouped into separate self-con-

tained classrooms, traditional divisions into tribal and sub-tribal and moiety groupings, and traditional avoidance relationships built into the kinship system, are shattered (McConnochie, quoted in Sherwood, 1982:75).

In 1976, the Senate Select Committee on Aborigines and Torres Strait Islanders agreed with the proposition that "to date the school system has failed Aborigines very badly by its inappropriateness and inadequacy." This conclusion was supported by evidence collected through surveys conducted in Queensland, the Northern Territory, New South Wales, South Australia, and throughout the other states and territories.

> Aboriginal people have not been the passive recipients of this confusion. The history of Aboriginal responses to white society is a history of Aboriginal people attempting to reduce discontinuity and to modify their culture in order to retain coherence and an Aboriginal identity in the face of a set of external constraints, demands and impositions. As part of this struggle, Aboriginal people have been attempting to modify their world view, the various expressions of this base, and the socialisation processes which provide the central mechanisms for the re-creation of Aboriginal culture in new generations. However, in all of this, the communities have been seriously hampered by:
>
> i) the arbitrary and often contradictory demands of the powerful outside society;
>
> ii) their lack of control over many aspects of the situation (economic frameworks, land usage, legal constraints, etc.;
>
> iii) their lack of control over elements of the socialisation systems which are central to the maintenance of Aboriginal culture (SACAE, 1983:12–13).

Response to a Need—
The ANTEP Programme

The Anangu Teacher Education Programme (ANTEP) was originally conceived to meet the needs of predominantly Pitjantjatjara people who reside in the Homelands of Northwest South Australia. The history of Aboriginal education in the Homelands reveals some unique features: From the outset it was recognized that children learn literacy best in their first language, because it is the language of initial concept development. When formal schooling was introduced in 1940, the teaching of literacy commenced in the vernacular. Secondly, Aboriginal teaching assistants have had an important part to play in the development of Aboriginal education since the mission days, and education in the Homelands has, to some very real degree, depended on the involvement and commitment of the Aboriginal community. In the early days of the establishment of schools in the Homelands, there were few white teachers available to service the educational needs of such a vast area, and Aboriginal people were frequently solely in charge of classes of children.

Rationale for the Development of the Programme

With the pressures for increasing self-management, Aboriginal people recognize the need for literacy, numeracy and technical skills in order to manage their own affairs effectively. Traditionally, the government response to these needs has been to establish schools for development of these skills. However, government schools reflect the values of the dominant culture and tend to offer a monocultural approach to addressing these educational components.

In a bicultural setting, which is the context in which Aboriginal schooling is occurring today, Western-style schooling provides services for children from a significantly different culture. The question that arises is what represents an appropriate educational service. We are faced with the complex issue of whether the process of attaining literacy, numeracy and technical skills can occur in a manner which supports the children's culture and primary Aboriginal identity or whether it conflicts with and disrupts it:

> Aboriginal communities are faced with increasing pressures to modify the fabric of their society in order to deal with the impact of Western society. If those changes are to be coherent, and consistent with the most important elements of their society, then they must be able to control them. Schools, for their part, must keep in step with those changes if they are to avoid adding to the difficulties already faced by the communities. This places some very specific demands on the system:
>
> - The symbolic and knowledge structures of the school must be aligned as far as possible with the same structures in the communities. This may require modification in teaching strategies, temporal and spatial organization, authority structures, language usage and so on;

- The educational process must be sensitively aligned with both the changing world view and with the changing economic and cultural characteristics of the communities;
- The education system must concentrate on developing essential skills as determined by the practical demands of the cultural context;
- The education system must be closely involved in the construction of emerging concepts of Aboriginal identity. As a central aspect of the cultural reproductive processes, education cannot avoid such a role (SACAE, 1983:14–15).

These goals cannot be fully met by teachers who do not share the process of socialization into Aboriginal culture. Non-Aboriginal teachers cannot perceive the learning situation from the viewpoint of their Aboriginal pupils and are usually inadequately prepared through conventional teacher education programmes for teaching in a cross-cultural situation. Too frequently, state departments of education appoint recent graduates to work in Aboriginal communities. Faced with developing their teaching skills in a culturally unfamiliar environment, often geographically isolated and with insufficient professional support, these teachers often withdraw from the community as soon as possible, destabilizing the fragile balance which the formal education system has in the community:

> Only Aboriginal teachers can provide schools with accurate, immediate information on the cultural environment to which the schools must respond; translate this response into culturally compatible teaching strategies and teaching styles; recognize and provide directions for the reduction of dissonance between educational and socialisation processes; provide children with teachers to whom they can relate immediately as familiar adults and provide communities with points of access for direct control over the essential reproductive processes within their culture (SACAE, 1983, in French-Kennedy, 1985).

The access of Aboriginal people to teacher education programmes has become an important issue. The National Aboriginal Education Conference points out the need for a variety of Aboriginal teacher education programmes to accommodate the different types of Aboriginal communities existing in contemporary Australia, identified as:

- traditionally oriented, geographically isolated;
- rurally located, not traditionally oriented;

- urban located, socially isolated; or
- urban located, embedded in mainstream Australian society.

The NAEC argues that indigenous teachers from one sector of Aboriginal society are not necessarily effective when working in a different sector. Therefore, specially designed teacher education programmes for Aborigines from traditionally oriented backgrounds are necessary if there is to be effective intervention in reducing cultural dissonance in the education of Aboriginal children within the formal Western system.

Organizational Features of the Programme

The development of teacher education courses for traditionally oriented Aboriginal people must respond to the educational needs of the community, as perceived by the community itself. Graduates must be adequately prepared to teach appropriately in that situation and to use their training as a baseline for developing a programme "without preconceptions or the precedent of present... teacher education courses" (Sherwood, 1982:47). Sherwood describes the features of a potentially "realistic alternative model," which would have to be offered within the community of the learners; it would require differing "exit" points, modified academic requirements, and appropriate structure, style, organization and content for teaching in the communities.

The ANTEP programme operates from the South Australian College of Advanced Education at Underdale, in Adelaide. At the campus base are located the course coordinators, the clerical staff, the curriculum writers, graphic artists, A/V technicians and many of the Lecturers-in-Charge of course units. Some of the Lecturers-in-Charge, and members of the Course Planning Committee, are from other Colleges of Advanced Education and the Adelaide College of TAFE.

The programme offers two courses and three potential "exit" points; at the completion of the first stage of study graduates should be at Level Two of the proposed industrial award for teacher aides in Aboriginal schools in the Homelands. After two stages of fulltime study, graduates receive the Associated Diploma in Anangu Education. The successful completion of three stages of study qualifies the graduate for the Diploma of Teaching (Anangu).

The programme is offered "on site" in the community of the learners, partly because traditionally oriented Aboriginal people find it difficult to leave their communities for long periods. Their social and religious obligations must be upheld if their cultural integrity is to be maintained.

In particular, Aboriginal women today are often found in equal proportion to men on community councils, land councils, and on the policy-making and decision-making boards of independent Aboriginal organizations such as health, legal and child welfare agencies and educational bodies. Most of these organizations have been established at a grassroots level to cater to local needs, and the ongoing participation by members of the local community is essential for their continuity and success. Extended absence of people who are undertaking study outside the community robs the community of the very people who, because of their skills and status, are often among the most valuable members.

The on-site model appears to be a relatively successful innovation because:

- there are sufficient students drawn from several communities to justify a fulltime on-site lecturer;
- the students can keep contact with their family obligations and community responsibilities;
- all of the participating communities share long-established cultural, social and linguistic features;
- the host communities (Ernabella and Alice Springs) are large enough to provide on-site lecturer housing, teaching space and parttime tutors (French-Kennedy, 1985:6).

On-site personnel include a community-based lecturer (usually referred to as an on-site lecturer) who is involved in the implementation of the programme in the local community, instruction and evaluation of course materials, assessment of students, local administration and community liaison. Supervising teachers are responsible for the supervision of lesson preparation, observation of teaching practice, and the evaluation of school experience sessions. The community based clerical officer is responsible for the secretarial services required by the on-site lecturer, supervising teachers, visiting lecturers and tutors.

The on-site programme has also enabled the local language to be used as a vehicle for instruction, a vital factor in a cross-cultural understanding of the concepts and language encoded in the discipline which we term "education." As importantly, if Aboriginal teacher trainees are to address the problems which Aboriginal children face in school, they must be facilitated in investigation of alternative teaching strategies which, grounded in Aboriginal experience, can more effectively encourage learning among Aboriginal children. Research must investigate the concepts and knowledge Aboriginal children bring to the school situation and how this knowledge can be built upon to bridge the gap between the "known and the unknown." To this end, Aboriginal teacher education students need opportunities to investigate Aboriginal domains of knowledge, in an Aboriginal context: to clarify, for example, how Aboriginal people conceptualize what Europeans term "mathematics" and what language Aboriginal people use to encode these concepts. These investigations can only be successfully undertaken if the students have access to those members of the Aboriginal community who have the right to impart such knowledge.

"Rights" to certain types of knowledge reside within designated members of the community, and not all Aboriginal learners are privy to all sections of traditional knowledge. For example, traditional sex-role demarcations play a part. During a research workshop at one location of the programme, the aim of which was to clarify how Aboriginal people perceive the natural environment, the female Aboriginal teachers involved in the workshop were unable to speak with authority on many issues. In this case, the appropriate men, many of them traditional owners and tribal elders, had to be contacted before this information could be acquired and openly discussed. This could not have occurred if the learners were not studying in the same community as the appropriate people with access to that particular knowledge.

The programme is attempting to be bicultural in approach, locating and clarifying each new concept in the Aboriginal domain before bridging to the Western perception. To achieve this aim, a Participatory Research Model has been adopted as an organizing principle for the development of course units. Learners are encouraged to commence the study of any area of the primary school curriculum with an initial investigation into the way in which

Aborigines conceptualize the area. For example, Curriculum Studies in Mathematics begins with the students locating mathematics concepts in an Aboriginal context, discussing the way in which Aboriginal people conceptualize mathematics, and recording the language in which the ideas are encoded.

The Social Information unit aims toward developing an anthropological analysis of white Australian society and its institutions—particularly their effect on traditionally oriented society. This initially involves students in an oral history project, interviewing community members about the impact of European institutions on Aboriginal society since contact. One on-site lecturer has commented that learners found this approach meaningful, because they could immediately apply newly learned skills in a real-life context. An additional effect of the Social Information Unit is to stimulate community involvement and interest generally, and this enthusiasm for reflecting on and "owning" their uniquely Aboriginal history, and "naming" it in their own way, has continued beyond the original project.

Consultation and Negotiation

Continued Aboriginal input is essential if this principle of biculturalism is to be implemented in practical terms. On the one hand European people involved in the programme cannot "know" Aboriginal culture, its total world view, its concepts and its "domains" of knowledge in the depth required to design a course of study which is truly bicultural. In addition, Aboriginal culture itself is changing from within, adapting and modifying in response to its changing environment. To be responsive to these cultural developments, and to plan a teacher education programme which takes into account the implications of change and "emerging concepts of Aboriginal identity" (SACAE, 1983:15), access and negotiation with the local Aboriginal community for which the programme is planned must be ongoing.

Aboriginal involvement in the decisions affecting the development of the programme has been identified as having crucial long-term importance. Without this involvement, a programme might be created which would not only not satisfy the "needs, wants, and desires of the community" but would actually conflict with them, with the possible consequences that:

- the students may not be able to look forward to support from the community, e.g., be denied positions of responsibility at the conclusion of the course;
- the community may disapprove of the implementation of the course and dissuade students from attending;
- essential advice and assistance may not be given (French-Kennedy, 1985:12).

Extensive consultation with the local Aboriginal community was undertaken prior to the development of the accreditation document for the programme to prevent this situation.

Having derived the broad parameters of the programme from the initial series of consultations, ANTEP has had to develop other mechanisms to ensure ongoing Aboriginal involvement in its development. At the suggestion of the current students at one location, an ANTEP Council has been formed, with two members nominated by the local community, one ANTEP student, and one of the visiting Lecturers-in-Charge of course units. This council acts as a "funnel" between the College and the community for all issues associated with the programme; it looks at a variety of issues including student attendance, research undertaken on behalf of the programme, negotiating contracts with students "at risk," and informing the local community about the programme.

An extension and refinement of the ANTEP Council has occurred at the more recently established second location of the programme. A Joint Management Committee is comprised of the members of the College (an ANTEP Planning Committee nominee plus the Faculty Dean or nominee), the learners, and their potential Aboriginal employers—who are also people of status in the local community. This committee's mandate is to negotiate an appropriate curriculum, monitor student progress, collaborate on funding submissions, and report directly to the College Principal on any matters associated with the programme.

The recent innovative decision by the ANTEP Planning Committee to undertake a "negotiated" model of curriculum development includes the following procedures:

1. the ANTEP Course Coordinator seeks advice from the employers of the potential graduates about the responsibilities the graduates will be expected to undertake as teachers in Aboriginal schools;

2. this advice is taken to a local community meeting, the objective of which is to ask the community representatives to assist the Course Coordinator to clarify the broad aims and parameters of each stage of the programme;
3. the information received is discussed with the Lecturers-in-Charge of units who, in consultation with the learners, determine the aims, content and activities of the particular units for which they have responsibility;
4. the Curriculum writers receive the information and proceed to develop the required resources;
5. the material is tested by the Curriculum writers with the learners on-site;
6. the on-site lecturer and the ANTEP students negotiate the work required to complete the unit satisfactorily.

Yet to be determined is a model for ensuring ongoing community evaluation of the programme, although locating the programme in the community enables the local Aboriginal people to monitor the progress of students in an informal way.

Conclusion

The programme providers and ANTEP course development team cannot yet identify the long-term implications for curriculum units developed through negotiations with the predominantly female students undertaking this study. We are left with the question of whether the curriculum would be altered significantly if predominantly male learners were negotiating the curriculum. At this early stage, however, it appears that the twin principles of ongoing consultation with the Aboriginal community and negotiating the curriculum with each successive group of learners have provided a model which appears to be flexible enough to respond to the developing needs of the local Aboriginal community.

Note

1. Katrina Tjitayi, speaking to Carol Scott, June 7, 1986.

References and Bibliography

Bell, Diane. (1983). *Daughters of the Dreaming*. North Sydney, N.S.W., Australia: McPhee, Gribble Publishers, in association with George Allen and Unwin.

Christie, M. (1985). *Aboriginal Perspectives on Experience and Learning: The Role of Language in Aboriginal Education*. Deakin: Deakin University Press.

Christie, M. (1985). *The Classroom World of the Aboriginal Child*. Ph.D. diss., University of Queensland.

Christie, M. (April/May, 1986). "Formal Education and Aboriginal Children." *The Aboriginal Child at School, 14*(2), 40–44.

Cole, M. and S. Scribner. (1974). *Culture and Thought*. New York, New York: John Wiley and Sons.

Coombs, H.C., M.M. Brandl and W.E. Snowdon. (1981). *A Certain Heritage*. Canberra: Centre for Resource and Environmental Science.

French-Kennedy, A. (1985). *Teacher Education For Traditionally Oriented Aborigines and Torres Strait Islanders*. (In press)

Grimshaw, P. (1981). "Aboriginal Women: A Study of Culture Contact." In Norma Grieve and Patricia Grimshaw. (Eds.). *Australian Women—Feminist Perspectives*. Melbourne: Oxford University Press, 86-106.

Groome, H. (1986). *To Break Through the Wall*. Pitjantjatjara Post-Primary Education Report. South Australia: Participation and Equity Program.

Hamilton, A. (1981). "The Complex Strategical Situation: Gender & Power in Aboriginal Australia." In Norma Grieve and Patricia Grimshaw. (Eds.). *Australian Women—Feminist Perspectives*. Melbourne: Oxford University Press.

Harris, S. (1980). *Culture and Learning*. Darwin: N.T. Department of Education.

Harris, S. (1985). *Constraints on Effective Use of Language for Learning in Aboriginal Schools*. Armidale, N.S.W.: Plenary Address to the Working Conference on Language in Education

Hughes, P. and E. Wilmot. (1982). "A Thousand Aboriginal Teachers by 1990." In John Sherwood. (Ed.), *Aboriginal Education: Issues and Innovations*. Western Australia: Creative Research.

Kaminsky, J. (1985). *The Directed Transmission of Culture.* Armidale: University of New England.

Parliament of Australia. (1984). *House of Representatives Standing Committee on Aboriginal Affairs.* Canberra: Monday, April 30, 1984. (Official Hansard Report).

SACAE. (1983). *Submission to the Tertiary Education Authority of South Australia for Accreditation of Two Courses Comprising the Anangu Teacher Education Program (ANTEP).* Vol. 1. Underdale: Aboriginal Studies and Teacher Education Centre.

Scott, C.A. (1985). *Developing a Paradigm for Cross-Cultural Research: A Case Study in Eliciting Arrernte Science Concepts.* (In press)

Scott, C.A. (1985). "Negotiation and Renaming Teacher Education Programs for Participation by Traditionally Oriented Aborigines." Paper presented to the ANZCIES Conference: Adelaide, December 9–11.

Scott, C.A. (1986). "Adult Aboriginal Perspectives on Formal Learning—Implication for the Design of Tertiary Programs." Paper submitted for the Diploma of Continuing Education, University of New England.

Sherwood, J. (1982). "Traditional Aborigines as Full Teachers: Towards the Development of a New Model." *Wikaru,* May.

Stalwick, H. (1985). "Reform as the Creation of New Usages." *Taking Control: A Review of the Indian and Native Social Work Education in Canada,* 2.

Welch, T. (1985). "Aboriginal Education As Internal Colonialism." Paper presented to the ANZCIES Conference: Adelaide, December 9–11.

FACING
NEW CHALLENGES

Editor's Introduction

Since the early 1970s, women's studies programmes have proliferated in many western nations. Such programmes have contributed significantly to the intellectual work of the feminist movement, and many programmes have also supported feminist cultural and political activity. The challenges posed by women's studies teachers and scholars to patriarchal hegemony in the university has engendered lively debates across disciplinary boundaries. Women's studies students and faculty have also often succeeded in creating a climate of community with one another, replacing competitive, hierarchical and elitist value structures with feminist principles of cooperation and consensus. Such achievements, however, have not been gained without great difficulty, and there are still many universities in the world which are not friendly to women's studies.

In Chapter 16, Jo Boon and Gerry Joosten document reasons for the value of women's studies through their study of enrolment patterns at the Dutch Open University. The Dutch OU, like the FernUniversität in West Germany, has had significantly lower female than male enrolments. As a step toward identifying the reasons for this imbalance, Boon and Joosten compared the backgrounds of male and female students and analyzed their study choices. The underrepresentation of women at the Open University was evaluated in terms of Dutch women's overall lower educational attainment level and their low status within the sex-segregated labour market. The factor of high national unemployment was also considered, with the hypothesis that the motivation of women to enter university is reduced by the knowledge that education will not significantly increase their employment opportunities.

Boon's and Joosten's study raises the important question of how a distance learning institution can attract and satisfy the needs of a student constituency which has been heretofore discouraged from entering higher education. Their colleague at the Dutch OU, Nelly Oudshoorn, follows their discussion with a consideration of the role of women's studies in meeting this challenge. In Chapter 17, Oudshoorn reviews the "integration vs. autonomy" debate, wherein the question is whether women's studies materials should be added to the curriculum of traditional disciplines or should instead be developed as separate courses through an independent programme. The OU took the integrationist approach and Oudshoorn identifies some of the problems that weakened this initiative, including reluctance or resistance on the part of most faculty and administrators to revise curriculum. The university opted for an integrationist approach, rather than for an autonomous women's studies programme, because it was predicted that a separate programme would attract only certain students and would ghettoize women's studies, while leaving the university's predominantly "womanless" curriculum unchanged. However, the "add-women-and-stir" approach, to the extent that even that minimal concession was granted, only served to reinforce the idea that there are "exceptional" women worth studying. Oudshoorn argues persuasively for a critical feminist analysis, which would challenge status quo perceptions that women at large have contributed little to society, and concludes that both integrated curriculum and separate women's studies courses are needed.

* * *

The final two chapters in this section focus on the practice of women's studies at two universities: Massey University in New Zealand, and the Open University in England. In Chapter 18, Shelagh Cox and Bev James, of Massey, discuss their pioneering course on "Women in Society," which has been taught at a distance for several years. Using an interview/dialogue conversational format, they discuss the substantive content of the course and the effects of the course on their students and on themselves. The students cover a wide age and experiential range and include male students. With a focus on theory, cultural imagery of females and material conditions of women's lives, the course is an exercise in critical thinking and consciousness-raising and lays groundwork for major reconsiderations of what would constitute a genuinely democratic pedagogy.

* * *

To many distance educators worldwide, the Open University of England represents the prototype of excellence in the field. At any conference, or in any publication, the OU is well represented. OU staff travel to other institutions as international consultants, and professional visitors likewise go to the OU for information and inspiration. As a single-mode institution, the OU has expertise in course design and development, the uses of technology in course delivery, and the benefits of carefully developed counselling and tutorial services. The university has also produced important theorists; Gill Kirkup, the author of Chapter 19, is among them.

There has been considerable activity at the OU on behalf of women's interests, and Kirkup details several examples of these programmes. These achievements have not been realized without a struggle, and Kirkup analyzes the challenges as well as the forthright successes of women's initiatives. She covers a wide range of issues that commonly surface in the development of women's programmes at a distance:

- transformation of course content;
- recruitment of female students;
- open access, barriers to access and compensatory quotas;
- gender disparity in course choice;
- family/job complications for re-entry women;
- programme funding—government? corporations?;
- non-traditional vocational skill programmes;
- faculty's lack of support from male colleagues;
- the importance of student support systems;
- geographic diffusion and sociological diversity of students; and
- conceptual reconstruction of the nature of knowledge.

Kirkup weaves an intricate portrait of the multi-faceted challenges faced by women who are actively acknowledging the interests of female students and constructively addressing the existing inequities. Her paper provides a blueprint for distance educators elsewhere who are planning women's programme initiatives.

— K.F.

A RECONSIDERATION OF THE ATTRACTION OF THE DUTCH OPEN UNIVERSITY FOR FEMALE STUDENTS

by

Jo Boon and Gerry Joosten

Jo Boon, born in Belgium in 1951, studied sociology in Antwerp. Since 1983 she has worked at the Open universiteit as a member of the research staff. She is mainly concerned with the analysis of student backgrounds and different aspects of achievement and is also studying the relation between labour market perspectives and motives for participation in distance education.

Gerry Joosten, born in the Netherlands in 1944, graduated in sociology at the University of Nijmegen. Since 1985 she has worked as a researcher at the Open universiteit, where she is responsible for studies of different aspects of distance education. She recently conducted research on the motives of different groups of students who take part in the Open universiteit.

Introduction

At the start of the Dutch Open University (OU), in September 1984, a high rate of participation by female students was anticipated. It was expected that distance education, and especially the extensive freedom offered by the Dutch system, would meet the needs of women in particular. The expectation of high female participation was based on the experiences of other institutions of higher distance education, notably the British Open University on which the Dutch OU was modelled. The history of the British OU led us to believe that 1) the proportion of male and female participants would become more equal in time; 2) the rate of female students at the OU would surpass the rate of female students at the traditional universities; and 3) there would be an annual rise in the percentage of female students.

The Netherlands has a rather exceptional international position in terms of the participation of women in education. By 1980 it appeared that women were overrepresented in adult education,[1] and especially in most forms of basic adult education, indicating a desire on the part of women for general skill upgrading. In most of the OECD-countries (Organization For Economic Co-operation and Development), the overall rate of increase of new entrants to higher education has diminished in recent years, but the rate of growth for female entrants has increased. In these countries women now take up more than 40% of the places. This is, however, not the case in the Netherlands. In 1982, the female fulltime school attendance at the undergraduate level was approximately 32% of total fulltime enrolment, compared to 47% in both Canada and the United States and about 50% in France and Finland (OECD, 1984). In 1978, when the Dutch OU was conceptualized, the percentage of female fulltime students at Dutch universities was only 27%; at institutes for higher professional education, females represented 40% of enrolments. By 1983 these percentages had been raised to 35% and 43% respectively, confirming growth rate expectations.

The arrears in educational levels achieved by Dutch females are greater than in other western countries. However, it has been perceived, in light of a strong women's liberation movement in the Netherlands, that many women would like to rectify this imbalance. Female students were an important target group for the Dutch OU because of a growing consciousness of the relevance for women of both higher education and entry into the labour market. However, this concern has been mainly expressed rhetorically and is not supported purposefully by governmental education or labour market policy. After two years of operation, we now have some basis for reevaluating our initial optimism. In the mid-1980s approximately 10,000 women and 20,000 men are studying at the Dutch OU. Although the gap between male and female participation grows with age, even younger cohorts show a significant imbalance: the smallest difference exists in the group aged 21 to 25, where 60% are men and 40% are women. This ratio differential also exists at the traditional universities where, relative to the share of women in the Dutch population, female students are likewise clearly underrepresented. In other words, the division between male and female students is as uneven at the OU as at any institution for higher education. The statistics do not show any trend indicating the lessening of enrolment disparity according to sex at the OU, although the short period of the OU's existence precludes a viable analysis of trends to date (Boon and Joosten, 1986).

Female Enrolment by Age, Education and Employment

About 80% of the students at the Dutch OU, both men and women, are younger than 40. However, there is a relative overrepresentation of young women aged 21 to 25. The largest portion of this young female group has achieved an educational level that would qualify them for access to the traditional universities or institutions of higher vocational education. They are generally better educated than the male OU population of the same age. Sixty-two percent of this group are employed, of which 50% work in administrative positions. Our hypothesis is that this group is seeking to improve its educational qualifications for the purpose of gaining better positions within the labour market. If the hypothesis were confirmed it would mean that for some groups the OU and other parttime institutions for higher education function as screening institutions for the labour market.

In general, female OU students are well-educated relative to the Dutch female population as a whole but have a lower average educational level than OU men. If we compare the proportions of men and women with higher educational levels who are studying at the OU with the proportions as they exist for the total Dutch population, the relative overrepresentation of women with higher education in the OU becomes clear.

Table 1: Highest Education of OU Students and of Total Dutch Population (percent)

	OU-M	OU-W	Total M*	Total W*
Secondary general lower stage	14	17	55	71
Senior vocational training	17	12	28	18
Secondary general higher stage	26	35	3	3
Vocational colleges university education	43	37	13	7

Note: fulltime students excluded.
Source: CBS, arbeidskrachtentelling 1979, in Oudijk, 1983:160.

When considering educational levels of adult students, we have to take age into account. The trends for both women and men seem to indicate that the gap between the educational level of OU participants and the Dutch population as a whole widens with age. In comparing the proportion of men and women with a university degree or a higher vocational educational level for several age groups, the following division appears.

Table 2: Proportion of Men and Women at Higher Educational Level

	<25 M	<25 W	25-34 M	25-34 W	35-44 M	35-44 W	45-54 M	45-54 W	>55 M	>55 W
Nl*	5**	4**	14	8	13	6	10	4	8	4
OU	19	21	43	41	47	37	50	36	52	40

* *Note*: Fulltime students excluded.
** *Note*: Forty percent of this age group is still studying.

Source: CBS, arbeidskrachtentelling 1979, in Oudijk, 1983:160.

Table 2 supports the following conclusions:

- The representation of highly educated women at the OU with respect to their share in the total population is stronger than the representation of highly educated men in the total population.

- This overrepresentation increases for both women and men by the rise in age.

In the Netherlands, 32.7% of the female population aged 15 and older participate in the labour market (1981), 36.2% of the single women and 29.2% of the married women. By comparison, women in the OU population who are active in the labour market are overrepresented at 57%, comprised of 61% of the single women and 52% of the married women. Thirty-five percent of the employed women in the OU population are parttime workers (thirty hours or less), and 65% are fulltime workers (thirty hours or more). This percentage lies well above the median weekly working time for women (46% of the Dutch female working population are working in parttime jobs).

Study Plans, Choices and Motives

The education offered by the OU consists of several course choices, and each time a student subscribes for a new course, he or she must outline new study plans. Table 3 shows the differences between male and female students in this regard. Female students seem to be slightly more careful or more insecure in the expression of their study plans. Somewhat more often than men, they say they don't yet know the goal of their studies.

Table 3: Study Plans of OU Students According to Sex (percent)

	M	W
I want to follow only one course	11.5	14.5
I want to get a degree	61.7	53.0
I am not sure/don't know	26.8	32.5
	(N=20300)	(N=9816)

A traditional pattern emerges in the content of study choices. As Table 4 shows, female students are strongly represented in cultural and social sciences. In all other disciplines they are underrepresented. Almost no differences exist in the study achievements of male and female students: about 55% of the students take examinations and 75% of them succeed.

Table 4: Study Choices According to Sex (percent)

	M	W	N
Business/Public administration	78.9	21.1	4878
Cultural sciences	40.5	59.9	5554
Economics	81.0	19.0	6821
Law	70.6	33.9	10355
Natural Science	66.1	29.4	1658
Social Sciences	40.2	59.8	2694
Technical Sciences	87.7	12.3	4542

Comparisons on participation between fulltime and parttime university or higher vocational education are difficult to make, in part because of disparities between fulltime and parttime enrolments of male and female students. We have tried to minimalize this problem by choosing three study choices that have fulltime and parttime equivalents (Table 5).

Table 5 indicates that segregation according to sex is stronger in parttime university and higher vocational education than in the fulltime equivalents.

Table 5: Proportion of Female Students in OU, Fulltime and Parttime Studies (percent)

	OU	University Education FT	University Education PT	Higher Vocational Education FT	Higher Vocational Education PT
Economics	19.1	10.0	7.4	31.5	17.7
Law	29.7	38.0	34.9	—	—
Technical and Nat. Sciences	18.0	13.0	—	10.2	10.4

Source: CBS, Zakboek onderwijsstatistieken 1985 and OU-studenten-statistiek-rapport 7.

Study motives are largely dependent on employment status. The extent to which women are involved in the labour market (measured by weekly hours of work) affects the extent to which career goals provide motive for study. Female students without paid jobs more often cite the development of intellectual capacities and general interest as their motive for entering higher education (Joosten, 1987).

In sum, the general picture of the female OU population as shown in the preceding figures is as follows:

- related to the total Dutch female population and related to the proportion of women expected to be interested in studying at the OU, female students are quantitatively underrepresented;

- the study pattern of male and female students is traditional: women choose cultural and social sciences, including those who study in order to facilitate their opportunities in the labour market;

- most students (both male and female) are younger than 40;

- compared to the Dutch female population, the educational level of female students is relatively high; and

- compared to the total Dutch female population, OU female students are more often involved in the labour market; the OU seems especially attractive to young, highly educated women who are employed.

Discussion

In search of explanations for these patterns, five elements are of central importance.

1. Although the OU doesn't require entrance certificates, a certain educational attainment level is necessary to facilitate study in higher education. Dutch women have a much lower average educational level than Dutch men, therefore fewer women than men are able to study at the OU.

2. University study (even the study of one course) is an investment in human capital (even if the student declares that studying is primarily an interesting way to spend leisure time). The costs of this investment are proportionate to a) the educational level (and the learning skills) obtained; and b) the "distance" between daily activities and the study enterprise. Women with an educational level below the pre-academic level need strong motivation to study at an academic level. We often assume that the capacity to make the most of fragmented pieces of time is one of the characteristics that attracts housewives to distance education. However, this argument can play only a minor role in explaining womens' participation in distance education at a university level, where a concrete study goal must compensate for a lack of educational qualifications. The gap between daily activity and university study is considerable for women who do mainly housekeeping. Housekeeping is primarily manual, blue-collar work, and blue-collar men are also underrepresented at the OU.

3. The more concrete the study goal, the more motivation one can muster to realize study plans. The desire to obtain or advance in a job is more concrete than a desire to develop talents. The present high unemployment rates, and lack of demand for new employees in the Dutch labour market, make an investment in one's education in order to get a job a precarious enterprise for older adults. The large numbers of unemployed people who are younger, better-trained, and more recently educated place adult job-seekers, especially females, at a disadvantage. In addition, research results indicate that women have less money to spend on courses than men (Boon and Joosten, 1986). Overall, the labour market position of women is worse than that of men irrespective of their educational level. This means that women, more often than men, are confronted with the "useless-

ness" of education for the labour market, generating not only a "discouraged workers effect" but also a "discouraged student effect." This offers an explanation for the overrepresentation of working and well-educated women among females who enrol at OU. It surely does not mean that all the women who have jobs are studying in order to get better jobs, but it does mean that involvement in the labour market offers a concrete motive for study.

4. A strongly sex-segregated education and labour market consolidates risk-avoiding behaviour in adults' study choices. The general rise in the educational attainment of women in Dutch society in recent years has not resulted in an equal widening of study choices. The Dutch labour market is strongly segregated, and women are largely confined to domestic and nurturant tasks inside and outside the home. Occupations are divided into "male" and "female" jobs. In 1979, 57% of the employed female population were working in professions where 60% or more of the employees were women (Van Mourik *et al.*, 1983), and occupational segregation is reflected in educational choices at secondary and higher levels. Certainly the two phenomena are related, although narrow educational choices on the part of the female population cannot fully explain segregation in the labour market.[2] Women who choose non-traditional study programmes have to compete against men in the labour market. It is entirely plausible that most adult women who are motivated to advance their education for employment purposes deliberately choose the "safe" study programmes. Their difficulties are great enough without venturing into study areas for which they have not been previously oriented.

5. Some features of distance education, contrary to common assumptions, do not yet appear to meet the needs of women. Theoretically the educational flexibility at the OU (for example, no entry requirements, freedom of choice in regard to study pace, starting time, place of study and course selection) could facilitate female participation, particularly for housewives. Our research results indicate, however, that women, more than men, prefer or need structure in their study. In a survey of potential students, respondents were questioned concerning study regulations by fixed schedules, set examination dates, and planned data for tutoring. Sixty-six percent of the poten-

tially interested females and 56% of the potentially interested males answered that they would appreciate a firm structure in these areas (Boon and Joosten, 1986). We can hypothesize that the pressures toward conformity and external discipline within rigid secondary school systems renders students less confident within a study system which demands individual choice and initiative.

An assumption that females in the Netherlands participate less than males in correspondence education because of lack of contact with teachers or with other students is not clearly supported by research results. Only 14.4% of potentially interested women (and 9.5% of potentially interested men) mention lack of contact as a reason for non-participation at the OU (*ibid.*).

Conclusion

The effects of the Dutch Open University on increasing the participation of women in university education have been limited in these first years of operation. Several interactive factors have had conservative effects on female participation. The less frequent involvement of women in the labour market, and their position of subordination therein, have had demotivating effects and have contributed to concentration in traditional study choice areas. Moreover, women's lower average educational level makes their participation more difficult. The Open University cannot change the current realities of women's position in Dutch society, but it can begin now to broaden women's choices by more explicitly taking these factors into account.

Notes

1. Statistics on adult education, however, are not complete.

2. Other theoretical explanations are: the theory of statistical discrimination (Schippers, 1983), the dual labour market theories (Vissers, 1977), theories on relative labour markets (Rijk and van de Velden, 1980), theories based on motivation and attitudes (Doorne-Huiskens, 1980), and Kanter's theory about segregation between men and women in organizations (Kanter, 1977).

References

Boon, J. and G. Joosten. (July 1986). *Belangstellenden voor de Ou van somer 1984 tot eind 1985.* Heerlen: Open universiteit.

CBS. (1985) *Zakboek Onderwijsstatistieken 1985.* 's Gravenhage: Centraal Bureau voor de Statistiek, Staatsuitgeverij.

Doorne-Huiskens, A. van. (1980). "Kinderen of carriere." *Intermediair, 11,* 37.

Joosten, G. (1987). *Studiemotieven en motieven voor de Ou.* Verschijnt binnenkort. Heerlen: Open universiteit.

Kanter, R. (1977). *Men and Women of the Corporation.* New York: Basic Books.

OECD. (1984). *Educational Trends in the 1970s. A Quantitative Analysis.* Paris: OECD.

Oudijk, C. (1983). "Sociale atlas van de vrouw." *Sociale en Culturele Studies—3.* 's Gravenhage: Sociaal en Cultureel Planbureau, Staatsuitgeverij.

Rijk, T. de and G. van de Velden. (July/August 1980). "Wie weet de veg naar een vrouwvriendelijk arbeidsmarktbeleid?" *Ars Aequi.*

Schippers, J.J. (February 1983). "Werkgelegenheidsdiscriminatie van de vrouw in Nederland." *Sociaal Maandblad Arbeid, 38,* 2.

Van Mourik, A., Th.J. De Poel, and J.J. Siegers. (1983). "Ontwikkelingen in de beroepssegregatie tussen mannen en vrouwen in de jaren zeventig." *Economisch Statistische Berichten, 6–7,* 597–601.

Vissers, A.M.C. eo. (1977). "Sociale ongelijkheid op de arbeidsmarkt." *Sociologische gids,* 1–2.

Chapter 17

TOWARDS A MORE WOMEN-CENTRED APPROACH FOR DISTANCE EDUCATION CURRICULUM

by

Nelly Oudshoorn

> **Nelly Oudshoorn**, born in the Netherlands in 1950, graduated from the University of Amsterdam in 1983 in Biology. She has worked at the Open University in the Netherlands on developing a policy for the emancipation of women in distance education. At present she is working at the Department of Women's Studies in Biology at the University of Amsterdam on a research project concerning the role of gender in the development of biological theories about women and men.

Introduction

Female students are an important target group of the Dutch Open University. In this paper we will focus on the question of how to develop a distance education curriculum which is relevant to women's interests and needs. In her article "Toward a Women-Centered University," Adrienne Rich suggests two categories of women's needs that would, if genuinely met, change the nature of the university. The first category includes both the content of education and the style in which it is treated. The second category includes institutionalized obstacles that effectively screen out large numbers of able women from engagement in higher education (Rich, 1979). We will focus mainly on the first category, with emphasis on the content of education and some attention to questions of pedagogical style.

The Challenge to Male-Biased Curriculum

As women (after continuous struggle) have gradually been admitted into the academic world, they have been educated in a male intellectual tradition. In 1938 Virginia Woolf was one of the first intellectual women who questioned the very nature of academic education.

> The questions that we have to ask and to answer about that [academic] procession during this moment of transition are so important that they may well change the lives of all men and women for ever. For we have to ask ourselves, here and now, do we wish to join that procession, or don't we? On what terms shall we join that procession? Above all, where is it leading us, the procession of educated men?... Let us never cease from thinking—what is this "civilization" in which we find ourselves? What are these ceremonies and why should we take part in them? What are these professions and why should we make money out of them? Where in short is it leading us, the procession of sons of educated men? (1963:62–63).

Woolf suggested that women entering the academic world should bring with them the education of their female experience (Rich, 1979). In the reemergence of feminism in the past fifteen years, female students accepted this challenge. Feminists started the enormous task of analyzing and re-thinking the content of the curriculum, and they discovered that there is no discipline that does not obscure or devalue the history and experience of women. In disciplines where women are considered, women are studied as a special category, as objects deviating from the male standard.

Feminist scholarship globally has revealed the extent to which the male academic tradition and the knowledge which it has created is only a partial definition of reality and has proffered ways in which feminist approaches can transform androcentric bias. This new scholarship was named Women's Studies, and many universities in western Europe, North America and the Pacific now have special Women's Studies programmes.

However, Women's Studies is a rather new phenomenon and the curriculum suffers from male bias. If we want a more women-centred curriculum in distance education, we must develop strategies to change the male tradition in the curriculum in the same way as at the traditional universities. This position is not unproblematic.

Is it possible to introduce Women's Studies in distance education? Should we aim at introducing separate Women's Studies courses or should we try to modify the curriculum by integrating the knowledge of Women's Studies in the mainstream courses? We will analyze two strategies for the introduction of Women's Studies into distance education curriculum, based on experiences in England and the Netherlands, looking at both content and style of curriculum.

Women's Studies Courses in Distance Education

In 1983 the British Open University presented its first Women's Studies course, *The Changing Experience of Women*. The course deals with issues and questions about women's position and sex differences, psychological and physical explanations of female sexuality, historical analysis of women's employment and economic dependence, health, and violence (Kirkup, 1983).

The course team had to face some serious problems. Some questioned the academic validity of the course, but with the cooperation and support from more "heavy-weight" academic women, they could convince university authorities that the Women's Studies course was academically credible. Financial needs represented another obstacle. No university funds were made available to them and they had to start with a small EEC (European Economic Community) grant.

Women in the British Open University fought hard for the establishment of a Women's Studies course because they knew that feminist scholarship was not given enough recognition anywhere else in the curriculum. They did not choose the strategy of modifying the mainstream curriculum because it was not apparent in 1982 that Women's Studies could be integrated into the general university curriculum *(ibid.)*

In choosing this position, they followed one of the trends in the women's movement in which it is argued that, in order to develop as a strong academic field, Women's Studies should be established as a separate discipline. The attempt to integrate Women's Studies within existing disciplines is in this opinion very risky, because faculty are already strongly committed to the present structure and content of their disciplines. The advantages of a separate Women's Studies course are clear. Feminist academics could direct their energy towards a project that would produce concrete results, instead of spending all their time trying, with unsure results, to convince their colleagues of the importance of Women's Studies. Another advantage is that women working on the course are gaining more experience in developing women-centred course material. This can strengthen them in developing material for new courses in their own disciplines. Most important, however, is that the *Changing Experience of Women* has made this material available for the first time to a whole body of female and male students *(ibid.)*

But there are also disadvantages in developing a separate course. In times of economic crises, Women's Studies courses run the risk of being cancelled for financial reasons. This risk will exist as long as Women's Studies is not accepted by academic authorities as an indispensable part of curriculum content. Another disadvantage is that students who don't choose this course will never be confronted with the enormous amount of new thinking that emerges from feminist scholarship. Probably only those people (mostly women) who already took some interest in the changing position of women and men will take this course, and Women's Studies will never become an integral part of the distance education curriculum.

Integration of Women's Studies

I arrived at the Open University (OU) in the Netherlands in 1983, before the first students started their studies. The development of this new educational institution had been the topic of political discussion and policy-making with regard to women's emancipation and "second chance" education, and women were identified as one of the most important target groups. These ideas were successfully incorporated into the legislation of the OU as a result of efforts by women working in the governmental Department of Education backed by lobbying from the women's movement. A special advisory committee comprised of both students and staff was established at the OU to develop a policy of outreach to women. This committee focused on items like creating facilities for childcare, equal representation of women and men in the organization, tutoring and counselling of female students, and an emancipatory curriculum content. For me this was an ideal situation to start my job as a staff member, specifically charged with the task of developing a more women-centred approach to the courses of the OU.

One of the policy aims of the Open University was to stimulate new development in higher education and to develop a pluralist curriculum which would be relevant for students of different social and religious backgrounds. Within this framework, it was easy to argue for the inclusion of Women's Studies in the curriculum, and all the requisite conditions seemed present for integrating Women's Studies with the OU course offerings. As a new organization, we were not beholden to the androcentric biases of the traditional universities, and most of the course material still had to be written. The curriculum structure was designed with a more flexible division in disciplines, which linked up perfectly with the interdisciplinary character of Women's Studies. Within this innovative educational climate the academic staff were expected to be more idealistic and less bound to tradition than their colleagues at the other universities.

From the outset we focused our attention on claiming a structural place in courses which seemed of particular relevance for Women's Studies. In this way the knowledge developed in Women's Studies programmes in other universities could be integrated with the planned courses of the OU, ensuring that Women's Studies would not be ghettoized but rather would become an integral part of the curriculum. We did not campaign for the development of a special Women's Studies course, because such a course could easily become an alibi for OU authorities to exclude Women's Studies from the mainstream courses. Instead we concentrated on advising staff members and authorities, organizing discussions with professors, and informing the academic staff about recent developments in Women's Studies. After two years of this activity, during which we had to face some major problems, it is evident that integrating Women's Studies is an enduring and complicated process.

Predictably, most academic staff members of the Open University did not have in-depth knowledge of Women's Studies or feminist theory. Everyone who applied for a job was questioned about her or his opinion about women's emancipation, but even so the faculty has the same traditional ideas as other university faculties. Most academics had a strong commitment to the present content of their discipline, and working in a new organization with emancipatory goals did not change this commitment. In order to gain acceptance as an academically viable institution, the OU exercised cautious conservatism in course development. Thus, the positive political climate which characterized the beginning of the Open University was short-lived.

Structural reorganizations in the OU, combined with financial problems, resulted in an attitude of protecting disciplinary territory, which minimalized the willingness of faculty to integrate new areas of knowledge. Although they continued to express concern for women's issues, most were not willing to give priority to integrating relevant new material with the curriculum. In our strategy we had focused our attention on the university authorities, who supported our plans for Women's Studies. However, the autonomy of the academic staff made it difficult to develop a central policy for integrating Women's Studies. The very idea of control over content by people not directly involved in the development of the courses conflicted with the notion of "academic freedom." And as it turned out, even the university authorities had never been very enthusiastic about the idea of Women's Studies. They had mainly accepted the integration idea to avoid the development of a separate Women's Studies course and now expressed doubts about the quality and academic viability of Women's Studies. Nevertheless, a few staff members were willing to integrate Women's Studies in their courses, and I will now consider how these courses differ from mainstream courses.

In traditional courses, women are invisible: we have a Womanless History, a Womanless Literature, and a Womanless Economics (McIntosh, 1984). Many staff members tend to solve this problem by adding a few famous women to their courses. Gerda Lorenz has named this the "add-women-and-stir-approach" (Vander Haegen, 1985). The OU course on Literature is an example of this approach: in this course some paragraphs address female writers through the history of literature. This type of curriculum revision can be easily accomplished and is by and large accepted by the scholarly community as a reasonable response to the demand of women for curriculum change. At first glance it seems to be an improvement over the traditional courses, but for feminists working at curriculum revision this approach was perhaps even worse than the traditional exclusion of female-centred content (McIntosh, 1984). It pretends to include women but really shows us only a famous few; the lives and works of most women remain invisible to us. Women don't really exist unless they make something of themselves in the public world and in the spheres of power. Scholars choosing this type of curriculum revision tend to be sympathetic to some feminist goals but to assume that their disciplines are basically functioning well. They were willing to think about the problem of why so few female students choose to study economics or technology, but they would not consider the possibility of changing the content of those courses.

It is precisely the content of the disciplines which is challenged by feminists. Curriculum change has to involve more than simply identifying the existence of a few notable women while leaving the vast store of traditional knowledge untouched. In the last fifteen years, feminist analysis of the content of many disciplines has shown that women, if included at all, have been traditionally seen as an anomaly or a problem. In biology, medicine and psychology, women's bodies and behaviour are seen as deviations from the male standard, and women's physiology and psychology are regarded as having pathological tendencies (Fausto-Sterling, 1985). The need for a critical feminist analysis and reinterpretation of traditional knowledge is increasingly clear.

It is here that the real transformation of the curriculum begins, with the questioning of basic concepts and methodologies across all disciplines. The Open University course in Epistemology—the development of scientific thinking—deals with these questions. Traditional courses on epistemology consider science to be the domain of men and believe in the sex-neutral character of knowledge. Feminist philosophers have criticized this belief and are addressing questions as to what extent the overrepresentation of men in the academic world has affected scientific thinking. Scholarship which reflects on the masculine character of epistemology, philosophy and methodology addresses questions such as:

- the relation between objectivity and masculinity;
- the focus of scientific thinking on mastery and control; and,
- the impact of female experience on scientific thinking.

To its credit, the OU team that developed the epistemology course has integrated parts of this new scholarship into the course.

Another example of this approach is the OU course on staff management. Traditional courses on staff management focus on people working in the organization, without differentiation between men and women. A critical reader soon discovers that the authors are in fact only talking about men. For the development of the OU course on this subject, I proposed to the team that they focus attention on the position of women in the organization, to deal with topics like the traditional placement of females in subordinate (often lesser paid) jobs, the position of female managers, affirmative action, parttime jobs, childcare facilities, and "feminine" styles of management. This approach to curriculum change is not easy to establish, because it requires agreement from faculty that their disciplines are not functioning well and challenges them to rethink their basic assumptions and redefine the extant body of knowledge in their discipline.

Integration Versus Separate Courses?

Reflecting on the first years of the Open University, I have to conclude that the positive governmental policy with regard to women's emancipation did not have much impact on the development of the organization. The idealistic plans were left stranded for the most part because they were not translated into structural and policy decisions and did not have sufficient support from academic staff and university authorities.

During the integration project we had to adjust our optimistic expectations, and in fact we misjudged some major factors. We gave too much value to the renewal power of a new organization. The extent to which changes can take place depends on the beliefs and commitments of the people working within the organization and the general opinion set by people in related organizations (in this case the traditional universities). We highly misjudged the extent to which the staff, mostly men, still value the traditional male-biased university system. At the beginning of the OU, the climate seemed favourable for creating a more women-centred organization. Everyone agreed, rhetorically, that the new organization would seriously consider the educational needs of women, but the political climate changed. The grim socio-economic reality of our times promotes this male-dominant way of thinking, i.e., why should women be educated at a time of great unemployment?

The strategy of integration is not an easy one. Although we achieved some desired results, we are still a long way from reaching a balanced curriculum. For this reason we have reconsidered the possibility of developing special Women's Studies courses, with the realization that developing separate Women's Studies courses versus integration of Women's Studies in the overall curriculum creates a false dichotomy. Why shouldn't we aim at both? With this vision the integration of Women's Studies in the curriculum does not take the place of Women's Studies; different strategies have different aims and results. Women's Studies is developing into an area of research with its own disciplinary identity and scholarly status and clearly requires a structural place in the academic curriculum. Students who want to pursue the fundamental intellectual questions surrounding gender inequality should have the opportunity to choose special Women's Studies courses as well as receiving instruction in other courses which do not exclude or distort the female experience (Spanier, 1984).

The success of the integration strategy is highly dependent on the status of Women's Studies in the academic world. As long as Women's Studies are considered to be of no academic value and marginal to inherited knowledge, this strategy will be a continuous struggle. But it is worth the attempt at a time when Women's Studies is making progress and establishing an international position in academic research. Likewise, accepting the challenge of developing separate Women's Studies courses is worthwhile at a time when there is an increasing interest on the part of students. Eventually, university authorities will become interested and even supportive, if only because of the market value of such courses. And with either strategy, the enthusiastic and continuous involvement of feminist distance educators is necessary in order to generate a community within which we can learn from each other's experiences.

Pedagogical Style in Distance Education

Changing the content of the curriculum is only one of the strategies for developing a more women-centred approach to distance education curriculum. The question is not merely *what* you teach but also *how* you teach. In the past decade, feminists have developed ideas for new approaches to learning based on experiences in the women's movement, in which style and content are inseparable.

One of the central features of a feminist approach is the valuation of personal experience as a basis from which to build theory. This approach implies a different way of treating academic knowledge, making it less abstract and obliging students to test it against their own individual and group experience. It also implies a changed relationship between teachers and students in which teachers function more as expert resources than as infallible pedagogues (Kirkup, 1983). In women's courses a style has evolved which is more dialogic, more exploratory, and less given to pseudo-objectivity than the traditional mode. This style is more personal and by nature antihierarchical (Rich, 1979).

The structure of distance education makes the adoption of a women-centred approach rather difficult, but there are means by which we can advance certain essential principles, including increasing tutorial hours, encouraging more active student participation and creating contexts for interpersonal explorations between students. Recognition of the need for more interaction between students was the prime reason that the distance educators at the Open University in England organized a one-week summer school for their Women's Studies course (Kirkup, 1983). Tutors and counsellors can also adapt themselves to a less hierarchical, more personal approach to their work while encouraging students to form their own discussion groups.

Even with conscious efforts at change, structural obstacles remain in the mode of teaching in distance education. Tutoring and counselling are often marginal aspects of the instructional design. At the Open University in the Netherlands the rate of tutorial hours is low, and this component of distance education is an easy target for financial cutbacks. The role of teacher in distance education has been largely replaced by self-instructing course material, which for feminist educators requires a closer scrutiny of course design. Is it possible to develop courses that incorporate aspects of women-centred teaching styles as well as content? Special techniques are being developed to render the materials "student active," such as in-text questions and non-directive, personalized writing styles.

The pedagogical/didactic theories underlying the development of most course materials are characterized by an unexamined assumption of sex-neutrality, and a differentiation in learning styles between women and men is virtually ignored. The introduction of a more women-centred pedagogy will have to come from distance educators experienced in and committed to feminist teaching styles, drawing on knowledge gained from involvement in the women's movement and applying that knowledge to the evolving curriculum and methodologies of Women's Studies. Without question, a lot of work has yet to be done.

References

Fausto-Sterling, A. (1985). "Myths of Gender." *Biological Theories on Women and Men.* New York: Basic Books.

Kirkup, G. (1983). "Women's Studies 'At a Distance': The New Open University Course." *Women's Studies International Forum, 6*(3), 273–82.

McIntosh P. (1984). "The Study of Women: Processes of Personal and Curricular Re-vision." *The Forum for Liberal Education, 6*(5), 2–6.

Rich, A. (1979). "Toward a Woman-Centered University." In *On Lies, Secrets and Silence: Selected Prose 1966–1978.* New York: W.W. Norton.

Spanier, B. (1984). "Inside an Integration Project: A Case Study of the Relationship Between Balancing the Curriculum and Women's Studies." *Women's Studies International Forum, 7*(3), 153–59.

Vander Haegen, E.M. (1985). "Integrating the Curriculum: Women's Studies as Social Change Agent. Exploding Myths About Women." *Current Issues in Education and Human Development, 4* (1), 31–41.

Woolf, V. (1963). *Three Guineas.* New York: Harcourt, Brace & World.

Chapter 18

EXTRAMURAL TEACHING AND WOMEN'S STUDIES: "WOMEN IN SOCIETY" COURSE

by

Shelagh Cox and Bev James

Shelagh Cox was educated in Great Britain, the United States (Washington, D.C.) and Canada (Toronto) before emigrating to New Zealand in 1966. Her first degree was in Philosophy and English Literature, from Reading University. While she was primarily at home, housekeeping and bringing up three children, she did freelance writing. Within the last twelve years she has trained in Sociology and has a M.Phil. in the Sociology of Literature. She is currently employed as a lecturer in the department of Sociology at Massey University; her academic interests include Sociological Theory and Women's Studies. She writes fiction and wants to work toward blending imaginative and intellectual understanding in both her creative and academic work. She is contributing editor of a book to be published by Allen and Unwin (New Zealand) entitled *Public and Private Worlds: Women in Contemporary New Zealand.*

Bev James has lectured at Massey University, Palmerston North since 1979. During that time she has been involved in teaching at a distance in courses on New Zealand society, the family and Women's Studies. She gained her D.Phil. in 1985; her research was based on a single-industry town and her topic the effects of men's occupations on women as wives and mothers. Her research interests cover the areas of feminist theory and methodology, family policy, community studies and race and class inequalities. She is currently embarking on a study of economic and social changes in the community in which she did her D.Phil. research. She is also interested in comparative research. In 1985 she spent six weeks in China, where she studied the position of women and family policy. In 1986 she was a teaching scholar at OISE, Toronto, for two months. There she pursued her interests in family policy and equality rights legislation.

Editor's Note: In 1978, a course entitled "Women in Society" was developed by the Sociology Department of Massey University, in Palmerston North, New Zealand. The course was offered only to on-campus students until 1984, when it also became available to distance learners through the university's Extramural Department. At the end of that year two of the course lecturers, Bev James and Shelagh Cox (who also served as Course Convenor), taped a discussion between themselves in which they describe and evaluate the teaching of women's studies at a distance. Their dialogue, as presented here, offers insights into collaborative teaching and learning about women's own lives.

Shelagh: Let us talk first about our own interests in the course...

Bev: I started off in the Sociology Department teaching in the area of the family, but my major interest has always been gender relations, and I've found it really exciting to get into the Women in Society course... which I've been teaching now for three years. My main research interest is the relationship between family and work. I am currently writing a doctoral thesis which looks at women's experiences of "home" and "work," particularly how they cope with the effects of their husbands' jobs on their lives. My study was carried out in a one-industry town, and the women are wives of mill workers.

Shelagh: My interest in feminism, and in the Women In Society course, has grown very rapidly and very markedly in the last few years. We find that we've really changed through the course, with the course, in lots of ways... it's been that way for both of us. My own interests include Sociological Theory, and the Sociology of the Arts; I also enjoy writing short stories.

The Women in Society course was started in 1978 by Ephra Garrett, who is a New Zealand feminist. She taught it on campus until 1982, when three of us took over—Robyn Leeming, Bev James and myself. Robyn Leeming has left the university, so now it is Bev James and I who teach it. It's been taught internally for some years, and it was taught extramurally—that is, distance teaching—for the first time in 1984. (Massey University is the officially empowered university in New Zealand to do distance teaching.)

Bev: Our students stretch from the very north of New Zealand right down to the south of the South Island. Massey itself is situated in the southern part of the North Island, and it is quite central in that respect, but it has to take in an absolutely huge constituency of students. New Zealand is really a long, thin country, and communication can be rather difficult. A lot of people are isolated in rural areas, a long way from any further education. There aren't many tertiary educational institutions in provincial centres, so people very much rely on the Extramural Department of Massey University to obtain continuous or further education. And we do have quite a number of rural women who are enrolled in the course. Shelagh, you were going to comment on the composition of the students.

Shelagh: We haven't done an official survey but yes, there were a large number of rural women. We could have expected that, because if they lived in the cities they could go to internal courses at other universities. Many are farmers' wives, running the house and living in small communities—many of them apparently housebound with young children. This is all rather impressionistic, gathered from their work where they make reference to their own experience. We also have women who are working in the paid work force, and our impression is that these women are primarily nurses, teachers, social workers—the service professions. We also had a fair number of men. There really were quite a surprising number of men—many of whom find women's issues arise in the course of their jobs. A couple of the men were head teachers, some were in government service—that sort of thing. The internal course has no male students. Also, the internal students tend to be a lot younger (18-22 years of age) whereas extramural students range from the young student to beyond retirement age. You get a far wider age range of students doing the extramural course than doing the internal course, and overall an older student group.

Bev: They also vary in that some are rather seasoned extramural students who have been around for maybe ten years. This is perhaps the last course that they are doing. Some may be completing a degree. We also have students who have had only one year of extramural work prior to taking our course. So we have that kind of experiential range as well.

Shelagh: Prior to enrolling in this course they either have to complete a Sociology prerequisite or other academic papers; everybody who comes into the course will have had some experience of university work. We usually start off with about sixty-five students and those who make it through to the end and take the exam number about fifty, the dropouts apparently finding it too difficult to combine studies with work and family.

Bev: As to the content of the course... Developing the materials for extramural students has forced us to make all the connections in the course explicit, and to firm up the conceptual framework that we were trying to put across to the internal students. We've looked at the experience of women from three angles and have tried to integrate them—that is, the material conditions of women, ideology and women's consciousness. Those are the three aspects that we're continually looking at, through all the different issues and areas that we cover. We have a contemporary emphasis, based on New Zealand society in the context of modern western society; therefore we are looking at women's experiences in the context of capitalism, in terms of economic and material relations, and in the context of patriarchal relations and how these affect culture and society.

Shelagh: Although we do focus primarily on a contemporary point of view, we also use nineteenth-century European developments as a comparative framework—especially in reference to the development of capitalism and industrialization. This emphasizes and makes very stark the whole patriarchal ideology. But your part of the course, the theory part, is much more contemporary than mine.

Bev: I'm aware of a criticism that one or two students have put to us about the emphasis on western culture in the course, and I'm hoping to do something about this—to get a more Polynesian element into the course and to look at Maori and Pacific Island women's experiences in New Zealand. We also encourage students to apply the ideas that are presented to them, to think for themselves, to develop their own perspectives and really to pursue their own interests. That is very much an implicit aim in the course, wouldn't you agree?

Shelagh: Yes, within the framework we've set up; it is a sociology course with the emphasis on theory particularly, and we set up certain theoretical frameworks within which the students pursue their interests. Thus it is an academic course that allows students to pursue personal interests.

Bev: The course is divided into three areas: theory, images and social conditions. I've had responsibility for developing the theory area, which is divided into several sections. First of all, the students take a critical approach to sociological theory. I'm taking the point of view of Dale Spender, looking at the politics of knowledge and how sociology puts forward a dominant view of the world which ignores the experience of women. We introduce this idea to students at the beginning of the course—that women are invisible, not only in society but within sociology as well. The way that sociology has been conceptualized, the sorts of sociological theories that are used, the concepts, the methods, and so on, are all very male-dominated. So we sensitize students to that and make them aware of the way that women have been left out of sociological accounts.

Then I proceed to what I call some of the intellectual roots of feminism. We look at Mary Wollstonecraft, and John Stuart Mill, as examples of the liberal tradition, and Marx and Engels as examples of the socialist tradition. In later lectures most of the theoretical emphasis is on contemporary feminist theories that have developed since the inception of the women's movement of the 1960s; we look in some detail at radical feminism, socialist feminism, contemporary liberal feminism and also lesbian feminism and black feminism. These last two areas in particular provide a critique of what you might call the mainstream of feminist perspectives, because they point out the way that feminist theories tend to ignore, or distort in some ways, the experiences of minority women. It is particularly in this light that I'm hoping to look at the experiences of Maori women in more detail.

Shelagh: Following from the theoretical framework comes the section on images of women. This is very much taught within the conceptual framework we have been discussing. In fact, I take as my starting point a patriarchal view of images, as they are defined within the patriarchy and reflect the interests of the patriarchy, certainly traditionally, and this is where I go back to the nineteenth century. I combine this with a Marxian view of the dominant ideology, wherein women are an underclass whose views and knowledge are not represented. This links in with Dale Spender's ideas on the politics of knowledge—considering whose interests knowledge serves, and whose experience it reflects. Within this framework we look at images of women, particularly in literature and the visual arts. We study images of women in film, and students also look critically at advertising and other images of "femaleness" in their own clubs and throughout society. We encourage them to take the theoretical framework and develop it in the specific areas that are of interest to them. Different perspectives are obviously developed within the different feminist theories, and we encourage people to find ways of breaking down the old patriarchal way of looking at things, by using feminist theory and developing what Annis Pratt has called "apatriarchal lore."

The third part of the course has to do with material and social conditions. When Robyn Leeming left we enlisted the help of several women and took a collective approach to teaching this section.

Bev: We started off with health issues. A nurse, who had previously been a student of the course, had developed a feminist perspective on nursing and women's experiences of medical institutions. We also had two women talk about women and work in New Zealand, and another woman focused on education, using Dale Spender's framework and referring to socialist-feminist work in this area.

Shelagh: All of this blended very well with what we'd both been doing concerning the politics of knowledge, which was a very integral part of the course.

Shelagh: The final area of this section was women and violence, contributed by a woman who took the course years ago when it started off, and who also has a background in sociological theory. She talked about violence in New Zealand society, and particularly her personal concern with setting up women's refuges—which she has done in Palmerston North. This brought in a strong activist element. The collective approach worked very well, as it should in a feminist course. We want to build on this, and we hope that we can develop an even more collective approach in our teaching. We particularly want to use the expertise of women who are not necessarily credentialled but who often have great skills.

The three areas of theory, images and material conditions interrelate very naturally, and we don't have to force them into shape too much. They flow together in many ways, and many of the students are able to work out interrelationships for themselves.

Bev: For their major essay, at the end of the year, many of the students have looked at some of the areas that we have discussed in lectures; for example, Shelagh's images section bore fruit in many students' essays, which analyzed things like advertisements on TV or New Zealand novels.

Shelagh: There was one fascinating essay by a Maori man, who talked about images of women in his tribal history and the way they perpetuated patriarchal images.

Bev: Other students have also brought their own experiences to bear, by looking at institutions in our society—for example, one woman who is a dietician did an essay on that profession and how it reflected the traditional role of women. Also, we have had some very good essays on nursing as a "female" profession.

Shelagh: Some of the rural women have talked about their day-to-day lives in terms of both theoretical perspectives and images—images of the "good woman" in what is called, in New Zealand, the "wop wops" (or back-blocks, i.e. very isolated areas). One woman wrote about images of barren women and childlessness. We've had some very interesting uses of this material. Compared with Canada, Australia and the United States, feminism in New Zealand is really very new and undeveloped, and there are patriarchal assumptions behind the way that most people live. It is a great struggle for many women to come out of the closet, as it were, and there is remarkably little material, so our students in their own way are developing their own written work. I think a lot of them are aware of this, that they are really doing pioneering work.

Bev: The extramural students receive study guides that go into considerable detail and follow closely the lecture material that the internal students receive. The first study guide covers the administrative aspects of the course. The study guides include things that we have written, to explain ideas and to link and clarify other material. We include readings from other authors, and we illustrate them with cartoons, line drawings and photographs. We have a good extramural department that helps us with the technicalities of that. The study guides supplement textbooks and other readings and also provide the structural basis of the course. The study guides blend the purposes of a text and an instructional guide, with directive questions and exercises. It introduces them to readings they wouldn't get by just having a textbook. I feel very strongly that it is important for extramural students to be provided with a great quantity and wide range of material, even if it looks a bit daunting to them at the beginning, because of the difficulty some of them have in getting to distant libraries. The study guides are useful as reference books which can be used long after they have finished the course.

Shelagh: Certainly in this course that is particularly true. In other academic subjects there is an established body of knowledge, and students can easily obtain books. However, because of the pioneering nature of the women's studies enterprise, the study guides are particularly important. The second study guide, *Hidden from History*—pinching Sheila Rowbotham's title—applies the theme of the invisibility of women under patriarchal rule to all three areas that we've been talking about—images, social and material conditions and a theoretical framework. The other three study guides were devoted specifically to these three areas. We have also supplemented the study guides with audiotapes. One of the first things we did was record an excellent two-woman lecture: Jennifer Waelti Walters and Mair Vethuy, from Canada, visited us during the year and did a presentation on women in fairy tales. We taped it and sent it out to the extramural students, which they appreciated. We also sent out a taped conversation I did with the women who taught collectively with us. And on national radio, last year, I talked about images of young girls, mothers and older women, and the students could send for that tape. So there's been regular input on tape during the year.

Bev: We've had very good feedback from the extramural students about the tapes; they talk about listening to them while doing the washing, or preparing the dinner...

Shelagh: We sent out a questionnaire at the end of the course asking people how they thought it had gone, and we got some really delightful answers, didn't we?

Bev: Yes, and several of them did talk about doing the ironing, for example, while listening to the tapes. The tapes are an informal supplement that underscore essential points; they're not as heavy-going as the study guides, so students can listen while doing other things. In an enjoyable way they are still learning.

Shelagh: A third component of our communication with distance students is a "vacation course."

Bev: We schedule it for two days during the May holidays. We require the students to come onto campus for this intensive course in which they receive lectures from us during the two days. It's a great opportunity for them to ask questions, have discussions about the course, and bring up any problems they are having, such as with assignments. We also show them videos and films. We pack as much in as we can. It's a very high-pressured couple of days and I think they're pretty exhausted after it; we certainly are. But as mature students, many of them older, they're very highly motivated, and they come in here wanting to get their money's worth.

Shelagh: Yes, one of them actually said, "I am going to get as much out of you as I possibly can." That's exactly how it feels at the end, when we are exhausted but exhilarated. It's very rewarding. It really does seem to be an important thing to be doing.

Bev: The reaction to the vacation course was a little mixed from the extramural students. On the whole they appreciated what we were doing in the course, but some of them thought there was too much emphasis on reading material and study guides, which we thought was a valid criticism. We did formal lectures covering the study guide material, emphasizing points, explaining concepts and ideas—which they probably found quite useful. But some of them wanted to have more small group discussion, perhaps tutorial sessions where they could get together more with other students and start applying and interpreting their own ideas and those presented in study guides. This is a major problem that we have—the lack of tutorial personnel.

Shelagh: In the vacation course it wasn't always clear if they came to listen to us or if in fact they came to talk to each other.

Bev: I think it is a conflict we have in organizing the vacation course. To a certain extent we got around it, because they had a wine and cheese social evening held at Shelagh's place—just a general social get-together. That was the first evening and it was very good; they made friends with each other. We talked about work, and about the course, but we also got to know one another pretty well that evening. Some of them said that they really appreciated that evening, and having it at someone's home was quite a change from other courses that they had been involved in. They found it very humanizing and quite an egalitarian approach.

Shelagh: We hurtle through this course at such a pace that we keep on getting new ideas, even in conversations like this, and say "what do you think about so and so?" If we get more people to help, I'd very much like to do regional courses throughout the country, and get discussion groups and local groups going. I do that in the theory course that I teach, and I think for this course it would be terrifically useful. They can work on things in their own communities which might be stimulated by but aren't necessarily included in the course.

Bev: Some of the students feel isolated because they don't get much direct feedback. They come in for the vacation course, but that is only once. They get written feedback on their essays, but that is only three times in the year, and it's only in writing. If they want any more communication with us they really have to write us letters. We have also put out a couple of newsletters, which they appreciated very much, and I think we might develop that further.

Shelagh: On one of the returned questionnaires was a suggestion for a newsletter. In fact, we might get some of the students to do a newsletter or journal; they could do the work and coordinate it. I think that we could use the goodwill and energy that so many of the students have, when we are really very much overworked. There's a limit to what we can do.

Bev: One of the issues that this course has raised for me is how important teaching is, and how communication through a course like this can raise people's consciousness—not only women, but also men. Courses like this in an academic setting are a way of reaching a very wide mixed audience—people who have experience in tertiary education, people who are very new to it, rural women, urban women, young, old, Maori, Pakeha (New Zealander of European descent), home-bound, in the work force, a variety of occupations—the whole range.

Shelagh: One can begin to break down distinctions that seem, at first, to be very rigid.

Bev: Many students have said that this course has changed the way that they have thought about their own experiences and has made them much more questioning about the situations that they're in, whether it's in the work place, or talking to their husbands about who's going to do the dishes that night—very basic aspects of life. Some of them said that they share their study guides with friends and neighbours, so we're expecting quite an increase in student numbers. Others have talked about how it's made them more critical of other university courses, that they're now looking at those courses in terms of how they are promoting a patriarchal view of the world.

Shelagh: Yes. One student wrote and said that this was her ninth year of extramural study, and it was just as well she hadn't come in and done this right at the beginning because she probably wouldn't, as she put it, have found herself accepting male-defined knowledge so meekly. It might have made her start to question all her other courses as well. Another one wrote... I don't think she actually said we had a responsibility to do the course supremely well, but she certainly implied it, because she said that the consciousness-raising that Bev was talking about can be really quite upsetting and difficult. I would imagine this would especially apply to students from some of the more reactionary rural communities that I know exist in New Zealand. It would be really very difficult and isolating. As she said, this paper disturbs and disrupts old ways of thinking and being. So women are moving on in spite of themselves, and they need support and information. This is why support groups of students could be so important in this course. I do think that the consciousness-raising aspect is very important. It's primarily an academic course, and we hold to high academic standards, exactly the same as for any other courses we teach in the second year, such as the course I do on Nineteenth-Century Sociological Theory and Bev's course on Structural Inequality. But we do realize that consciousness-raising, and personal development and knowledge, are going to be a part of what goes on in women's studies. Teaching this course, in my own experience and in the way we have developed it, and certainly from what we hear from the students, really brings home the idea that the personal is political, particularly in an emerging women's movement. And it still is emerging in New Zealand as a new phenomenon, certainly in the social circles of many of our students.

Another student talked about what she calls the "filtering" effect of a course like this. She talks to other people and it filters throughout the community, spreading these new ideas. Another student said something about how, when she started the course, she was very ambivalent, and she was very wary about being labelled a feminist. She didn't want to be that at all, and she said she was almost ashamed to be doing the paper to begin with. Now she feels that to be a feminist isn't to be an ogre, and she now says that she is a feminist even though there is still in New Zealand the feeling that feminists are some kind of bra-burning viragos—it is definitely not a complimentary term in our society.

Bev: Let me read an extract from one of the questionnaires that we got back from an extramural student, showing how a very busy woman, coping with a paid job and also running a household, manages to fit in extramural study as well. She starts off: "Textbooks and housework don't mix. Last week I was carrying Mitchell around (that's Juliet Mitchell's book, *Women's Estate*) and swotting as I went. One morning I couldn't find it until I went to hang out the washing, and there she was—washed, rinsed and spun. Missing chapters at either end, and soggy scraps everywhere, not to mention an entire load of washing that now leans to the left!" Not only the washing, but some families and neighbourhoods have been irrevocably changed by our course through these women.

Shelagh: It certainly is a tremendously rewarding experience, though tiring, emotionally taxing, and politically hard work.

Bev: We do feel that we are a little bit on show and really have to stand up and be counted over these sorts of issues—both within the university and also out there. What we do has to be of a high quality because it is going out to so many areas of New Zealand.

Shelagh: I think that we both feel that we have to do it as responsibly as we can, not to be too extreme, and not to push our own barrows too much—without sitting on the fence or selling ourselves short. It's a very difficult balance to strike, that one.

Bev: We have to develop a very solid product.

Shelagh: Yes, that's the main thing. It's not really a tub-thumping thing for ourselves at all.

Update: March 1987

Since we taped this interview, Kay Saville-Smith has joined us. We are in the process of rewriting and reorganizing the course; it will be taught in its new form from 1988. The course will have as its text a forthcoming book which Shelagh has edited and to which Kay, Bev and Shelagh have contributed: *Public and Private Words: Women in Contemporary New Zealand* (New Zealand: Allen and Unwin).

— *S. C. and B. J.*

Chapter 19

SOWING SEEDS: INITIATIVES FOR IMPROVING THE REPRESENTATION OF WOMEN

by

Gill Kirkup

> **Gill Kirkup** is a Lecturer in Educational Technology in the Institute of Education Technology at the Open University. Her work has increasingly concentrated on aspects of women's education, and the uses of information technology for distance education, but she also does work on course evaluation in general. She has been active in women's campaigns since the early 1970s. She had a son in 1982 and another in 1985 and since then is less active outside her work. Having children herself has made her much more conscious of the invisible problems faced by women studying at a distance.

Introduction

When thinking about any distance education institution and its women students—potential as well as actual—it is useful to separate out issues of access from issues of content. A critical analysis of the institution should examine why women are unequally represented in sectors of the traditional curriculum and should also examine this curriculum to see how women and women's experience has been marginalized. We don't simply want to make higher education a place where more women are more comfortable; we want to change the nature of what has previously constituted the disciplines so that we are in the content as well as in the institution, in the lecture as well as in the lecture theatre. Or in the case of distance education, in the text as well as in the armchair studying it.

Issues of access are often seen as issues of recruitment, but they also incorporate issues of content; a course designed to address issues that women find interesting or important will recruit a large number of women. The issue of access also relates to delivery systems, with content presented in new ways that will make it more accessible to women, through the way that it is written, with new examples and different perspectives, or through the design of delivery systems, for example scheduling tutorials to take into account family responsibility.

It is possible to put the issues crudely on a continuum, with a radical position at one end concerned with examining the nature of knowledge and the content of academic curriculum, and a reformist position at the other which is concerned with increasing the numbers of women enrolled in any particular course. However, most of us who are engaged with practical initiatives in our own institutions will find ourselves operating at a number of different points on the continuum, depending on the particular course or student group.

In this chapter I will first discuss access as a general concern of the Open University (OU) in England and then review three specific OU initiatives, two of which broadly address issues of improving the access of women to traditionally male areas of study and employment, technology and management, and a third which focuses on a women's studies course. In terms of both access and content, I will evaluate the success of these initiatives and look at their ripple effect on other aspects of the university. Finally, I will deal with some new, important issues of access for women raised by the introduction of information technology systems as a tool for distance education.

Applicants and Access

The key educational principle of the Open University, alongside its distance teaching methodology, is equality of opportunity through open access. This policy was stated in the government White Paper *A University of the Air* (1966) which laid out plans for the university:

> Enrolment as a student of the University should be open to everyone on payment of a registration fee, irrespective of educational qualifications, and no formal entrance requirement should be imposed (quoted in McIntosh *et al.* 1977:3).

It was elaborated further in the inaugural address of the Chancellor Lord Crowther in 1969:

> The first and most urgent task before us is to cater for the many thousands of people, fully capable of a higher education, who, for

one reason or another, do not get it, or do not get as much of it as they can turn to advantage, or as they discover, sometimes too late, that they need (quoted in *ibid.*, p. 6).

As far as the undergraduate programme and most of the other programmes are concerned, all British adults are equally eligible for a place on a course, if they can pay the course fee. But even from the beginning it was seen that some way of monitoring and even controlling access was needed in order to ensure that some groups were not being unfairly underrepresented. Theoretically, the personal and demographic data collected on application forms can be used to group applicants according to factors such as sex or previous educational qualification, and to then place entry quotas on such groups. However, this has not been a straightforward policy in the history of the OU.

Certain population groups have always been underrepresented in the OU; these groups, mainly working-class men and women, are those which might benefit most from university study, both for personal fulfilment and for usefulness in acquiring educational qualifications. The reality is that structural factors deter some people from applying to the university and from particular areas of study. In an extensive piece of survey research, McIntosh investigated who the students were in the first five years of the OU's operation and identified barriers to access. These, she discovered, ranged from simply not knowing what the university provided to questions of "availability of time, money, access to educational support systems... assumptions about verbal and numerical facility, and the use of language and the cultural background that are embedded often unconsciously in the way that courses are structured" (McIntosh *et al.*, 1977:30).

An open access system on a strict queuing basis ignores these questions, but any system which attempts to offer special assistance to one group of students is seen as discriminating against another. For example, in the early years women were roughly 45% of applicants to the undergraduate programme. However, because they applied mainly to arts and social science courses, where there were many more applicants than places, fewer women applicants got places, (roughly 40% of total enrolments). A simple occupational quota was in operation but men and women have different occupational patterns and this was not acknowledged in the quotas. Attempts were made in the admissions procedure to juggle with the male/female ratio to give women places proportional to their applications. This effort was argued to be a contravention of Equal Opportunities. Such resistance to operating quotas has led the university to abandon all quotas except those based on geographic location and those which give priority to students with no prior degree. The debate about quotas remains basically unresolved, and any attempt at positive discrimination on behalf of women is open to attack as an apparent contradiction of the open access principle.

When the Open University accepted its first batch of undergraduates in 1971, approximately 25% were women, the smallest proportion of women in the history of the university. By 1975 the proportion of women undergraduate students had reached 42.3%; it has remained close to this level ever since, and the 1986 figure was 42.9%. (This compares with 41.5% of undergraduates in other British universities [UGC, 1986]). But undergraduates are, in the mid-1980s, only 81% of the university population of registered students. Other areas of course provision have expanded rapidly. These range widely, including, for example: low-level, short and inexpensive courses and self-study packs on pregnancy or the countryside, produced by the Continuing Education Sector, which people buy without registering as students and which have sales of roughly 40,000 packs per year; and expensive, high-level specialist courses for technological upgrading or business studies requiring at least one year of study. The university has expanded these self-financing areas of course production at a time when the government has cut back its contribution to the subsidized undergraduate programme, causing that programme to contract relative to overall student numbers. To clarify the provisions the Open University is making for women in Britain, the following details how women are represented in several areas of the university:

The Undergraduate Programme

In the OU undergraduate programme, there are gender disparities in different faculties similar to those in any institution of higher education.

Table 1: Women Undergraduates Studying in Different Faculties, as a Percentage of all Students, 1985

Arts	Social Science	Technology	Maths	Science	School of Ed.	Interdiscip.
66	54	16	26	37	67	72
(11,371)	(7,654)	(2,702)	(3,395)	(4,246)	(3,283)	(1,884)

The figures in brackets in Table 1 show the actual numbers of women students. Although there are large proportions of undergraduates studying in the arts, education, and in interdisciplinary studies, women are seriously underrepresented in technology, maths and science.

Continuing Education

The Continuing Education sector contains a widely disparate selection of courses at different levels. Those which approximate the undergraduate level have lower proportions of women students, whereas short courses in personal development attract a higher proportion. These short courses are developed and maintained by separate academic units such as Personal and Cultural Education, Health and Social Welfare, and Community Education. For example, the study packs and short courses prepared by the Community Education section of Continuing Education appeal mostly to women, with topics such as The Pre-school Child, Healthy Eating, and Planning Retirement. Table 2 shows the sale of study packs and courses from the Community Education programme between 1980 and 1983, demonstrating a very different gender profile from the undergraduate programme.

Table 2: Sex of Buyers of Community Education Materials as a Percentage of all Students

	1980	1981	1982	1983
Total numbers	17,149	12,000	15,792	12,760
Sex				
Female	79	86	84	87
Male	21	14	16	13

Table 3: Women Open Business School Students as a Percentage of all Students

Course		percent
P670:	The Effective Manager	23
P671:	Accounting and Finance for Managers	15
P672:	International Marketing	15
P673:	Personnel Selection and Interviewing	36
P677:	Marketing in Action	22
P678:	Start up your own Business	30
All OBS courses		22

Open Business School

The Open University Business School has 22% women students as reflected in course enrolments cited above in Table 3.

Postgraduate Studies

The university runs an extensive postgraduate programme with a number of taught masters' degrees and degrees by research. Overall, women are only 30% of postgraduate students.

The unequal representation of women has never been an issue meriting an institution-wide initiative. The few initiatives which have been adopted have been designed and set up by individual women, or by small groups, and directed at particular perceived problem areas. However, their effects on the rest of the university have been subtly very influential. The following sections contain discussion of three such initiatives.

Women into Technology

The most well-established efforts to provide special help for women to enter courses where they have been previously under-represented have been in the technology faculty. In the early 1980s the proportion of women students entering the foundation course of the technology faculty was about 13% and was much lower in the higher level courses. Apart from a small number of enthusiastic female staff, the faculty was not actively committed to changing that situation. Although some members of the faculty were concerned, few had suggestions about changes, and fewer still seemed willing to try. It was a parttime member of the university's regional staff, in collaboration with a member of the Centre for Extension Studies at Loughborough University, who designed a scheme which used distance teaching materials to retrain women who have had a career break, usually for family reasons, and who now want to return to work.

In 1978, Swarbrick (1980) surveyed women technology students during their residential summer school period. She found that, in general, women were given poor advice about course choice and were sometimes even discouraged by university staff from studying technology. When they began studying they lacked confidence, especially about mathematics, but those who persisted became very enthusiastic. Swarbrick's work did not generate positive initiatives from the faculty, so she herself explored what schemes could be implemented if external funds could be obtained.

The first Women in Technology Scheme (WITS) addressed the needs of women already qualified in science and technology who had taken a career break and needed their skills updated to re-enter employment, a clearly defined group with specialized educational needs. The authors of the scheme describe their rationale for wanting to use distance education to reach these women:

> The retraining needs of experienced women engineers who wish to retrain and return to work after several years at home are not necessarily the same as those of the young male trainees who are normally found in college classes. There are problems of distance and travel to college, lack of childcare facilities, inconvenient timetabling, apart from the inappropriateness of courses. Distance learning methods along the lines pioneered by the Open University seemed to offer a solution....

> Although the number of women qualified in engineering and technology who could benefit... from such courses would not be vast, there must nevertheless already be a substantial number. Either they do not realise it is possible to study a single OU course, do not perceive it as a career strategy, or at a time when family budgets are most stretched, simply cannot afford the fees (Swarbrick and Chivers, 1985).

The aims of the scheme are described in the programme's publicity leaflet:

> The Women in Technology Programme is for women who left work for family reasons and are now considering returning. It is designed to encourage women into technological areas by:
> - either acquiring basic technical knowledge, or
> - broadening and updating previous technical knowledge, and
> - promoting confidence, knowledge and skills in career planning through a continuing education programme while they are still at home.

The scheme is primarily funded by the Manpower Services Commission (MSC), (an unfortunate title), a government agency which funds schemes of education and training to improve the individual student's chances of employment, as well as providing training for sectors of the economy with a shortfall in skilled labour. Although "Manpower" connotes an unconscious ideology, the MSC has been a major source of funding for various training and retraining projects for women. It provides the bulk of the funding for the scheme and the Open University provides staff resources and facilities. The scheme initially provided bursaries for thirty women to study a higher level undergraduate course. These bursaries pay all the course fees as well as the costs of a specially designed preparatory weekend and students' travelling expenses.

The first group of bursary students began their studies in 1982. Although the project was originally designed as a one-year experiment, there was such a demand for places that the MSC renewed funding for 1983 and 1984. In those first three years 118 women received bursaries. A report on the project (Swarbrick, 1984) identifies some of the positive outcomes of the scheme:

> *The flexi-study home-based approach of the OU is very appropriate to the women at time of application....* The relatively small numbers, their geographical distribution and their varied specialisms can be catered for satisfactorily by a proven nation-wide, distance-learning system.... Part-time home-based study also enables them to begin looking for work before the end of the course, and can be combined with a job if necessary....
>
> *Participation in the project has a positive effect on the students in a variety of ways.* If looking for work is not an immediate possibility ["within three years" was specified in the criteria] either because of family commitments, geographical location, or the levels of local unemployment, WITS women do not allow their newly refurbished skills to languish again. Technicians continue to degree studies, graduates embark on research, skills are put to good use in the community or in free-lance home based consultancy work.
>
> *WITS women become more confident about seeking work.* The [preparatory] weekend provides opportunities for discussing advertisements, for local interview simulation, for assessing non-vocational experience positively. Successful progress through the chosen OU course restores confidence in knowledge and skills thought forgotten (pp. 57–58).

Swarbrick (1986) also analyzes the reasons for the success of the students in terms of the extra support mechanisms provided. For example, the scheme was administered by a small enthusiastic staff in the Leeds regional office. They engaged in a lot of counselling with applicants and students and were frequently phoned by students needing support. The scheme also had a special compulsory residential weekend at the beginning of the course, something which does not occur in any other OU course. This seems to have been a source of great motivation for most students, especially during those early weeks of a course when getting to grips with distance learning can be a struggle.

Unfortunately, the benefits of the flexibility provided by distance learning for women with family commitments do not continue when they look for employment. In that sense, distance teaching does not provide any solution for women coping with multiple commitments; it only postpones the problem. Because of the nature of the scheme, the majority of women had children under the age of ten. Many felt that it would be extremely difficult to fit their childcare responsibilities in with the demands of a fulltime job in industry; this perception caused them to look for teaching or research jobs in education.

In the 1984 report, Swarbrick argued for an extension of the scheme to include a *conversion course* for women who had been deterred from studying science and maths in their earlier education and would like to do so now. The MSC were convinced by her arguments and in 1985 the scheme was extended to include thirty women who had left work for family reasons and were considering returning but who wanted to *enter* technology for the first time. These women, whose educational and work backgrounds were non-technical, received bursaries for two years. In the first year they study the foundation course in technology; if successful they proceed in their second year to a more specialized, higher level course of their choice from the areas of technology and maths.

Both schemes have been popular, and a large number of applications are received every year from women who fulfil all the criteria for a bursary. Few women fail to complete the course, and women completing the course who are actively looking for jobs are finding them. A couple of the successful students from the first scheme now help tutor the weekend course for students in the "conversion" scheme.

The scheme is now well known within the technology faculty and perhaps even better known outside it. The year 1984 was declared Women Into Science and Engineering (WISE) year by the British Equal Opportunities Commission, and the publicity this generated was used to establish a WISE group within the Technology Faculty (Carter, 1987). The WIT scheme was, and remains, the core initiative around which other smaller initiatives have been developed. Its obvious success provides a fertile environment receptive to suggestions for further schemes, and issues and problems identified through monitoring the scheme have stimulated new initiatives. For example, it has been extremely difficult to find career information for the WITS students. Career publicity for engineering, directed at school leavers, was perceived by WITS students as inappropriate for them, even discouraging, since it did not address their most important problem, how to organize a career and extensive family responsibilities. Therefore, the group has produced a careers booklet directed specifically at mature women, Career-Wise (Kirkup, 1986), partly funded by a grant from the Equal Opportunities Commission.

The WISE group is continuing work in three particular areas: tutors, course content, and teaching methods. It is looking at what can be done to recruit and support women as tutors on technology courses: at the moment these are a small proportion of all technology tutors and there would be clear benefits for staff and students if there were more. In 1987, for the first time, there will be a day meeting for women tutors of technology and computer science courses, in the hope of providing the stimulus for a network to develop among women tutors. The university will fund tutors to attend this meeting.

In the case of content, the priority is to make sure that the new technology foundation course is at least non-sexist and at best reflects the fact that hopefully over a quarter of the students may be female. Members of the group have engaged in discussions with the course authors and have been asked to operate as critical readers.

In the case of teaching methods some of the most enthusiastic tutors have expressed doubts about the appropriateness of their own teaching, because of the different experiences that women students bring to the course. Most study examples used to help explain difficult concepts in physical science presume "male" knowledge, such as about car engines and central heating systems. Tutors need help to develop new ideas that will be more applicable to the experience of either sex. The WISE group is exploring how to get access to the expertise that now exists outside the university in special women's Technology Training schemes and apply it to distance teaching.

Unfortunately, despite the far-reaching positive effects and enthusiasm for the programme, a large portion of the male staff of the technology faculty have remained personally unaffected by and uninterested in the scheme. Perhaps the best that can be hoped for is authoritative backing from a few key members of the faculty, such as the Dean, and in-principle support from the major university committees. Those of us with a primary commitment to women's issues must now get on with the job, and each successful achievement, such as the Women in Technology scheme, gives us a firmer base for meeting that challenge.

The next scheme I will discuss, Women Into Management, used the example of WITS as a lever within a completely different area of the university, the Open Business School, to convince the Director of the School that a scheme for women students could get external funding and internal and external recognition. The initial idea for the Women into Management scheme was based on WITS but includes new aspects suggested by experience with WITS.

Women Into Management

In 1983, the OU presented its first management course, *The Effective Manager,* the foundation course for the rest of the management programme. A self-financing unit called the Open Business School (OBS) has been established to develop and manage a whole programme of business and management courses. From the beginning its courses recruited few women, a fact that was remarked upon by those of us who noted such things but did not seriously concern the school as a whole. It was felt that the number of women students reflected the proportion of women in management. It also reflected the pricing policy of the courses, which were priced with companies in mind as buyers (in 1987, *The Effective Manager* sells for £495, the foundation course in the undergraduate programme for £158, plus a summer school fee of £99). Companies were buying for their aspiring (male) employees, and although the school's overt policy was to provide management education to fulfil the needs of individuals, the economic power of company sponsorship has affected programmes and pricing policy.

In 1984, a small group of women met to discuss the poor representation of female students in Business School courses. The only area of the country with a 50% representation from women was

London, where the Greater London Council, a self-declared equal opportunities employer, had made a block-booking. At our meeting we discussed alternatives for promoting access for women. For example, did we want a course on management for women? If so, which women? Or did we want to add "women" to the present content of the Business School, perhaps by writing a course for male managers about their female employees? We decided that the best place to begin was with women who had the capacity to become managers but lacked either the confidence to try or recognition or training from their employers. A short course which would enable women to build up their confidence seemed a good way to begin. The successful outcome of the WITS bursaries, especially the "return to study weekend," provided an excellent model.

One problem for female students in distance learning courses in traditionally masculine areas is that, as the minority gender, they may be very isolated for their whole period of study. A student can end up as the only woman in a local tutorial group and, more crucially, she may be in a group where her male counterparts already have successful unbroken career patterns, an experiential disparity which can contribute to a woman's lack of confidence. Early experiments with group entry schemes (Peacock et al., 1978) had demonstrated the importance of mutual support for students with common characteristics such as childcare responsibilites or no paid work. When a group of such women were kept together as a tutorial group for the whole year, they were much more likely to complete the course than were similar students assigned to a more typically heterogeneous group. Swarbrick (1984, 1986) found that her students valued the preparatory residential weekend they attended at the beginning of their year of study as the most valuable part of the scheme. For some who lived in sparsely populated regions of the country this was their only contact with other bursary students and almost their only contact with other women studying the same course; they met other women who shared their problems and their worries, and this camaraderie fired their confidence and enthusiasm. Any scheme for women in the business school would have this "grouping" aspect as a priority.

At first there was little encouragement from within the OBS, and it was suggested, for example, that market research among managers was needed to assess their wishes and their likely response.

On the face of it, such suggestions are intended to be helpful, but in reality they are not, since money is never forthcoming for this sort of research. If a group is to take it on themselves voluntarily, they will spend at least as much time and energy on the background research as they will on actually developing their initiative. Indeed, sometimes such suggestions look suspiciously like attempts to keep us harmlessly busy. However, when it was appreciated quite how much money the MSC was giving to the technology faculty in the form of bursaries, the environment of OBS became much more supportive. The MSC did decide to fund a scheme, one which is a step more ambitious than the WITS scheme, for producing a short course, *Women Into Management* (WIM), to include a residential component as well as a complete multi-media package. Illustration I gives the structure of the course.

The course as it was finally written had an optimistically broad spectrum of potential students in mind. The Course Guide states:

> This course is not exclusively for women, but it was designed for women and, in particular, for women in the following categories:
>
> - women seeking to return to work and enter a management career after a career break, either immediately or in the future;
> - unemployed women seeking a management post;
> - women currently in paid work, full or part-time, who want to move into management either within or outside their organisation;
> - women who are contemplating taking a career break but wish to return to work thereafter at a managerial level; and for,
> - training and personnel officers and anyone with responsibility for organisational training.

The suggestion that men could take the course could be seen as a failure of nerve. Although it is possible to have special bursary schemes for one sex, the general open access aims of the university have been used to block any developments of single-sex courses. (This is a difficult issue, especially in regard to the women's studies course, discussed later.)

Forty students would be funded for the pilot *Women Into Management* course, before it became available publicly, and these forty would then receive bursaries to continue with the next course, *The*

Illustration 1: Components of the Women into Management Course

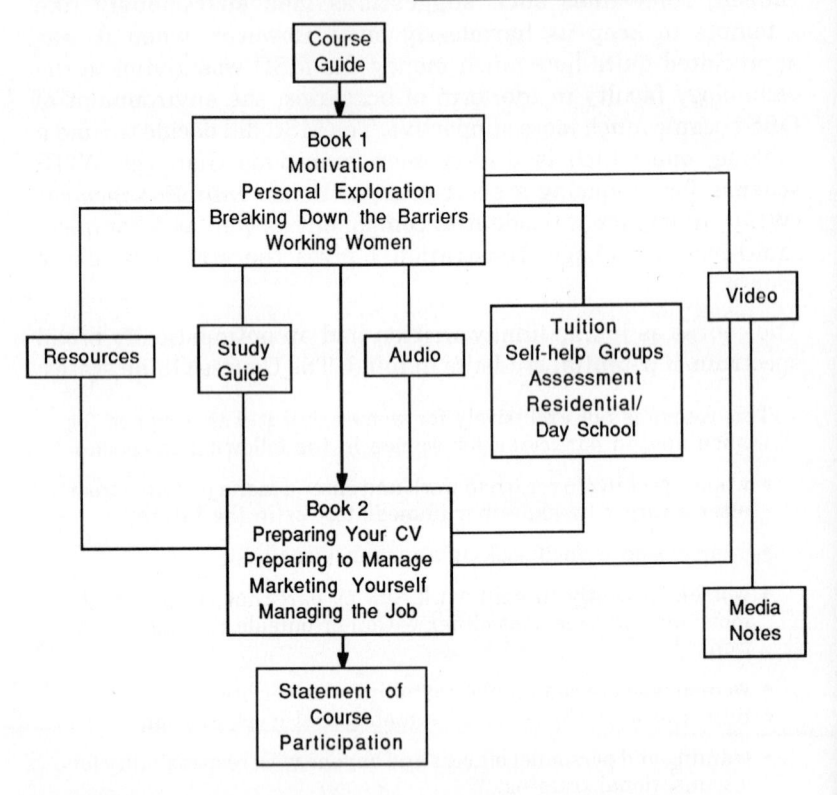

```
                    ┌─────────┐
                    │ Course  │
                    │  Guide  │
                    └─────────┘
                         │
                         ▼
              ┌────────────────────────┐
              │        Book 1          │
              │      Motivation        │
              │  Personal Exploration  │
              │ Breaking Down the Barriers │
              │     Working Women      │
              └────────────────────────┘

┌──────────┐  ┌────────┐  ┌───────┐  ┌──────────────┐  ┌───────┐
│Resources │  │ Study  │  │ Audio │  │   Tuition    │  │ Video │
│          │  │ Guide  │  │       │  │Self-help Groups│ │       │
└──────────┘  └────────┘  └───────┘  │  Assessment  │  └───────┘
                                     │ Residential/ │
                                     │  Day School  │
                                     └──────────────┘

              ┌────────────────────────┐
              │        Book 2          │
              │   Preparing Your CV    │
              │  Preparing to Manage   │
              │   Marketing Yourself   │
              │    Managing the Job    │      ┌────────┐
              └────────────────────────┘      │ Media  │
                         │                    │ Notes  │
                         ▼                    └────────┘
                  ┌─────────────┐
                  │ Statement of│
                  │   Course    │
                  │Participation│
                  └─────────────┘
```

Source: Smith, 1986.

Effective Manager. The first course would be seen as a preparatory course for women who would then study other management courses, although only the bursary students will be committed to both the *Women Into Management* course and *The Effective Manager* when they initially register. Other students will be able to register only for WIM if they wish. The pilot went ahead September to November 1986. Although there was no official publicity during 1986, word got around and there was a flood of requests for places, primarily from employed women who had already begun their management careers. Few came from unemployed women—a group the course team especially hoped to reach. There was also a surprising amount of interest from private industry, surprising since they had previously appeared loathe to send their female employees on management courses. One private company and one Local Education Authority asked to be part of the pilot in 1986, and were taken on a fee-paying basis in addition to the forty bursary students. Interest expressed by specific sectors of industry and the public services suggests that there would be a place for supplements to the course specific to these sectors.

The pilot scheme has been evaluated, and it is hoped that a longitudinal study of the bursary students will be funded to monitor the more long-term effects of the course. The initial evaluation suggests that the course has a successful future. Students commented extensively on all the teachings materials, and the unit texts in particular are being modified to take account of their comments. Many students had no idea what to expect and were initially surprised at the amount of material which dealt with personal development. But their comments at the end of the course indicate that this aspect of the material was very successful. It is heartening to know that it is possible to teach such skills at a distance. We have decided that in future we must tell students that even if they decide not to enter management or paid employment, the kinds of personal skills that they learn in the course have applicability across a wide range of areas. We have redefined our own objectives to the extent of saying that our most important concern is to open up choices for women, so that with the help of the course they should be better able to pursue further management training and work, *if they choose to do so.* But the course should provide enough honest information for a woman to decide not to do so, without any sense of guilt or failure.

Students who were least successful in completing the course were students who were not in work—the group which was difficult to recruit in the first place. This highlights the difference between this scheme and WITS, where a criteria for the bursary was not having been in paid employment for at least two years. The content material of the technology course was not overtly vocational although the intention was that women should use it to establish a career. It is possible while studying it to postpone thinking about a later career. On the other hand, much of the course content of WIM deals with work experience and practical exercises on how to deal with work-related events such as an interview or producing a curriculum vitae. This would appear to be the major reason for the failure of the course for unemployed women.

Finally the success of the pilot with industry may turn out to be a mixed blessing. It is gratifying that training officers in companies find the OU course to be of good quality and are willing to buy it. However, as I said earlier, group bookings of courses by companies can strongly affect various aspects of course development and policy, such as pricing policy. And it seems that WIM is likely to cost students almost £100 each for the first few years of its life and is therefore likely to be too expensive for students on low incomes who do not have some form of financial sponsorship. The course team is exploring the possibility of OU-subsidized bursaries for some women, since the MSC bursary scheme has a limited life.

At the time of writing the effect of this course on the Open Business School programme is still uncertain. The group which produced the course material is well aware that the publicity and impetus of such an initiative should not be lost and hopes that a *Women Into Management* group will be established, similar to the WISE group, with an interest in monitoring the situation for women in OBS in general and the course content in particular, and even perhaps beginning new research in this area.

An Interdisciplinary Women's Studies Course:
The Changing Experience of Women

As I discussed in the introduction, at the Open University we are not just concerned with gaining access for women to courses for which they have not applied in the past; rather, we have more radical notions about the nature of content and the creation of knowledge. The outcome of this aspect of feminist work has been seen most obviously in the second level interdisciplinary course: *The Changing Experience of Women.*

The course was first presented in 1983, late in the day to be presenting a women's studies course relative to similar developments in regular universities. As with the initiatives described above, the course was established by a small number of very junior academic staff members. In face-to-face universities, students, often the most radical members of the institution, can make their needs and demands felt. In a distance teaching institution like the OU, the student body is scattered, and student groups find it more difficult to recruit active members and to exert pressure on the institutions. Students are older and their studies are only one part of their responsibilities. This seems to contribute to general passivity over issues other than those immediately related to courses or to financial issues such as fees, grants and media costs. Therefore, those of us working for change have no forceful student body to provide leadership or support. Unfortunately, although priding itself on breaking new ground over issues of teaching and student recruitment, and despite occasional accusations of Marxist bias, the OU has been criticized as very conservative in terms of course content at the undergraduate level:

> The debates about democratising education tended to centre upon the question of access. The kind of education which was to be offered was not seen as requiring any modification. The curriculum in particular was seen to be unproblematic, with natural "levels" and "subjects"... it followed that the Open University naturally had to have a conventional university curriculum if it was to maintain "standards" and receive the support of the academic community—a university with any other kind of curriculum was almost a contradiction in terms. As a result, despite some experimentation with multi-disciplinary courses or with new specialisms, the content of courses at the OU tend to reflect the conventional views of what counts as university knowledge. The implications for openness and social mobility are clear—OU curricula embody many of the characteristics that seem to be connected with the failure of "working-class" students in schools in the first place (Harris and Holmes, 1976:80).

For our purposes, the argument is just as valid if "working-class" is replaced by "women." If the Harris and Holmes argument is true (and I think many of us hope that the situation is not really as bad as all that!) it is imperative that we develop courses and research methods which embody the theory and practice which have been developed in the last twenty years of the Women's Liberation Movement.

The history of the course and some of its inherent problems have been described by Kirkup (1983) and Leonard (1984). Its aims are described in the 1986 Course Handbook as follows:

> *The Changing Experience of Women* is an inter-disciplinary course which focuses mainly on women in British society. The course aims to encourage students to reflect on the changing experience of women, to inform them about the position of women in Britain both contemporarily and historically, and to engage them in analysing the situation of women and thinking about the possibilities for change.

The course is worth one-half credit towards a B.A. degree (one twelfth of a degree) and includes sixteen text units, a one-week summer school component, eight television programmes, and three 60-minute audio cassettes. Illustration 2 shows the components of the course and how they fit together.

The Changing Experience of Women course attempts to cover widely diverse content in some depth. It begins by looking at some of the issues most frequently raised in the press and in general conversation about women's position and sexual differences in society. It goes on to look at biological explanations for sex differences, the links between sex and gender, and the psychological and physical explanations of female sexuality. Students are then introduced to women's descriptions of their own experiences, using extracts from prose, poetry, and diaries, and a complete novel: *Daughter of the Earth* by Agnes Smedley. They examine both the text and the illustrations of a woman's magazine, to analyze its presentation of a woman's world. They are introduced to historical material on the family to give them some understanding of how the modern family has developed and to examine the family as a social organization and an economic and ideological structure dependent on women's unpaid work. Students are also introduced to an historical analysis of female employment in the U.K. and an analysis of women's economic dependence vis-à-vis state policy. The final units cover three distinct areas where feminist analysis and activity have been very strong: education, health and violence, ending with a review of some of the most current questions and debates in the women's liberation movement and some indication of future concerns.

Open University in the United Kingdom

Illustration 2: Course Components of The Changing Experience of Women

Unit No.	Unit Title	Course Readings, Set Book & Supplementary Readings	TV Program	Casette No.
1	The Woman Question	[Allin and Hunt]	TV 01 Introductory Programme: Women Speaking	
2	Biology and the Development of Sex Differences	Bartels	TV 02 Women and Spott	
3	Women as Part of Nature	Arditti Brown and Jordanova Rose		
4	Sexuality	Freud Bland	TV 03 Sexual Identity	AC592, side 1 (30')
5	Reading Women Writing	Smedley Grimm Lessing		
6	Femininity and Women's Magazines	Woman's Own		AC593 (60')
7	Women in the Household	Scott and Tilly		
8	The Development of Family and Work in Capitalist Society	Hall Hall	TV 04 Public Space and Private Space	
9	The Family: Daughters, Wives and Mothers	Edholm Rich Comer [Bose] Stott	TV 05 Working for Love	AC592, side 2 (30')
10 11	Women and Employment	Alexander Bruegel Braybon Morgall	TV 06 An Office Career	AC 594, side 1 (30')
12	Economic Dependence and the State	Barrett and McIntosh Brophy and Smarr		
13	Educating Girls	Stanworth Deem Kessler and McKenna	TV 07 Raising Sons and Daughters	AC594, side 2 (30')
14	Health and Medicine	Lennane and Lennane Graham and Oakley		
15	Violence Against Women	Russell Dobash and Dobash		
16	Moving Forward		TV 08 Everyday Violence	AC595 (60')

Source: Whitelegg, 1984.

Illustration 2 shows that the eight TV programmes and cassette tapes are closely integrated with the text material. There is also a book of set readings which students are expected to buy and a compulsory summer school where students engage in practical work such as film analysis. They have about seven hours of face-to-face tutorials throughout the year and are encouraged to set up their own study groups. To gain the half-credit they must satisfactorily complete both the continuous assessment and the final exam.

The Changing Experience of Women course was evaluated during its first year and proved successful with students and tutors; external examiners were particularly impressed by the ability of students to range coherently across disciplinary boundaries. Student numbers each year have remained high (Table 4).

Table 4: Registration Figures for *The Changing Experience of Women*

	1983	1984	1985	1986	1987 (predicted)
Undergraduates	544	563	472	525	512
Associate	174	119	140	160	162
Total	718	682	612	685	674

In 1986, there were thirty-seven tutors working regionally on this course, most of whom have had experience in teaching women's studies. Their commitment to the course is high and so is the enthusiasm for writing a new women's studies course. And, although the course has aroused some controversy, those university staff who feel it should be removed from the undergraduate programme constitute a tiny minority.

It is hard to trace the effects of this course on different aspects of the university. Certainly it has affected some students dramatically: they report having changed their whole view of life as a result of the course. I don't wish the course to sound like an exercise in political conversion since personal changes often occur as a result of any successful experience in education, in whatever field of study. Most women's studies courses report similar comments from their students (see Kirkup, 1983), but most university courses are taught through group work, using shared experience and elements of consciousness-raising which facilitate intense personal involvement. This is harder to achieve in distance education and accounts for the great success of the one-week residential summer school.

Within the academic body, the course has had a number of effects. Since the course team began work on the course more feminist academics have joined the university and some were recruited specifically to work on the course. The course now provides a focus for meetings of female staff interested in a variety of issues to do with women, as well as an instant network for new female staff. The academic credibility of the course has helped make feminist research and women's issues a valid area of inclusion in other areas of course content, across all the faculties, whereas women's issues were previously not considered properly "academic." There is now a women's studies research group in the university, made up of a small core of academics, most of whom were originally women's studies course team members. The group attempts to provide a focus for research in aspects of women's studies within the university. However, women's studies in the wide academic sense has been so successful in generating new research questions in a variety of disciplines that it becomes harder over the years to focus onto one academic unit or research group. Writing an interdisciplinary course was both difficult and exciting for the Course Team, and we feel that working across disciplines has produced a better course than any which might have been produced by one faculty alone. The course is now coming to the end of its life. It has been so successful that in principle the university is committed to producing a new course, twice as long, worth a full credit rather than a half credit. However in practice the economic climate within the university is such that people are under great pressure to make their first commitment to mainstream courses, and finding staff who are able to be involved in interfaculty, interdisciplinary courses of any kind is increasingly difficult.

New Information Technology and Access

The new initiative for change in distance education, unlike other changes, is neither small scale nor the work of a few committed women; rather it is large-scale, technology-driven, numbering among its most enthusiastic supporters a disproportionate number of men. On the surface, this is does not sound like good news for women.

At the Open University, we have made extensive use of all forms of media, especially electronic media: television, radio, and the telephone. There is enormous potential for new information media, such as satellite and cable communications and the various applications of microprocessors, to affect our course design and delivery. At present such developments also appear to be inevitable. Whether we are enthusiastic "hackers" or pessimistic "luddites," we must assess the effect of such new technology on our female students in particular. Microcomputers are being seen as potential vehicles for computer-assisted learning, using commercial software such as statistical and spreadsheet packages as well as specially designed teaching packages. Microcomputers are also seen as general purpose tools for the student, providing the possibility of using word processing as well as new forms of communication via modem links. Rumours abound amongst the student body about whether or not it will be necessary to own or have access to a microcomputer to do some OU courses and, if so, when, and which machine will do. Articles like the following have been appearing in the student newspaper:

> *MICRO CRUNCH TIME NEARER*—*but don't rush to buy just yet*
>
> CRUCIAL negotiations with Government departments and computer firms are bringing the OU's new policy on home computing nearer to reality—but students will have to wait for next Spring for firm details.
>
> **Best Deal**
> One positive step in the right direction is the appearance of a computer which meets the OU's specifications and is nearer the price target which the University has set.... "We are still actively seeking external funding," said Deputy Vice-Chancellor Norman Gowar. "It will be the Spring of next year before we can advise students about the best deal we have been able to negotiate" (*Sesame*, December 1986).

Whatever ultimate deal is struck with the government or suppliers, and whatever financial arrangements are agreed upon, such as loan schemes or discount buys, students will have to make a financial investment. In early 1987 the university had almost finalized plans with a particular manufacturer. But, because of the volatility of the microcomputer market in Britain I have avoided specifying the outcomes of these decisions on the principle of "don't count your chickens until they have hatched." The wording of the above article suggests that students are poised, waiting for a decision so they can "rush to buy." Our knowledge of women and their present use of computers suggests that *they* won't be rushing.

Research on computing use in schools has shown that girls are less enthusiastic than boys (Culley, 1986), and that experience with a microcomputer is more likely to *reduce* the girls' enthusiasm, while the boys' is *increased* (EOC, 1983; Collis, 1985). The psychological reasons for this have been explored to some extent by Turkle (1984), who postulated that the sexes have completely different ways of reacting to the machine. However, social reasons seem more obvious and relate to the association of computers with other machine-based "masculine" activities (often known as "tinkering with"), and with "masculine" school subjects such as science and maths. Boys are also much more likely to have had experience with computers outside school. The authors of the EOC Report (1983) claim that boys are nine times more likely to have the use of a home computer. The data that is available about who buys microcomputers in Britain suggests that the family most likely to have a machine is one with a teenage boy in the house (Culley). Collis and Culley asked school children who had a machine who in the family would be least likely to use it. In both surveys over 90% replied "mother."

The information we have about OU students and their access to microcomputers is taken from a survey done in 1984; the following table shows the sample grouped by occupational category and gender.

Table 5: Access to Microcomputers by Sex and Occupation

Occupational category	Female % access	Male % access	Difference F:M
Housewives	44.0	—	—
Admin. & management	43.9	56.6	-12.7
Primary Teachers	52.2	71.3	-19.1
Secondary Teachers	61.0	70.8	-9.3
Higher Education Teachers	61.1	82.8	-21.7
Other Teachers	29.2	53.9	-24.7
Medical	34.5	37.3	-2.8
Social Services	28.2	46.0	-17.8
Other Professions	26.6	49.5	-22.9
Qualified scientists & engineers	72.7	68.5	x-+4.2
Tech Person	57.4	68.4	-11.0
Clerical & Office	28.1	39.9	-11.8
Sales & Service	34.2	47.0	-12.8
Retired	11.4	34.1	-22.7
Total	42.2	59.3	-17.1

Table 5 shows quite clearly that in all occupational groups, except educators and "qualified scientists and engineers," women are much less likely to have access to equipment. At present, OU courses which include compulsory computing have been lending the student a kit or providing access through a terminal in a local study centre. Even so, women have been much less likely to take these courses. In 1985, women constituted 27% of all students studying a second level mathematical computing course, 24% of those studying a third level mathematical computing course, and 14% of those studying a second level electronics and computing course. It is in fact in courses in the technology and social science faculties that a policy of compulsory ownership/access will be implemented first. The technology faculty is at the moment negotiating such a policy for their foundation course, which will then enable them to presume access, eventually, for students doing higher level courses. It is in the area of technology and mathematics that women are already underrepresented.

A policy on home computers could drive women back into choosing courses in more traditional female areas of study. If a home computer linked via a modem ultimately becomes the major delivery system for all components of distance teaching, as predicted by the most optimistic futuristic hackers, women may find distance teaching much less attractive. In their eagerness not to be left behind in the new technological revolution, the OU is taking less than seriously the fact that some student groups, women among them, might be disadvantaged. Although the issue of economic disadvantage is now being taken seriously in attempts by the university to get the government to subsidize equipment, decision-makers do not take seriously the issue that this technology might be gendered in a way that our other distance teaching technologies were not. This leaves those of us working on improving access for women with more problems, and we must begin now to prepare new initiatives for our female students.

Conclusion

For most (male) academics at the Open University, the student is still "he." However, female distance educators, in developing the three successful initiatives described above, have done a great deal to improve the receptiveness of the university for further initiatives. Common themes can be seen in those already in operation, such as the students' enthusiasm for opportunities to meet other women students studying the same subject and with similar domestic backgrounds, and the enthusiasm of many women to study in traditionally male areas if they are given a special invitation and even a slight amount of special support. However, the overall conclusion must be that we dare not rest on our laurels. The seeds that we have planted are growing well, but they are still seedlings and, if not tended carefully, will either wither away or be thoughtlessly trampled on by others.

References

Bowles, Gloria and Renate Duelli-Klein. (Eds.) (1983). *Theories of Women's Studies,* London: Routledge and Kegan Paul.

Carter, Ruth. (1987). *WISE Women at the OU.* Paper given at the Fourth International Arts and Science and Technology Conferences, University of Michigan, Ann Arbor, 1987 (in conference proceedings).

Collis, Betty. (1985). "Reflections on Inequities in Computer Education." *Education and Computing, 1*(1), 179–86.

Culley, Lorraine. (1986). "Gender Differences and Computing in Secondary Schools." Report published by Department of Education, Loughborough University of Technology, U.K.

Equal Opportunities Commission. (1983). "Information Technology in Schools: Gudelines for Good Practice." London: London Borough of Croydon for the Equal Opportunities Commission.

Harris, Dave and John Holmes. (1976). "Openness and Control in Higher Education: Towards a Critique of the Open University." In Roger Dale *et al.* (Eds.). *Schooling and Capitalism.* (pp. 78–87). London: Routledge and Kegan Paul.

Kirkup, G. (1983). "Women's Studies 'At a Distance': The New Open University Course." *Women's Studies International Forum, 6*(3), 237–82.

Kirkup, G. (1986). "Career-wise: A New Start in Technology—Women Tell Their Stories." United Kingdom: Open University, Walton Hall, Milton Keynes.

Leonard, D. (1984). "The Changing Experience of Women at the Open University." In M. Hughes and M. Kennedy. (Eds.). *Breaking the Mould.* London: Routledge and Kegan Paul.

McIntosh, Naomi E., with Judith A. Calder and Betty Swift. (1977). "A Degree of Difference." In *The Open University of the United Kingdom.* New York: Praeger.

"Micro Crunch Time Nearer—But Don't Rush to Buy Just Yet." *Sesame*. No. 110. Open University, Walton Hall, December 1986.

Peacock, Geraldine, with M. Susan Hurley and Jonathan F. Brown. (Summer 1978). "New Opportunities for Women: A Group Entry Project at Newcastle Upon Tyne." *Teaching at a Distance, 12,* 33–42.

Smith, Rosemary. (1986). "Course Guide for Women into Management." *Open University*.

Swarbrick, Ailsa. (Spring 1980). "To Encourage the Others: Women Studying Technology." *Teaching at a Distance, 17,* 2–14.

Swarbrick, Ailsa. (April 1984). "Women in Technology." A Report to the Training Division of the Manpower Services Commission on the Retraining Programme for Qualified Experienced Women Technologists. (Unpublished paper, from the author, *Open University*.)

Swarbrick, Ailsa. (1986). "Women in Technology: A Feminist Model of Learner Support on the Open University." *International Council for Distance Education, 12,* 62–66.

Swarbrick, Ailsa and Geoff Chivers. (1985). "Evaluation of the Women in Technology Scheme." Contributions to the Third Gasat Conference, April 13–18, 1985, England. London: Chelsea College University of London, Centre for Science and Mathematics Education.

Turkle, Sherry. (1984). *The Second Self*. London: Granada.

University Grants Committee. (1986). *University Statistics 1984–85.* Vol. 1. *Students and Staff,* Table 1 H.M.S.O.

Whitelegg, Elizabeth. (1984). "Course Guide to *The Changing Experience of Women.*" Open University.

PIONEERS IN DISTANCE EDUCATION

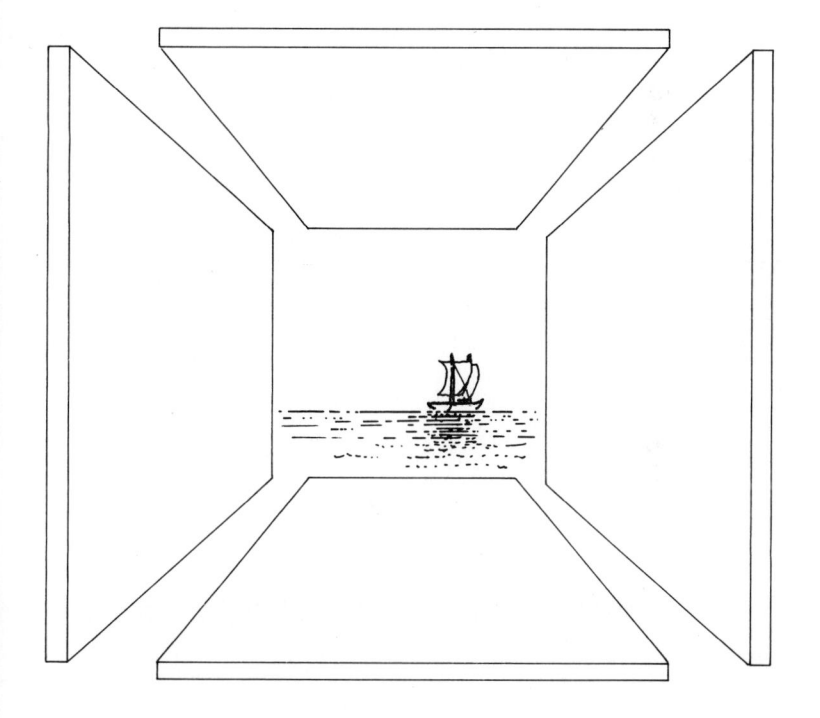

Editor's Introduction

Thousands of women are engaged in distance education, and most are involved in the kind of teamwork without which meaningful achievement is impossible. However, there are also individuals whose contributions to the field have helped chart the course for the rest of us, and these are the pioneers of our trade. Their creative initiatives and energies have set the stage, and they represent the beginnings of a wide network through which women in distance education have steadily expanded their links with one another. We have multiplied as new programmes have been developed but we are still at the nascent stage of our work, as this book has articulated.

In this final chapter, Diana R. Carl offers tribute to twenty-five pioneering women whose individual contributions to distance education have advanced international progress in the field. Representing myriad aspects of distance education administration and course delivery, the brief profiles of these educators remind us of the accomplishments of women in the past. In particular, Carl has highlighted the work of women who have been innovators in the use of educational telecommunications for distance learners. By identifying a portion of those women who have been in the vanguard, we can draw inspiration from their work while noting the continuing achievements of women in distance education who are now building on that inheritance. — *K. F.*

BRIDGING THE GAP: THE CONTRIBUTIONS OF INDIVIDUAL WOMEN TO THE DEVELOPMENT OF DISTANCE EDUCATION TO 1976

by

Diana R. Carl

> **Diana R. Carl,** Ed.D., is an assistant professor in the Education Department at Mount Saint Vincent University, Halifax, Nova Scotia (Canada). For more information on her work, please refer to Chapter 7 of this volume.

Author's Note: The author extends special gratitude to Anna Stahmer, who provided many leads for this study.

Dedication

This chapter is dedicated to those women whose names do not appear here but whose work has made a difference in the practice of distance education. Their work, too, must be recognized and remembered.

In recent years there has been an attempt to analyze histories, including histories of education, in terms of the presence and contribution of women. The roots and structures of earlier historical dogma have been questioned in the light of these investigations. Hubbard (1983), for example, argues that although research has been described as "value-free," in fact, all research is influenced by the politics, economics and sociology of the time and by the value system of the researcher. Most history has been researched by white males and reflects the values of this group. The absence of women from history is a symptom of this value-laden research and of the assumption that male-generated research speaks for all humanity. The absence of women from texts has meant more than just the failure to document works of specific women: entire philosophies and structures have been built on patriarchal assumptions, with inadequate attention paid to the impact of a significant female population. Dodson-Gray stated:

> It is clear and becoming clearer as women historians do their research in women's studies that patriarchal history works hard to make history the story of men, or literally *his* story! Women's accomplishments are *erased,* and when, like the UN Declaration of Human Rights, the accomplishment itself cannot be erased, the women's crucial role in giving it birth is simply *not remembered* (1982:76).

Searches of the literature and observations of distance education systems reveal surprisingly few women. The question arises as to whether histories of distance education are following the value-laden, androcentric tendencies described above. Given an absence of systematic documentation, distance education, as a field, may run the risk of following the same pattern as other histories. Women are noticeably absent from the literature, and little documentation exists to examine their impact on the development of distance education. This chapter is intended to stimulate others to examine seriously the field of distance education in the light of what individual women have accomplished.

The survey focuses on women around the world who have either worked in distance education or have influenced its development, with the objective of naming them and identifying their accomplishments. Lessing (1985) points out the difficulty of analyzing past works without placing some distance between the present and the past. The year 1976 was selected as a cut-off point to allow sufficient perspective to be placed on the work of the women cited in this chapter.

Many researchers (such as Martin, 1982; Lagemann, 1983; Dodson-Gray, 1982; Lerner, 1979; and Beard, 1946) have called attention to the influence of patriarchy on the classification of roles in history and in social structures. The field of education is said to consist of a set of characteristic elements. Contributions to education are judged according to how they "fit" with these pre-existing elements. Although distance education is a relatively young field, its literature is already filled with references to these elements of patriarchy.

An example of how these structures have affected the development of education in general will demonstrate the problems they pose for distance education. Martin (1982) analyzes Pestalozzi's description of Gertrude and her instructional activities with her children in the home. Pestalozzi concluded that while Gertrude's interactions with her children should be observed and emulated by educators, her practices were not considered education. Martin effectively demonstrates that Pestalozzi discounted the value of mothers as teachers, the home as an environment for learning, and the family as a unit for learning. Martin's caveat regarding acceptable avenues for investigation in education is important to this study. It is not enough to consider the contributions of women according to established criteria. The roots of these criteria and the assumptions surrounding the theory and practice of distance education are necessarily called into question (Lerner, 1979).

In conducting this inquiry, it was important to look beyond the existing definition of distance education. For example, some nominees technically did not work in distance education per se, but through their work educators were able to plan "educationally sound" distance education systems. The question also arose as to whether communities setting their own education agendas using distance techniques qualified as being distance education since technically the providers were also the learners. The "grey" area in which distance education overlapped with distance provisions of other services also presented questions regarding whether the activity was truly a distance *education* activity.

For this study, criteria for assessment of contributions were generated which allowed inclusion of activities which: 1) led to the further development of distance education systems; and 2) took into account distance education activities not undertaken by a formal educational institution but in which education was a primary motive. Therefore, some who may not have served traditional distance education functions have been included.

Authors appear to agree that present-day distance education had its origins in either 1840 or 1850 in England followed by the establishment of a French correspondence school in Germany (Wedemeyer, 1985; MacKenzie *et al.*, 1968; de Freitas *et al.*, 1986). No accounts mention the involvement of women in these establishments; however, they do describe the work of Anna Eliot Ticknor who founded the Society to Encourage Studies at Home in Boston, Massachusetts, in 1873. MacKenzie *et al.* (1968) said Ticknor had inquired into similar organizations in existence during that period in England, which leads the present author to question whether other women in England were instrumental in the development of these organizations. A search of relevant literature, however, revealed no clues. Researchers differ in their descriptions of the development of the history of distance education from that point onward. There is also variance between their accounts and information obtained as a result of this investigation. Several of the women listed here appeared to have had important impacts on the development of present-day institutions, yet these women, with the exception of Anna Ticknor, were noticeably absent from existing chronologies.

This paper could not possibly represent fully women's contributions to distance education. Only women whose work could be found and verified were included. Many of the women suggested for inclusion worked in the post-1976 period and, since we cannot yet know the long-term effects of their work, they are not included here. No doubt readers will know of candidates other than those listed. Although their names do not appear, researchers in distance education must recognize their contributions as part of the ongoing development of the field. This chapter is an incomplete sketch to which others are invited to add further information, in order to create a more focused and total picture of the impact of women on distance education.

Data was solicited in a variety of ways. An initial mailing list was compiled from membership lists of the Women's International Network and the International Council for Distance Education. Requests for nominations and further information were sent to these names. Networking played a significant role in the development of this paper, as one request for information would result in additional sources. Follow-up information about each nominee was requested via telephone or letter if the nominee was alive, or through inquiries to other sources if she was deceased. Verification of position held, functions and publications was obtained through those in a position to verify the work, through library searches, or through contacts with governmental and non-governmental agencies associated with the nation where the nominee did her work. Histories of education and, specifically, correspondence education were consulted wherever possible. Bibliographies and other publications which were particularly helpful are included in the reference section of this chapter; an appendix provides a selected bibliography of publications by women whose profiles are included here (see Appendix A).

The following, then, are brief summaries of the work of twenty-five women who have contributed significantly to distance education and whose pioneering efforts have set standards for new generations.

Beelitz, Anne
Deutsches Industrie-Institit, Köln, West Germany

Anne Beelitz had a decisive influence on the formation of international contacts between distance educators in Europe and on the establishment of qualitative standards in the private sector of the distance studies market. She worked to achieve cooperation between companies and their associations in the free market and distance study practitioners and theorists.

Bonness, Gertrud
Rustin Lehrinstitut, Berlin-Muenchen, West Germany

In the late 1940s, Gertrud Bonness reconstructed the oldest German correspondence school, founded in 1896 in Western Berlin, thus ensuring its survival.

Brock, Dee
Public Broadcasting Service, USA

Dee Brock was Director of Information and Marketing at the Telecommunications Center for the Dallas County Texas Community College District, where she was involved in all aspects of telecourse production. In 1974 Brock created the telecourse *Writing for a Reason* which has been used for first-year composition in hundreds of colleges. *Writing for a Reason* was considered a major stepping stone in the active involvement of higher education in using television for distance education.

Burns, Red
Alternate Media Center, New York City, USA

Red Burns has been involved in interactive telecommunications experiments for community education since 1971. In 1975, she directed the implementation of a two-way cable television system at Reading, Pennsylvania, and evaluated its community education uses. Earlier she was the evaluator of a similar system put into place for post-secondary education in Florida (Dayton-Miami Valley Consortium). Her publications in 1974 and 1975 included two books encouraging educators to use the education and community access channels of local cable systems. In 1975, she was a member of the Federal Communications Commission Advisory Conference on Research Concerning the Educational

Uses of Cable Television. Under the sponsorship of the U.S. Information Service, she conducted video workshops for teachers in France and Germany in 1974. She has distinguished between different video formats and their implications for developing educational programmes. A founder and director of the Alternate Media Center, Tisch School of the Arts, New York University, Burns was appointed Adjunct Professor of film and television for the school in 1974. She approached technological research and applications from a user perspective and worked to encourage the design of communication systems for education from the point of view of the user's needs and wants, as opposed to those of the producer of education.

Campbell, Audrey L.
University of British Columbia, Canada

Associated with the University of British Columbia Extension Department since 1957, Audrey Campbell was appointed Director of Credit Courses in the Centre for Continuing Education in 1972. She coordinated the Guided Independent Study Program which produced print-based and, later, video-based courses. Between 1974 and 1976 she obtained substantial grants for the expansion of the Guided Independent Study Program and the development of a criminology certificate programme for correspondence study. The first television course offered for degree credit in British Columbia was developed under her administration in 1975 and was offered over several cable television systems throughout the province of British Columbia the next year.

Carney, Pat
Gemini North, Inc., Canada

In 1976, as president of Gemini North, Pat Carney was asked by the provincial government of British Columbia to head the Distance Education Project, to explore distance delivery options for education in that province. She was a principle designer of the Satellite Tele-Education Project (STEP) which carried out experiments using the Hermes satellite. As Manager of the Distance Education Planning Group she authored the *Report of the Distance Education Planning Group on a Delivery System for Distance Education in British Columbia,* which became the underpinnings for the Knowledge Network in Western Canada.

Cross, K. Patricia
Educational Testing Service, USA

Since the late 1960s, Patricia Cross has researched and published on non-traditional learners in post-secondary education. Her work has influenced admissions policies of universities as well as methods used to teach the adult non-traditional learner, many of whom are distant learners.

Erdos, Renee
External Studies College of the New South Wales, Department of Technical and Further Education (TAFE), Neutral Bay, Australia

Renee Erdos's contributions date from 1944 when she was appointed to write correspondence courses for adult students. She was Head of the College of External Studies from 1959-69 and was the first woman appointed head of a section in TAFE. In 1970-71 she was appointed Head of Correspondence Study at the Francistown Teachers' Training in Botswana by UNESCO. From 1972-75 she was employed by the Swedish International Development Authority as Head of the National Correspondence Institution intended to be part of the Institute of Adult Education, Faculty of the University of Dar es Salaam, Tanzania. In 1976 she was employed by the Danish International Development Assistance as a consultant in correspondence education in the Extra-Mural Department of the University College of Swaziland. She was Vice President of the International Council for Correspondence Education from 1961-65 and President from 1965-69. In 1970, she chaired a seminar for the UNESCO Institute for Education on Correspondence Courses for in-service teacher training at the primary level in developing countries. Erdos's publications between 1974 and 1976 document experiences in setting up distance and correspondence education systems in developing countries.

Hudson, Heather
Canadian Department of Communications—Agency for International Development of Telemedicine, Canada and the USA

Heather Hudson has published on college curriculum-sharing, using satellite, telecommunications planning for rural development, the ATS-6 satellite Alaska experiment, and communications and development of rural areas. She helped formulate policy guidelines for development of northern communication services which have been used for education, community development, and health care. In 1970 she was a consultant to the Policy, Plans, and

Programmes Branch of the Canadian Department of Communications, studying the impact of computer technology and cable television on northern Native populations in Canada and assessing their communications requirements. From 1972–74, she was responsible for the planning and execution of the evaluation of the Northern Pilot Project for the Canadian Department of Communications. This project introduced communications media into Inuit communities of the central Arctic and Indian communities of Northern Ontario. From 1974–76 she evaluated the use of the ATS-6 satellite for telemedicine in bush communities in Alaska. She was consultant and acting manager for the Wa-Wa-Ta Native Communications Society and prepared broadcast plans for remote areas of Ontario, negotiating with common carriers and communication agencies. She helped to plan a satellite experiment using the CTS Hermes satellite and conducted studies for Alaska Telemedicine.

Jelly, Doris
Communications Research Centre, Ottawa, Ontario, Canada

In 1973, Doris Jelly worked on the planning and coordination of Hermes Communications Satellite, which led to the establishment of some notable Canadian distance education satellite-based networks. She was responsible for the scheduling of satellite resources through negotiation with NASA (the National Aeronautics and Space Administration of the US Government), the identification of resources and their allocation to meet the needs for proposed experiments on Hermes, and the development of experimental plans in coordination with experimenters and Department of Communications staff. Overall, twenty-six experiments by twenty agencies were completed. The accomplishments relative to distance education included: tele-education for the Federal Public Service Commission which employed the use of videoconferencing from St. John's, Newfoundland to other Newfoundland and Labrador locations for training purposes; the Telemedicine Project of Memorial University of Newfoundland, which experimented with the use of slow-scan video in health care and in continuing medical education; an interactive two-way video network between five campuses for tele-teaching undertaken by the Université de Quebec and the Quebec Ministry of Education; experiments with the Ontario Educational Communications Authority which led to the establishment of the TVO (TV Ontario) Academy via satellite; experiments with the British Columbia Ministry of Education in interactive video and library data transmission from Vancouver to four community colleges, testing the feasibility of satellite to meet B.C.'s distance education needs and the consortium model of programme development, production and delivery, and producing information used in planning further distance education courses and leading to the establishment of KNOW (Knowledge Network of the West); work with the University of Montreal resulting in plans for distant nursing education courses; plans for community communications between native groups in various provinces; and experiments which led to transmission of ACCESS Alberta educational programming via satellite. Jelly's role, on behalf of the Department of Communications, was to be a facilitator and catalyst by providing equipment, expertise, and limited funding as well as opportunities for meetings and discussions of results.

Kannila, Helle
The Correspondence Institute of the Society for Popular Culture and Adult Education, KUSK Institut, Helsinki, Finland

Affiliated with the Finnish Library Association, Helle Kannila was an advocate of the andragogical, social and occupational possibilities of the distance teaching method. She initiated distance education programmes (vocational training for "female occupations") for those with inadequate job-training and low status; females predominate in these categories. Helle Kannila had an active career, lasting over fifty years, as a distance educator. She died in 1972, and her life is documented in a book by Hilkka M. Kauppi (1976) which is availabe in Finnish.

Köernig, Helga
Ministry for Science and Research of North Rhine-Westphalia, Dusseldorf, West Germany

Helga Köernig's work provided the basis for the FernUniversität in Hagen, West Germany. She has been concerned with distance education and educational technology since 1973. She set out to improve, reform, and expand the distance educational system in Germany because of the growing number of enrolments at universities and the need for more opportunities for adult education. She travelled widely in the USSR, the USA and the UK, gathering information on distance studies and holding discussions with German distance study experts. This information was used in developing the FernUniversität. She elaborated a concrete plan and a feasibility study for the FernUniveristät as a comprehensive university for all comers. She wrote *Bildunsexpansion und Fernstudium Als Bildungs und Gesellschaftspolitische Aufgaben* (Munchen: Minerva Publ., 1979; translated as *Educational Expansion and Distance Education as an Educational and Social Task),* in which she developed and analyzed ideas concerning the philosophy and practice of distance education.

McIntosh, Naomi
Channel 4, London, England and Professor of Applied Social Research for the Open University, Great Britain

In 1970, Naomi McIntosh was a Senior Lecturer in Research Methods at the Open University. She became Head of Survey Research Department, Institute of Educational Technology, Open University in 1972. From 1974–78 she was Pro Vice-Chancellor (Student Affairs), Open University (OU). In 1975 she was a reader in Survey Research at the OU. She represented the OU on the National Foundation for Educational Research. From 1969 onwards, she ran research and evaluation projects for the OU. She was an SSRC grant holder from 1970–72, researching the social and educational consequences of the Open University. She served as a consultant on educational evaluation to the Council of Europe's steering group on educational technology from 1972–75 and as a member of the Research Advisory Board, Satellite Technology Demonstration for the Federation of Rocky Mountain States in the USA. Her publications on evaluation and media research are numerous. Several publications between 1972 and 1976 presented models for the evaluation of distance education and educational technology systems, concentrating on formative evaluation concerns and methods. Many of her publications presented detailed information on student populations at the OU and discussed their implications. She brought to the OU a market research orientation and understood students to be "consumers" of OU education.

McPartlin, Mary Louise
Loyola University, Chicago, Illinois, USA

Mary Louise McPartlin was employed by Loyola University of Chicago for thirty-eight years, first as a librarian, then as Director of the Correspondence Study Division from 1952 to her retirement in 1979. Students were enrolled from all parts of the world and included such groups as missionaries and military service personnel. She is particularly noted for her letters of encouragement to students in foreign countries, said to motivate them to complete their studies. She was active on the executive of International Council for Correspondence Education (ICCE) from 1969 to 1972. In 1970, she became the first editor of the ICCE Newsletter and from 1970 to 1973 Chairman of the ICCE Newsletter Committee. In 1975 she was elected Vice-President of ICCE and worked to further the cause of distance education. McPartlin served on accrediting and evaluation teams for the National Home Study Council and the North Central Association of Colleges and Schools, and she was the recipient of the Gayle B. Childs Award of the National University Continuing Education Association for outstanding service in extension education. McPartlin died in 1986.

Manwaring, Gaye
Dundee College of Education, Dundee, Scotland

From 1969 to 1975, Gaye Manwaring was a research fellow with the University of Glasgow where she was involved in the design, production and evaluation of self-instructional audio-visual programmes for first year biology undergraduates. From 1975 she has been a Senior Lecturer in Educational technology at Dundee College, where she is responsible for the planning, teaching and coordination of courses in educational technology, as well as writing packages, editing and acting as a tutor. Dundee College was an unsuccessful experiment in institution-centered resource-based learning. It was largely Manwaring who identified the problems and worked to change the system so that Dundee was able to provide a more effective environment for distance learning. Dundee College was, and continues to be, an exponent of distance learning both as a method and as a subject of study. Dr. Manwaring, as director of a course on educational technology conducted by distance learning, has made major contributions to both the theory and practice of distance education. Her publications during the early 1970s document course development procedures which were used to train university staff in correspondence education in Great Britain and in Southeast Asia.

Matiru, I. Barbara
College of Adult and Distance Education, Nairobi, Kenya

I. Barbara Matiru is a pioneer editor of distance education courses in Kenya. She trains writers in Kenya and Eastern Africa and has been a curriculum developer in distance education since 1967. She published and developed learning materials on curriculum development in developing nations, examining possible hybrids of traditional African education with imported educational concepts, and her work documents examples of course development in Tanzania, Kenya, the Cameroons, Botswana and Zambia.

Mody, Bella
Satellite Instructional Television Experiment (SITE), India

Bella Mody researched the diffusion of first-world educational technologies into Third World countries. She has compiled information on the effects of these technologies and articulated schema for appropriate organizational structures for use of these technologies in Third World countries. In 1972 she was hired as one of the first two social scientists by the Indian Space Agency where she worked until 1977. She conducted both formative and summative evaluations of the SITE project. She prepared life-style profiles to help SITE producers decide on communication strategies with villages. Mody pre-tested programmes and participated in the design of the multi-methodological approach to the summative evaluation of the SITE project. Her doctoral thesis was specifically concerned with the economic class of the viewer as a determinant of the impact of distance education during the SITE project. She introduced the team production system into India's four rural television stations and trained social researchers in formative evaluation techniques. Her publications are numerous and include discussions of media effectiveness, learner characteristics in response to media, reports on formative evaluations, proposals for organizational structures for communications technologies in India and elsewhere, women and communications technologies, and the impacts of First World technologies on Third World cultures.

Norquay, Margaret
Open College, Ryerson Polytechnical Institute, Toronto, Canada

In 1943, Margaret Norquay began working with Rural Adult Education Service of McDonald College, Quebec. This was the provincial branch of the National Farm Radio Forum which used radio for educational purposes. In this capacity, she wrote the weekly newsletter and prepared the ten-minute weekly feedback on the concerns of farmers. This was broadcast at the end of each national radio programme. In addition, she prepared a variety of "study group" courses. In the 1960s, she prepared a number of educational documentaries for the Canadian Broadcasting Corporation's programme *Take Thirty*. In 1970, Ryerson Polytechnical Institute hired her to prepare a two-semester credit course in introductory sociology. This distance course, offered in 1971 and using radio, was the first course broadcast over Ryerson's radio station CJRT. These first courses were the basis of what would become the Open College service of CJRT. From 1972–74 she was Director of Studies for Ryerson Open College. In 1974 she became Director of Open College. She was also Programme Director of CJRT-FM. From the beginning, courses offered over Open College were intended to be of a quality that would merit accreditation by other institutions. Norquay played a major role in ensuring this quality.

Okwata, Consolata
Linos, School for the Blind, Kisumu District, Kenya

Consolata Okwala was a blind girl who left school after sixth grade. She studied with a referee and through correspondence methods, did twelfth grade exams, passed, and joined a teacher training college to train as a primary school teacher. Her determination to pursue further education, despite her visual handicap, was considered amazing. While she was studying through distance methods, around 1975, she was also raising a family of three young children.

Shah, Smt. Madhuri
SNDT Women's University, India

Smt. Madhuri Shah was Education Officer of Bombay Municipal Corporation of Greater Majarastra from 1961–65 and became Vice Chancellor of Shreemati Nathibai Damodar Thackersey (SNDT) Women's University in 1975. Her flexible approach and noteworthy impact on education greatly encouraged the open university and distance education programmes associated with the SNDT. She introduced the open university programme to provide education to women irrespective of age and level of education. In her publications during the mid-1970s she argued that women working in traditional roles in the home deserve a higher education just as do working women.

Sheppard, Marlene
New South Wales Department of Education, Sydney, Australia

Marlene Sheppard was employed by the Department of Education as an Inspector of Schools for seventeen years beginning in 1969.

In her role as Inspector of Schools, she has raised an awareness of needs for distance education at the central level. She has been responsible for special staffing, has initiated and supported trials in communication technology, represented the isolated parents, and greatly influenced policy in distance education in the region. Sheppard represents a turning point in the policy application, focusing administrative attention on the needs and potential of distance education.

Stahmer, Anna
Canada, Department of Communications, Canada

Anna Stahmer was active in preparing policy papers regarding the use of communications satellites for education. She worked as a Policy Advisor for the Department of Communications from 1974–79, where she formulated the policy research programme for the Canadian Direct Broadcast Satellite Programme. She was a member of the management team of the Anik B and Hermes experimental satellite programmes with responsibility for policy analysis and evaluation. She developed project implementation and evaluation plans and a variety of reports and presentations on the use of satellite and telecommunications technology for both education and health care needs. These have provided grounding for present day use of these systems by education and health care.

Ticknor, Anna Eliot
Society to Encourage Studies at Home, USA

MacKenzie *et al.* provide the only detailed account of Anna Ticknor found during this investigation. She is considered the founder of the first correspondence instruction programme in the United States in 1873. The programme, known as the Society to Encourage Studies at Home, was intended as a charitable activity to enable women at home to obtain an education because "despite the progress made in providing equal educational opportunities for them, conservatism and individual prejudice still kept many women safely tucked away by the hearth" (1968:25). The school consisted of letters, guided readings, and tests in history, science, art, literature, French and German. Enrolment reached 1,000 in 1882. With the death of Ticknor in 1897 the society ceased to exist.

Valaskakis, Gail
Concordia University, Montreal, Quebec, Canada

Gail Valaskakis was active in the interactive satellite projects (Hermes, Malaakvik I and Anik B Inukshuk) with work that has been documented as a non-formal distance education system. She has worked in Native communications since 1971, as a member of the Arctic Institute's Man in the North Project, Communications Task Force, and as an evaluator, researcher and advisor. She was Coordinator of the CBC Northern Service radio programme "Winds of Change" which was based on lectures in the Native Peoples of Canada course (1971–73). She chaired a panel for the Canadian Council of Teachers of English on the Cultural Impact of Contemporary Media in 1971. She was the evaluator for the Second Report on the Adoption of Television by Native communities in the Canadian North, prepared for the Department of Indian and Northern Affairs in 1976, and presented papers on media and acculturation and communication patterns in 1975 and 1976. She has studied and published on the effective use of satellite television broadcasting on isolated northern populations and has treated the planning and delivery of social services using distance technologies.

Wilson, Martha
Alaska Native Health Services, Anchorage, Alaska, USA

Wilson was Director of the Alaska Native Medical Center from 1961–71. In 1971, when the ATS-1 satellite was launched, she stimulated the centre's involvement in an audio health communications network using the satellite. At her urging, the satellite was used for continuing medical education and direct patient consultation at the Tanana Hospital. Communications with villages were conducted primarily through medical doctors and school teachers. She later became the Director of the Office of Programme Development and worked in telecommunications using ATS-1. She was described by colleagues as a "forward thinker" who saw the need to link all services of health care of rural Alaska and make better use of health aides.

Conclusion

This study documents the contributions of selected significant women in the field of distance education. The influence of these women on female distant learners merits study. As a growing majority of distant learners are female, the question of the effect of male-dominated structures on these learners is relevant. Are women who take courses through such structures in danger of being perpetuated as a "subject" of distance education as opposed to playing an active role in formulating their own systems?

In her analysis of historical research on women in higher education, Graham (1975) indicates that when writing about successful women one is distorting the record of women's experience in higher education and thus the assumptions about the quality of the experience. A number of questions arise about women's experiences in distance education. Does the presence of women in decision-making roles affect the quality of the educational experience? Specifically, did the presence of these women as functionaries in the distance education system have an influence on the rate and quality of participation of women as distance learners? In looking at the work of successful women in distance education, does the researcher alter what is known about the experience of the female learner? Are the current definitions of distance education appropriate when examined in the light of women's contributions?

Hubbard (1983) suggests that women recognize themselves as part of the research and deliberately adopt an estrocentric (female-centred) approach to the investigation. She recommends the development of estrocentric theories, that is, paradigms which recognize the situation, values and experience of women and which provide a grounding for examination of events in distance education in this light. Secondly, women can pare away the myths from the raw data to see what new picture of women's reality emerges and what new questions are posed concerning the relationship of distance education to women's situations. Thirdly, existing male assumptions about distance education and women can be exposed and analyzed for their validity.

In sum, the presence of women in distance education is significant not only in the successes of women as functionaries in the field but also in the recognition of women's experiences as a basis for an adequate theory of distance education. Theories of distance education generated by men cannot speak for the experience of women. Women are necessarily central figures in developing appropriate theory and practice for a growing female learner population.

References and Bibliography

Astin, H.C. (1974). *Women: A Bibliography On Their Education and Careers.* New York: Behaviour Publications.

Beard, H. (1946). *Women as a Force in History.* New York: MacMillan.

Blumberg, R.G. (1980). *India's Educated Women: Options and Constraints.* Delhi, India: Hindustan Publications.

de Freitas, K.S., P.D. Lynch and R. Sweitzer. (September 1986). "Nontraditional Study Program: An Overview." *International Council for Distance Education Bulletin, 12,* 37–46.

Dodson-Gray, E. (1982). *Patriarchy As a Conceptual Trap.* Wellesley, Mass.: Roundtable Press.

Graham, P.A. (1975). "So Much to Do: Guides for Historical Research on Women in Higher Education." *Teachers College Record, 76*(3), 421–28.

Hubbard, R. (1983). "Have Only Men Evolved?" In S. Harding and M.B. Hintikka. (Eds.). *Discovering Reality: Feminist Perspectives on Epistemology, Metaphysics, Methodology, and Philosophy of Science.* Boston: D. Reidel.

Kauppi, Hilkka M. (1976). *Helle Kannila: Elämänpuut.* Helsinki, Finland: Otava. [Address: Kustannusosakeyhtio, P.O. Box 134, SF-00121, Helsinki, Finland.] (ISBN 951-9025-20-0.)

Kelly, G.P., and Y. Lulat. (1980). "Women and Schooling in the Third World: A Bibliography." *Comparative Education Review, 24*(2), 224–63.

Knowles, A.S. (Ed.). (1977). *International Encyclopedia of Higher Education,* Vol. 9. San Francisco, California: Jossey-Bass.

Lagemann, E.C. (1983). "Looking at Gender: Women's History." In J.H. Best, *Historical Inquiry in Education, A Research Agenda.* New York: American Educational Research Association.

Lerner, G. (1979). *The Majority Finds Its Past.* New York: Oxford Press.

Lessing, D. (1985). *Prisons We Choose to Live Inside.* Toronto: CBC Publications.

MacKenzie, O., E.L. Christensen and P.H. Rigby. (1968). *Correspondence Instruction in the United States.* New York: McGraw-Hill.

Martin, J.R. (1982). "Excluding Women from the Educational Realm." *Harvard Educational Review, 52*(2), 133–48.

Parker, F. (1979). *Women's Education: A World View.* Westport, Conn.: Greenwood Press.

UNESCO. (1972). *Growth and Change: Perspectives on Education in Asia*. Paris: UNESCO.

Wedemeyer, C.A. (1985). "Correspondence Study." In T. Husen and T.N. Postlewaite. (Eds.). *International Encyclopedia of Education*. Vol. 2. San Francisco, California: Jossey-Bass.

Westervelt, E.M. (1971). *Women's Higher and Continuing Education*. New York: College Entrance Examination Board.

Appendix A:

Selected Bibliography of Publications Authored by Distance Educators Profiled in Chapter 20

Brock, D. (1978). *Evaluation of a Telecourse: Writing for a Reason*. Dallas, Texas: Dallas Community College.

Burge, L., M. Norquay and J. Roberts. (1987). *Listening to Learn*. Toronto: OISE.

Burns, R. (1974). *The Access Workbooks*. New York: The Alternate Media Center, New York University.

Burns, R. (1975). *Public-Cable Handbook*. Washington, D.C.: National Education Association.

Burns, R. (1978). "Beyond Statistics." In M.C.J. Elton, W.A. Lucas and D.W. Conrath. (Eds.). *Evaluating New Telecommunications Services*. New York: Plenum Publishing.

Burns, R. (1978). *Two-Way Cable Television: An Evaluation of Community Uses in Reading, Pennsylvania*. [Available from Tisch School of the Arts, New York University.]

Burns, R. (October 16, 1981). "Technology is not Enough." Paper Presented at the *American Council on Education*. Washington, D.C.

Carney, P. (1977). *Report of the Distance Education Planning Group on a Delivery System for Distance Education in British Columbia*. Victoria, B.C.: Ministry of Education, Province of British Columbia.

Coll, D., H.E. Hudson, D. Lumb and P. Guild. (July 1975). "College Curriculum Sharing vis CTS." Paper Presented at the *Conference of the American Institute of Aeronautics and Astronautics*. Denver, Colorado.

Cross, K.P. (1971). *Beyond the Open Door: New Students to Higher Education*. San Francisco, California: Jossey-Bass.

Cross, K.P. (1972). *Explorations in Non-traditional Study.* San Francisco, California: Jossey-Bass.

Cross, K.P. (Ed.). (1974). *Leaders in Education.* New York: Jacques Cattell Press, Bowker Co.

Cross, K.P. (1974). *Planning Non-Traditional Programs: An Analysis of the Issues for Post-Secondary Education.* San Francisco, California: Jossey-Bass.

Cross, K.P. (1976). *Accent on Learning: Improving Instruction and Reshaping the Curriculum.* San Francisco, California: Jossey-Bass.

Elton, L. and Manwaring, G. (1981). "Training Teachers in Higher Education in Developing Countries." *Higher Education, 10*(2), 131–40.

Erdos, R. (1967). *Teaching by Correspondence.* London: Longman.

Erdos, R. (1975). *Establishing an Institution Teaching by Correspondence. (Experiments and Innovations in Education No. 17).* Paris: UNESCO Press.

Erdos, R. and J.H. Clark. (1971). *Correspondence Courses for In-service Teacher Training at Primary Level in Developing Countries.* Hamburg, Germany: UNESCO Institute for Education.

Hudson, H.E. (February 1975). "Transportation and Communication in Northern Development." Paper Presented at the *Symposium on Planning for Sub-Arctic Communities.* Sponsored by the American Society for Public Administration. Anchorage, Alaska.

Hudson, H.E. (May 1975). "Communication and the Development of Rural Alaska." Paper Presented at the *International Broadcasting Institute Seminar on the Role of New Communication Systems.* Ottawa, Canada.

Jelly, D. (1983). "DOC's role in the Development of Social Service Satellite Delivery Systems." *Proceedings of the First Canadian Domestic and International Satellite Communications Conference, 1983,* Amsterdam: North Holland Publishing Company.

Jelly, D. (1984). "The Role of Field Trials in Satellite Service Development." *Conference Proceedings of the Canadian Satellite Users Conference, 1984.* Ottawa, Canada: Telesat. 128–32.

Jelly, D. (July 1978). *Report on the Process of Implementation of Hermes Experiments. CRC Technical Note No. 694-E.* Ottawa, Canada: Department of Communications.

Kletter, R.C. and H.E. Hudson. (1972). "Video Cartridges and Cassettes." In C. Cuadra. (Ed.). *Annual Review of Information Science Number 7.* Washington, D.C.: American Society for Information Science.

Koernig, H. (1979). *Bildungsexpansion und Fernstudium als bildungs- und gesellschaftspolitische Aufgaben.* Munich: Minerva Publikation.

Manwaring, G. (May 1973). "Self-instruction Biology." *Visual Education,* 19–22.

Matiru, B. and P. Sachsenmeier. (1979). *Basic Training Course in Systematic Curriculum Development.* Nairobi, Kenya: German Agency for Technical Cooperation.

McIntosh, N.E. (February 1972). "Preparation for the Open University." *Home Study.*

McIntosh, N.E. (1972). "Research for a New Institution—The Open University." *Innovation in Higher Education.* London: Society for Research into Higher Education.

McIntosh, N.E. (1972). "The Response to the Open University—Continuity and Discontinuity." *Higher Education, 2,* 186–95.

McIntosh, N.E. (1973). *Evaluation Research for Out of School Multi-Media Educational Systems.* Strasbourg: Council of Europe.

McIntosh, N.E. (1973). *Evaluation Techniques of Multi-Media Learning Systems.* Strasbourg: Council of Europe.

McIntosh, N.E. (1974). "An Integrated Multi-Media Educational Experience?" *Educational Television International, 4*(3), 229–33.

McIntosh, N.E. (October 1974). "Evaluation of Multi-Media Educational Systems—Some Problems." *British Journal of Educational Technology, 5*(3), 43–59.

McIntosh, N.E. and A.W. Bates (1972). "Mass Media Courses for Adults." *Programmed Learning and Educational Technology, 9*(4), 188–97.

McIntosh, N.E. and A. Woodley. (1974). "The Open University and Second Chance Education." *Paedagogica Europeae, 10,* 85–100.

McIntosh, N.E., J. Calder and B. Swift. (1976). *A Degree of Difference—A Study of the First Year's Intake to the Open University of the United Kingdom.* London: Society for Research into Higher Education.

Mody, B. (December 1976). "Towards Formative Research in TV for Development." *Educational Broadcasting International, 9*(4), 160–63.

Mody, B. (April 1978). "The Indian Satellite Instructional Television Experiment: Its Origins, Organization, Messages and Effects." Paper Presented at the *International Communication Association Annual Conference.* Chicago, Illinois.

Mody, B. (1978). "The SITE Experiment: Messages for What?" *International Development Review, 2,* 51–54.

Mody, B. (1979). "Programming for SITE." *Journal of Communication, 19*(4), 90–98.

Mody, B. (April 1981). "Lessons for Third World Evaluators from the SITE Experience." *About Distance Education, 11,* 11–13. [Available through the International Extension College, 18 Brooklands Ave., Cambridge, England, CB2 2HN.]

Mody, B. and F. Basrai. (March 1980). "Evaluating TV in Third World Countries: A Retrospective on the Evaluation of the Satellite Television Experiment in India." Paper Presented at the *Conference on TV in the Developing World,* at the University of Winnipeg, Manitoba, Canada.

Norquay, M. (November 1985). "Educational Radio." Paper Presented on the occasion of receiving an Honorary Doctor of Laws from York University, Toronto, Ontario.

Parker, E.B. and H.E. Hudson. (December 20, 1973). "Medical Communication in Alaska by Satellite." *New England Journal of Medicine, 289*(25), 1351-56.

Parker, E.B. and H.E. Hudson. (Fall 1975). "Telecommunication Planning for Rural Development." *IEEE Transactions on Communications.*

Parker, E.B., H.E. Hudson and D.R. Foote. (February 1976). *Telemedicine in Alaska: The ATS-6 Satellite Biomedical Demonstration.* California: Stanford University Institute for Communication Research.

Shah, S.M. (1976-77). "Status and Education of Women in India." *Journal of Gujarat Research Society, 38/39, 4*(1), 15–24.

Stahmer, A.E. (1973). *Towards a Model for Satellite-Based Social Delivery Systems in a Developed and Developing Country: A Case Study of the ATS-6 Experiments in the United States and India.* Unpublished thesis, Washington, D.C., American University.

Stahmer, A.E. (1979). "The Era of Experimental Satellites: Where to go from Here." *Journal of Communication, 29*(4), 137–44.

Stahmer, A.E. (1979). "From Satellite Experiments to Operational Applications: Canadian Experiences and Plans." *Acta Astronautica, 8,* 87–99.

Valaskakis, G. (1971). *Communications Task Force, Man in the North Research Project.* Montreal, Canada: Arctic Institute of North America, 1 and 2.

Valaskakis, G. (Summer 1972). "Media, Native Peoples and Cultural Propaganda." *Alive, 3*(2). Guelph, Ontario.

Valaskakis, G. (March 1981). "Communication and Control in the Canadian North: The Role of Interactive Satellites." Paper Presented at the *7th Annual conference of SIETAR,* Vancouver, British Columbia.

INDEX

Aborigines; *See also* Native Indians, in Canada
Australia, 128, 229-47
New Zealand, 278-79, 281, 284
Advanced Studies for Teachers Unit, New Zealand, 82-92
Africa, distance education in, 7, 137-51, 322, 326-28
All India Radio, 176-81
Anadolu University, Turkey, 210
Anangu Teacher Education Program, Australia, 127-28, 229-47
Association of Colleges and Universities of Canada, 29-30, 37
Atatürk, Kemal, president of the Republic of Turkey, 126, 205-7, 212
Athabasca University, Canada, 28, 33, 127, 214-28
Audiocassettes, and distance education, 183-84, 306
Australia, distance education in, 126, 190-204, 281, 322, 328-29
Australian Council of Churches, 169
Australian Development Assistance Bureau, 170

Beaulieu, Claudette, distance educator in Canada, 118
Beelitz, Anne, distance educator in West Germany, 320
Bell, Diane, anthropologist, 234
Bolton, Geoffrey, historian, 5
Bonness, Gertrud, distance educator in West Germany, 320
British Columbia, Canada, distance education in, 21, 25-38
British Equal Opportunities Commission, 295
Brock, Dee, distance educator in the United States, 320

Burns, Red, distance educator in the United States, 320-21

Campbell, Audrey L., distance educator in Canada, 35-36, 321
Canada, distance education in, 9, 21, 23-24, 25-38, 107-20, 135, 214-28, 255, 281, 321, 323-24, 327-28, 329, 330
Canadian Association of Distance Education, 36
Canadian Association of University Continuing Education, 36
Carnegie Commission on Higher Education, United States, 14
Carney, Pat, distance educator in Canada, 321
Changing Experience of Women, distance education course, 266-73, 302-7
Children and childcare, women's responsibility for, 10-11, 45, 47, 51, 55, 71, 78, 87, 93, 104, 130-33, 185, 187-88, 215, 221, 223, 224, 230-31, 253, 277, 295
Classroom education, 6, 130-31, 134, 183-84, 188, 197-204, 214-28, 241-42, 282-83
College of Adult and Distance Education, Kenya, 137-51
Computers, and distance education, 308-11
Crocombe, Marjorie, distance educator in the South Pacific, 167
Cross, Patricia K., distance educator in the United States, 322

Distance education, benefits of, 6, 80, 86, 87, 94-97, 134; *See also* Classroom education

Distance education, course content, 27-30, 90-92, 154-55, 196-99, 220, 253, 287-312
   readability, 163-67
   sexism, 137-51, 288-91
Distance education courses; agriculture, 179; art, 71, 82-92; business, 110, 163-66, 185, 191, 291, 297-302; communication skills, 156-61; computer science, 41, 43, 51-55, 61; construction, 190-204; criminology, 33-34; economics and commerce, 41, 43-47, 50, 54, 61, 110, 183-84, 186; education, 41-43, 47-50, 71, 138-51, 163-66, 179, 210-11, 239-40, 243, 291, 295, 329; engineering, 41-43, 51-55, 61, 191; English language and literature, 156-61, 163-64, 185; family and child care, 11, 27, 124, 177-79, 291; German literature, 49-51; gerontology, 110, 291; health care, 27, 71, 114, 116-17, 119, 135, 179, 280, 291, 329, 330; insurance, 185; languages, 49; law, 45-46, 164-66, 185; mathematics, 41, 43, 51-55, 60-61, 243, 295; nutrition, 185, 291; personal finances, 185; philosophy, 49-50; psychology, 49, 186; rural studies, 191; science, 161-63, 295; secretarial skills, 185; social sciences, 41, 43, 47-49, 61, 119, 243; sociology, 27, 49-50, 110, 186; statistics, 164-66; study skills, 156-61; vocational and technical, 126, 190-204, 253, 292-97, 324; women's studies, 110-12, 186, 251-52, 264-74, 275-86, 302-7; writing, 185
Distance education delivery systems, 196-204, 218, 253, 287-312; educators, 89, 135-36, 217-18; flexibility of, 30, 76, 85-86, 133, 136, 187-88, 218, 261-62; origins of, 318-19; student motivation, 6, 10-12, 30-34, 39-65, 85-88, 93-94, 156-61, 219, 251, 257-59; study methods, 85, 134-35, 219-20; women-centred approach, 264-74, 330-31

Deverell, Gwen, distance educator in the South Pacific, 170
Distance University Education via Television (DUET), Canada, 109-13
Department of of Technical and Further Education, New South Wales, Australia, 190-204
Dutch Open University, Netherlands, 251-52, 254-63, 264-74

Education, and women, ix, xii, 4, 8, 10, 55-61, 63, 315-37; *See also* Classroom education, Distance education
Emily Carr College of Art and Design, Canada, 26, 28
Employment
and distance education, 33-34, 44-45, 61-62, 97-98, 102
and women, 31, 131, 158-59, 184-85, 192, 193, 195, 198-99, 215, 223-24, 253, 259, 277
England, distance education in, viii, 265, 287-312, 318, 325
Erdos, Renee, distance educator in Australia, 322
Everyman's University, Israel, 22, 67-81

Family and home, women's responsibility for, 6, 32, 40, 46, 55, 60, 63, 71, 75, 87, 94, 99-100, 104, 130, 158-60, 170, 184-85, 206, 221, 223, 253, 261-62, 277, 295; *See also* Children and childcare
Fellman, Anita Clair, distance educator in Canada, 28
Feminism, and distance education, ix, xii, 12-15, 251, 255, 264-74, 275-86, 304
FernUniversität, West Germany, 21-22, 39-65, 72, 251
Finland, distance education in, 255, 324
France, distance education in, 255
Fukofuka, Salote, distance educator in the South Pacific, 170

Gandhi, Mahatma, 182-83

Index

Garrett, Ephra, feminist in New Zealand, 276
Gender inequity, ix, 9, 11, 29, 49-50, 63, 72, 123-30, 137-51
Goodale, Jane, anthropologist, 234
Goodwillie, Diane, distance educator in the South Pacific, 169

Hudson, Heather, distance educator in the United States, 322-23
Howard, Dawn, distance educator in Canada, 36

Illiteracy. *See* Literacy
India, distance education in, 7, 125-26, 172-89, 327, 328
Indira Gandhi National Open University, India, 186
Integrated Child Development Service, India, 177-78
International Council for Correspondence Education, x, 325-26
International Council for Distance Education, x-xi, xii, 5-6, 11-12, 36, 319
Israel, distance education in, 22, 67-81

Jelly, Doris, distance educator in Canada, 323-24

Kaberry, Philis, anthropologist, 234
Kannila, Helle, distance educator in Finland, 324
Kenya, distance education in, 124, 137-51, 326-27, 328
Kirk, Pauline, distance educator in England, 32
Knowledge Network of the West, Canada, 26, 28-29, 321
Köernig, Helga, distance educator in West Germany, 324

Language, sexism in, x-xi, 25-26, 29, 144-45, 197-98
Leeming, Robyn, distance educator in New Zealand, 276, 280
Literacy, and women, 3, 126, 173-74, 179-81, 186, 206-8, 230, 238

McIntosh, Naomi, distance educator in England, 325
McPartlin, Mary Louise, distance educator in the United States, 325-26
Madurai-Kamaraj University, India, 175-76
Manwaring, Gaye, distance educator in Scotland, 326
Maoris. *See* Aborigines (New Zealand)
Marriage. *See* Family and home
Massey University, New Zealand, 252-53, 275-86
Matanimeke, Kesaia, distance educator in the South Pacific, 167-68
Matiru, I. Barbara, distance educator in Kenya, 326-27
Memorial University, Canada, 24, 114-17
Mill, John Stuart, and feminism, 279
Mody, Bella, distance educator in India, 327
Mount Saint Vincent University, Canada, 23-24, 108-14
Mysore University, India, 175-76

Nance, Margit, continuing studies educator in Canada, 36
Native Aboriginal Education Conference, Australia, 239-40
Native Indians, in Canada, 127, 214-28; *See also* Aborigines
Native Welfare Act, Australia, 235
Netherlands, distance education in, 254-63, 264-74
New Brunswick, Canada, distance education in, 24, 117-20
New South Wales, Australia, distance education in, 190-204, 237
New Zealand, distance education in, 22, 82-92, 275-86
Newfoundland and Labrador, Canada, distance education in, 24, 114-17
Norquay, Margaret, distance educator in Canada, 327-28
Nova Scotia, Canada, distance education in, 23-24

Okwata, Consolata, distance educator in Kenya, 328
Open Learning Institute, Canada, 26-29
Open University Business School, England, 292, 302
Open University Consortium of British Columbia, Canada, 26-27, 31-32
Open University of England, 30, 252-54, 266-67, 273, 287-312
Open University, Turkey, 127
Organization for Economic Co-operation and Development, 192, 255

Pacific Pre-School Teachers Programme, University of the South Pacific, 167-71
Papua New Guinea, distance education in, 123-24, 129-36
Patriarchy in society, 3-4, 8, 10-14, 29, 36, 195, 198-99, 230-33, 251, 281
Préfontaine, Marielle, distance educator in Canada, 118
Prince Edward Island, Canada, distance education in, 118
Prison, distance education in, 34

Queensland, Australia, 237

Radios, and distance education, 125, 176-81, 188, 307-8, 327-28
Rural areas, and distance education, 130, 133, 134, 159, 190-204, 215, 277, 281, 285

Satellites, and distance education, 153-54, 168, 171, 178-79, 308, 321, 322-24, 327, 329, 330
Saville-Smith, Kay, distance educator in New Zealand, 286
Schoeffel, Penelope, distance educator in the South Pacific, 167
Scotland, distance education in, 326
Scraton, Pamela, distance educator in the South Pacific, 171
Senate Select Committee on Aborigines and Torres Strait Islanders, Australia, 237

Sexual inequality, 3, 5, 7-10, 15, 29, 47, 150-51, 210-11, 231, 234, 242-43, 261; *See also* Gender inequity
Simon Fraser University, Canada, 26-37
Shah, Smt. Madhuri, distance educator in India, 328
Sheppard, Marlene, distance educator in Australia, 328-29
Shreemati Nathibai Damodar Thackersey (SNDT) Women's University, India, 126, 173, 181-87, 328
Sipolo, July, poet in the South Pacific, 159-60
South Australia, Australia, 237
South Australian College of Advanced Education, 133
South Pacific Commission's Women's Bureau, 168, 169
South Pacific, distance education in, 167-71
Spender, Dale, feminist, 12-14, 279-80
Stahmer, Anna, distance educator in Canada, 329
South Australian College of Advanced Education at Underdale, Adelaide, Australia, 240
Sweden, distance education in, 23, 93-106

Technology, and distance education, 292-97, 307-11, 324-29; *See also* Audiocassettes, Computers, Radios, Satellites, Telecommunications technology, Television, and Video technology
Telecommunications technology, and distance education, 24, 114-17, 118-19, 215, 217-18, 307-8, 320-21, 322-24
Television, and distance education, 23, 24, 27, 28, 109-13, 114-17, 118-19, 125-26, 178-80, 188, 306, 307-8, 320-21, 330
Ticknor, Anna Eliot, distance educator in the United States, 318, 329

Index

Tagoilelagi, Iole, distance educator in the South Pacific, 170
Thackersey, Premlila, founder of SNDT Women's University, 181-82
Thackersey, Vithaldas, founder of SNDT Women's University, 181-82
Tognivalu, Adi Davila, distance educator in the South Pacific, 170
Turkey, distance education in, 126-27, 205-13
Turkish Open University, Turkey, 205-13

UNESCO, 177
UNICEF, 170, 178
United States, distance education in, 255, 281, 320-23, 325-26, 329
Université de Moncton, Canada, 24, 117-20
University of British Columbia, Canada, 26-37, 321
University of Delhi, India, 174-75
University of Madras, India, 125-26, 175-76, 180, 187
University of Nairobi, Kenya, 137-38
University of Papua New Guinea, 132-33
University of the South Pacific, 124-25, 152-71
University of Victoria, Canada, 26-37
University of Waikato, New Zealand, 169
University of Western Ontario, Canada, 30

Valaskakis, Gail, distance educator in Canada, 330
Video technology, and distance education, 109-13, 188, 225-26, 320-21
Violence against women, 225-26

West Germany, distance education in, 21-22, 39-65, 210-11, 251, 318, 320, 324
Western Samoa Pre-School Association, South Pacific, 169
Western culture and education, in Australia, 229-47; in New Zealand, 275-86

Wilson, Martha, distance educator in the United States, 330
Women and Development Network, Australia, 167, 170
Women in Society Course, distance education course, New Zealand, 275-86
Women in Technology Scheme, distance education course, England, 293-97
Women into Management, distance education course, England, 297-302
Women into Science and Engineering, distance education course, England, 295-97
Women's International Network (WIN), i, x-xi, 12, 21, 36, 319
Women's studies, 251-52, 264-74, 275-86, 302-7
Women, self-esteem, 23, 86-87, 90-91, 93-106
Woolf, Virginia, viii, 4, 264-65

Young Women's Christian Association, in the South Pacific, 167-69

Zuckernick, Arlene, distance educator in Canada, 36

Ministry of Education, Ontario
Information Services & Resources Unit,
13th Floor, Mowat Block, Queen's Park,
Toronto M7A 1L2